America Goes to College

JOHN E. SEERY

A M E R I C A

———

G O E S   T O

———

C O L L E G E

political theory
for the liberal arts

STATE UNIVERSITY OF NEW YORK PRESS

Published by
STATE UNIVERSITY OF NEW YORK PRESS
ALBANY

© 2002 State University of New York

For information, address
State University of New York Press
90 State Street, Suite 700, Albany, NY 12207

Production, Laurie Searl
Marketing, Patrick Durocher

Library of Congress Cataloging-in-Publication Data

Seery, John Evan.
    America goes to college : political theory for the liberal arts / John E. Seery.
        p. cm.
    Includes bibliographical references (p.) and index.
    ISBN 0-7914-5591-2 (alk. paper) — ISBN 0-7914-5592-0 (pbk. : alk. paper)
        1. Education, Humanistic—United States. 2. Education, Higher—Political
aspects—United States. 3. Education, Higher—Aims and objectives—United States. I.
Title.

LC1021 .S42 2003
370.11'2—dc21   2002075882

10 9 8 7 6 5 4 3 2 1

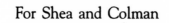

For Shea and Colman

Contents

COMPOSITIONS

COMMISSIONS

12   America Goes to College: A Manifesto of Sorts   193

     Notes   209

     Index   241

Acknowledgments

M any persons have read parts, or even entire drafts, of this book at various stages of completion, and for their generous help I am grateful beyond words. They include: Yishaiya Abosch, Joseph Acorn, Henry Adams, Benjamin Barber, Derek Barker, Richard Caperton, Brenda Carpio, Terrell Carver, Beth Cope, Daniel Conway, Wanda Corn, Devon Crie, Paul Dahlgren, Patrick Deneen, Laura Ephraim, Mario Feit, Alan Finlayson, Kathleen Fitzpatrick, Andrew Flores, Iselin Gambert, Sarah Jackel, Steven Johnston, Charles Junkerman, Joshua Karant, George Kateb, Grace Kim, Karl Kohn, Nancy Laursen, Bronwyn Leebaw, Nicholas Lewis, Diana Linden, Lee McDonald, Robert Meister, Matthew Moynihan, Frances Pohl, Chris Rocco, Laura Rosen, Aaron Sachs, Paul Saint-Amour, Jean Schroedel, George Shulman, Verity Smith, Jacqueline Stevens, Tracy Strong, James Sullivan, Daniel Wahlig, and Samuel Wineburg. I wish to extend a public thank-you to the many anonymous reviewers and journal editors along the way. I also am deeply appreciative of the supportive efforts of Michael Rinella, Laurie Searl, Michele Lamsing, and State University of New York Press. For all of the book's possible shortcomings, I alone am the culpable party.

A National Endowment for the Humanities (NEH) Summer Grant for College Teachers and a Graves Award in the Humanities for College Teachers helped support the research and writing of chapter 7, "Grant Wood's Political Gothic."

Permission to reprint material published elsewhere has been granted as follows: "The Demise of Western Culture" with Daniel W. Conway, *Curricular Reform: Narratives of Interdisciplinary Humanities Programs*, ed. Mark E. Clark and Roger Johnson Jr. (Chattanooga, Tenn.: Southern Humanities Council Press, 1991), 89–113, for a portion of chapter 1; chapter 5 originally appeared in the spring 2001 issue of *Polity* 33: 33: 345–64; "Nietzsche Contra Nietzcheanism: Philosophy in the Twilight of an Idol," *Journal of Nietzsche Studies* 16 (fall 1998): 80-86, for a portion of chapter 6; "Grant Wood's Political Gothic," *Theory & Event* 2: 1 (1998) (on-line Muse Project, Johns Hopkins University Press), for an earlier version of chapter 7; "Castles in the

Air: An Essay on Political Foundations," *Political Theory*, 24: 4 (August 1999): 460–90, with the permission of Sage Publications, for an earlier version of chapter 10; and "Twentieth Century Context," *Contemporary Political Theories*, ed. Alan Finlayson (Edinburgh: Edinburgh University Press, 2002), for reprinting chapter 11.

Cover art: Grant Wood, "Honorary Degree," 1937, lithograph on paper, permission granted for reproducing by Collection of Davenport Museum of Art, © Estate of Grant Wood/Licensed by VAGA, New York, New York.

Introduction

Political Theory for the Liberal Arts

T he basic material of this book consists of several essays that I wrote and
a few selected speeches that I delivered during the 1990s while teaching
political theory at Pomona College. On first pass these pieces may appear
to cover a range of topics suggesting little connection from one to another.
Explicitly they lack an overarching or unifying argument—and I well understand that many readers yearn for such customary coherence. Nonetheless, risking some complaint, I assemble these writings here not to argue
but to insinuate a claim that together they constitute (or enact) a subject
matter that merits attention. Perhaps it merits attention because it is a
subject that should always remain a bit understated, so it tends to escape
widespread notice. I also believe that it is a *fragile* matter that I am con-
sidering, so my approach, overall, must be circumspect and tentative, not
frontal and relentless.

By publishing these essays as a book, I hope to shed some light, more
flickering than glaring, on the enterprise of liberal arts education in America
today. Although many large research universities offer programs and degrees
in what is called "the liberal arts," my contention—which I leave unproved
but shall dangle for consideration anyway—is that a liberal arts education
flourishes best, or perhaps is pursued properly and effectively, only in America's
small liberal arts colleges.[1] At the same time, the survival of many of these
colleges is now at stake, which indicates, canary-in-the-cave-like, that the
survival of an entire mode of education may also be at stake.[2] This book
aspires to serve a double purpose then, namely, to limn the precarious successes of liberal arts education as they sometimes reveal themselves and also

to signal internal problems, and even a possible demise.[3] My view is that a liberal arts college education goes largely unappreciated, not mainly because the nation's employers routinely disparage the untrained "liberal arts gradu-ate," but because the nature and purpose of the liberal arts often are poorly understood and therefore falsely derided—or, maybe people have just gone looking in the wrong place.

Liberal arts education as it is practiced in many of our small colleges carries on in spite of all, in the trenches of the classroom, away from the national spotlight, even though it lacks high theoretical articulation. Liberal arts colleges operate on their own without a rallying manifesto or mission statement.[4] No poet laureate sings their praises. No public intellectual, pontificating from an Ivy League post, puts forth an impassioned plea on their behalf. Rather, these colleges operate in the shadows of the nation's prestigious research universities.[5] They are viewed by many, in and out of academe, as simply smaller and thus evidently less successful versions of the research university. Mom-and-pop grocery stores offer, to be sure, quaintly intimate services, a better person-to-person relationship with their custom-ers; but the modern economy now favors the Wal-Mart superstore, where cost and convenience trump quality and service. So goes the liberal arts college, a relic of the past, a *Gemeinschaft* operating in a *gesellschaftlich* world.[6] Accordingly, money and reputation flow these days to support the activities of the university scholar, not the liberal arts college professor. The Guggenheim Foundation bestows few of its grants on persons with college affiliations.[7] The National Endowment for the Humanities, the American Council of Learned Societies, and the Fulbright Foundation offer separate competitions for college teachers, a concession that their curricula vitae just cannot com-pete. It is no secret that young Ph.D.s often regard an appointment in a liberal arts college as a stint in the minor leagues, a way station or stepping-stone to the majors. Cutting-edge research is conducted in the universities, and thus careers and names are made there. If you cannot do, you teach, and thus many professors at these colleges labor under the unspoken stigma that, as failed research scholars, they must serve out their days—should the call up to the bigs never come—as glorified schoolmarms.

America's research universities, largely modeled after the nineteenth-century German university, are organized in pyramidal fashion, the upper-most aims of which are to conduct research and prepare graduates for careers in specialized scholarship. America's small colleges, in contrast, are widely viewed as sectarian experiments in undergraduate "teaching," where service-minded professors borrow the results of top-level research produced else-where and disseminate it in a hands-on and popularized, but derivative, manner. These teacherly instructors interact directly with undergraduates, whereas graduate student teaching assistants (TAs) perform the lion's share of "teaching" and paper grading at universities, freeing up precious time so their supervisory professors can investigate and profess some more. Although some universities have been attempting in recent years to offer something more than lip service with regard to undergraduate teaching, providing material incentives and recognition for exceptional teaching efforts, for the most part, the world of American academe is still divided quite starkly into research scholars versus classroom teachers. The two separate beasts more or less congregate in their respective institutions, the university versus the college.

Yet this functional division of labor affects the nature of scholarship produced at both kinds of institutions. It affects the nature of teaching, what is taught and how it is taught, at both kinds of institutions. Moreover, the divide indicates rival philosophies, diverging ever more, on the point and purpose of higher education.

The research university prides itself on producing state-of-the-art, specialized, professional scholarship, whereas a liberal arts education traditionally values some amorphous notion of "well-roundedness" that is admittedly hard to prescript, define, and pass on to others (because it must be appropriated independently and self-critically). However construed, liberal arts well-roundedness entails critical suspicion, almost an aversion toward preprofessional specialization. Liberal arts college students, we sometimes gently remind them, ought to put those workaday concerns in abeyance. Surely specialized training produces discrete marketable skills that usually are rewarded handsomely in the modern economy. So why would a liberal arts ethos actively eschew such preparation? The answer reveals a different philosophy of education altogether. Freedom of inquiry, the life of the mind, cannot be tethered to the freedom of the marketplace, spirited arguments to the contrary notwithstanding. Instrumentalism, gearing one's efforts toward producing persons and products serviceable to the marketplace of goods as opposed to the marketplace of ideas, kills the spirit of free education. Such freedom, by definition, cannot be productive, or at least cannot be expected to be productive. The freedom of free inquiry, a different concept and practice of freedom altogether, can be absolutely exhilarating when put into practice. Students, suspending their concerns about employment for a precious four years, can pursue ideas wherever they may take them. Their research need not produce immediate results in order to win another round of grants. They can read, brood over, and savor *long* books. They are free to ask probing questions of each other. They can be romantic, searching, or harshly critical of the prevailing norms of society. They are utterly free to be irresponsible, which makes their moments of commitment and responsibility all the more meaningful. More often than not, they act studiously and responsibly, albeit of their own accord. It works. The liberal arts ivory tower works if you structure it well, enlist the energies of the right people, trust that education still matters, and let it be.

In a world that espouses the benefits of efficiency, growth, productivity, and accountability, the liberal arts ethos seems out of place. But a market mentality must not triumph as the supreme value over all of our most important human interactions and enterprises. A few times I have told my students that if a lover of theirs calls them "efficient," that may not be a compliment (translation for the humor impaired: many forms of eroticism are wasteful expenditures of time that completely confound a cost-benefit analysis). To the extent that the market has infiltrated the normal operations of life at the American research university, with few firewall protections in place, the nature of scholarship produced will surely be affected.[8] Skewed toward specialization and productivity, such research has to cut corners elsewhere. If I belong to a philosophy department with fifty members, I might become the Plato specialist in that department—and my career may depend on my pursuing one particular Plato passage that has been slighted in the extant literature. Others in the department, out of professional courtesy, will probably cede that territory to me. Having a Plato ringer in their midst will probably discourage them from writing about Plato much at all. Possible connections between Plato and Goethe will probably not be broached, lest some Goethe specialist accuse the trespasser of dilettantish poaching. Likewise, free-ranging forays and cross-disciplinary transgressions fall, in due time under such rearguard conditions, largely by the wayside.

Where tenure and promotion depend almost exclusively on publishable productivity, the research scholar will naturally return, time and again, to his or her métier. Academic deans and faculty members serving on tenure committees themselves have little time to read an entire portfolio in order to glean subtle distinctions and sublime insights. The research university thus runs the risk of systematically producing tediously narrow and risk-averse Johnny-One-Notes whose research may be rigorous, but lacking in delicacy, hazard, or imagination. Small wonder that so many fields are producing scholars whose work emulates the drudging methods of natural science: hypothesis, data, test, conclusion. Niche scholarship has won the day, and academic publishers know that their intended audience ought to be established and well defined. Besides, who reads outside of one's field these days? For that matter, where are our polymathic public intellectuals who can speak across a range of topics?

The liberal arts college does not provide a panacea to the above ills, but it does embody an alternative view, a road not heavily traveled. At the college level, the criteria for promotion and tenure usually include teaching and community service contributions in addition to scholarship, a tripartite distribution that can relax somewhat the drumbeat pressures toward specialization and productivity. Such institutional ambiguity can occasionally foster creative, independent scholarly efforts that defy routine and convention. A liberal arts college professor and his or her students might just ask a question or two that no one else seems to be asking. As well, in practice, college teachers usually must become generalists in their field in order to provide some measure of disciplinary coverage within a smallish department. That expansive purview can, of course, work to one's detriment, as one scurries around trying to teach everything to all comers and thus does not teach anything particularly well. But especially in matters regarding "the crooked timber of humanity,"[9] should not *every* teacher/scholar be able to discuss *both* forest and trees?

I dare say also that liberal arts college professors, in order to be successful within their context, must cultivate a better sense of their *audience* than their university counterparts. Scale has a lot to do with it. Direct exposure to student constituents in small classroom settings makes "accountability" a day-to-day imperative. You cannot hide behind a lectern. As someone who has taught in both venues, small college classrooms and large university lecture halls, I can report that the latter can be deceptively flattering. In a lecture course of 400 students, even if only 10 percent find your jokes amusing, forty students nonetheless will fill the room with giggles—and you walk away from the podium with the impression that you are indeed funny. But in a classroom of ten students, one lonely snicker confirms that the joke bombed. Entertainment issues aside, a professor with a poor teaching reputation in a large university may still end up with enrollments of several hundred students (and TAs will rarely pass on bad news upstairs). Word-of-mouth student grapevines, for better or for worse, operate in every small college setting, and the word about a professor's methods spreads quickly. A bum teaching reputation spells disaster in such a setting. Students vote with their feet, and they are discerning consumers in such an anti-consumerist setting. The difference between enrollments of two students versus twenty-five students can speak volumes.

So too with writing. Many, many university research scholars, it seems to me, have lost sight of their main audience—college folks—or apparently have limited their reach to the cant of their professional peers. Whatever the reason, the vast majority of scholarly production these days is unreadable (or unpleasant). It cannot be assigned for undergraduates, even in advanced classes at the best colleges in the nation. One knows this by experience, the test of trial and error. In good part, I blame the American academic fascination with Michel Foucault and the poststructuralist movement (as much as I have welcomed many of the contributions following from this fascination). That movement should be held responsible, however, for producing a preponderance of passive voice constructions coursing through all academic discourse today. Instead of saying, "Mary hit Jane," one asseverates, "Power signifies the distillation of hierarchically interpolated imbalances." The passive voice, as it does in much scientistic writing, lends an air of authority in such constructions, because lines of causality and perspective are left implicit. (Mandarin, in contrast, often allows one to refer to verbal action without invoking a phantom subject, the doer behind the deed, but the speaker's perspective still informs the grammar of positioning characters into sentences.) In days of yore, one learned to write English for most purposes in the "active" voice, where the subject of the verb coincides with the subject of the sentence—but no longer. While I accept the broadside critiques of subject-centered reason, humanism, power, masculinism, and so forth that such contemporary writing presumes and performs, I must insist that smart undergraduates simply cannot follow the logic of those brave new convoluted clauses. The "subject" may be a grammatical fiction, but it makes for better prose. Moreover, the passive voice provides other deceptions, now deploying alternative grammatical fictions that also do not announce themselves as such. Action becomes slyly decontextualized. Global assertions sneakily get unsupported respect. "Indeterminacy" becomes the medium and the message. At least with the active voice you knew Mary was Mary and Jane was Jane and who was hitting whom. But who or what institutions or what mechanisms or what disciplinary practices are now signifying those hierarchical imbalances? Garbled grammar produces classroom mush. In contrast, the small classroom atmosphere forces liberal arts teachers to learn how to explain themselves eventually without the crutch of academic jargon. Small interactive classes also tend to disabuse one from relying on the "captive audience" mode of lecturing or its printed equivalent.

But all is not well. The American liberal arts college is under attack. It is experiencing both internal and external problems. Staffing those small classrooms with an attractive student-to-professor ratio is an expensive proposition. From a business perspective, a liberal arts education is a costly, labor-intensive enterprise. More and more, the liberal arts classroom is being scrutinized according to bottom-line business concerns. As costs rise, parents and students are asking for tangible returns on their educational dollars. Grant-giving foundations and other donors also are asking for measurable bang-for-the-buck results. Trustees and administrators are chipping away at the institution of faculty tenure. In addition to rising "labor" costs, colleges are experiencing a financial pinch due to the rising costs associated with the rapid pace of technological innovation. In order to stay competitive, every college must keep investing in new computers, new science equipment, new media equipment, and so forth. Large universities can defray some of these costs because of other lucrative revenue streams available to them: huge donations and research grants, spin-off patents and businesses, corporate sponsorships or partnerships, and revenue-producing professional schools and athletic teams. But, increasingly, in a changing high-tech world, the liberal arts college cannot compete, even as a smaller version of the mega-versity. Many American colleges have traditionally depended upon a regional student base for their survival, but today many of those colleges are losing local students to "distance learning" via the on-line virtual university. The top liberal arts colleges, ones that enjoy a national profile, are flourishing in this winner-take-all, the rich-get-richer environment, but other colleges are barely holding on. Clearly a shakeout is coming.

Facing these pressures, liberal arts practitioners are doing much internal housecleaning and soul searching. But some of the proposed changes represent a failure of nerve and threaten to compromise the very integrity of the liberal arts mission. Where college trustees rate success in endowment dollar increments, college administrators and development officers struggle to find ways to "sell" the liberal arts college experience in market-driven, economic terms—terms that all too often betray the spirit of liberal arts. A few years ago at Pomona College, for instance, we implemented a new curriculum that categorizes courses into various "skills" that students purportedly develop along the way (by the way, the debate, itself contentless, was never informed by a Deweyian understanding of skills). The skills involve "reading texts carefully," "learning some history," or "examining values critically"—hardly the kinds of technical expertise that one can highlight on a resume or in a job interview. But the whole apparatus, with its allusive promise of providing marketable trade skills, allows top college officials to put forth a favorable public relations spin regarding the "value-added" economic benefits of a liberal arts education. Hypocrisy is one thing, but such outward concessions also tend to erode the mission internally. As managers and administrators make greater claims on and take greater control of the curriculum, the magic of the classroom tends to recede in importance. Some people start believing the hype and along the way somehow forget what really matters.

Under such conditions, college professors are liable to lose heart. Usually the joys of teaching provide ample sustenance in periods of darkness, but occupational indignities can, over time, take their toll. One's teaching load in a small liberal arts college usually is quite heavy compared to that of a university professor, which means that one is less likely to be able to pursue a high-flying, enormously prolific scholarly career. One writes, one publishes, but an appointment in a small liberal arts college can produce bumps in the road to gaining standing in one's field and recognition among one's professional peers. Again, as someone who has taught in both research universities and small colleges, I can report anecdotal but strongly telling evidence that institutional letterheads matter immensely in the world of academe. Calls are returned sooner, publishers are more responsive, and panel invitations are more forthcoming, depending on one's home affiliation as announced at the top of one's stationery. I suspect that almost every college professor in the country can provide additional testimony along those lines. For a host of reasons, it becomes difficult to keep pace with one's field; after a while, it becomes difficult to maintain an active professional profile. I have seen it time and again: bright young stars burn out in college positions. Over time, they lose confidence, drop out of professional circulation, and become embittered. The joys of teaching do not always compensate for the attendant loss in

stature. Put a bunch of such resentful also-rans together on the same academic committee, and you are asking for bickering, small-town infighting.
Suffice it to say that a liberal arts college is not always a happy place. The
adage about academic politics—where the fighting is fierce, because the stakes
are so low—applies with even greater ferocity wherever folks view their lot
as lowly. When that happens at a small college, life can become especially
unbearable. Quarrels occur in large universities, too, but at least one can
more easily avoid daily combat by retreating to one's research cubicle. At a
small college, one is forced to share many pathways, not just the parking lot,
with colleagues, friend and foe alike.

But wait! I do not intend this to be a downer book. I have a
countervailing story to tell. I see hope. All is not lost. I want to propose
another set of largish claims to offset the downward spirals I have tracked
above. My corollary contention is that there is at least one pocket of
activity in American academe today, whether research university or college
setting, wherein liberal arts learning persists and perpetuates. It happens to
be in my own field—political theory—and ruthless honesty prevents me
from withholding that truth. Some may see my claim as self-serving, but I
really do have a larger point to make, which is more compelling to me than
self-promotion. Once upon a time the proper custodians and purveyors of
the liberal arts would have been housed in various humanities departments—philosophy, the classics, English, religion, history, theatre—but now
that role has been assumed, in academic institutions across the country, by
political theorists.

In order to do respectable political theory today one must be broadly
educated—more so than most any other field I know. There is no single
point of entry or prevailing methodology the quick mastery of which will
allow start-up operations to commence. One cannot just carve out a small
corner, for instance, in the Hegel literature; one first needs to know Aristotle.
And then Nietzsche. And then Derrida. And the list goes on. The parameters of what count as "political theory" keep expanding, and old-guard practitioners expect the initiates to keep adding new contributions and not just
to return to already covered territory. One must know a fair bit of history.
One must have sharp analytic tendencies. One must be well versed in literature. One must have healthy empirical leanings. One must have multiple
language facilities. One must know some case law. Political theorists are
expected to be able to engage in careful textual exegesis as well as address
the topical questions of the day. They are expected to be generalists and
specialists, at home in high culture and pop culture, adept in both erudite
and diurnal matters. Today, it is taken for granted that a political theorist
must be steeped in feminist, queer, multicultural, poststructuralist,
postmodernist, postcolonial, and other contemporary debates and literatures.
The entire field has been receptive, not resistant, to these trends, while also

keeping canonical torches burning. The field has valued independent, critical, contestatory thinking but also has avoided some of the excesses of theoretical speculation characteristic of some other fields.

"Theory" plays a unique role in political theory compared to the way "theory" operates in other academic fields. Theory in the natural sciences connotes hypothesis formation. In literary criticism, it refers to contemporary approaches toward interpretation. In sociology, it refers to a field of inquiry that arose only in the early part of the twentieth century. In politics, however, theory refers to a separate and distinct field of study that dates back to preclassical Greece (*theorein*). Thus one studies not only the politics and history of the Peloponnesian War, one also reads the theoretical works of Thucydides, Plato, and Aristotle. In art history, in contrast, one studies Caravaggio's paintings as well as contemporary commentary on how to interpret Caravaggio's paintings. But there was no comparable "theorist" of Caravaggio writing as Caravaggio's contemporary whose own writings deserve separate scrutiny in the same way that Machiavelli deserves close scrutiny along with and in addition to the study of Florentine politics in his day. The point is that political theory has a long history that behooves careful and ongoing study from a contemporary vantage—and all theorists must have an expansive, not a restricted, grasp on the field as a whole. Few texts or issues fall into desuetude. Many psychology departments no longer teach Freud and few physics departments teach Galileo, but political theory feels itself obliged to continue teaching Marx. The texts keep accumulating, and the scholarship keeps growing. Yet political theorists typically avoid scholarly obscurantism by keeping worldly concerns in view.

In sum, if one wants to rehabilitate the liberal arts tradition at one's school, one should first consult the resident political theorist. That person will be able to help think through the problem, probably without being overly polemical or predictable. Political theory is the one field that necessarily fashions a bridge between the humanities and the social sciences, and many political theorists today address issues of natural science as well. Political theorists have traditionally been busybodies, meddlers, voyeurs, eavesdroppers, encyclopedists, and wayfarers who have made a point of learning what others are doing. In academe, this means that they are likely to take the trouble to find out what people in other disciplines are doing rather than accede to the fragmentation that characterizes much of scholarly life today. Moreover, political theorists have already been thinking about education as part and parcel of what they have been doing all along. The political theory canon is replete with authors who wrote explicitly on education: Plato, Confucius, Christine de Pizan, Rousseau, More, Mill, Wollstonecraft, and Dewey. Today, a good number of political theorists have written directly on educational matters: Benjamin Barber, Allan Bloom, Peter Euben, Amy Gutmann, Stephen Macedo, Martha Nussbaum, Michael Oakeshott, Alan

Ryan, and David Steiner (to name a few). As democratic theorists are wont to point out, Thomas Jefferson and the American founders thought education was crucial to the functioning of democracy, and thus one naturally and necessarily takes up the topic.

Political theory's influence sometimes spills beyond the classroom. If American academe today is producing individuals who count as "public intellectuals," chances are those persons will have a considerable background in political theory. One thinks of, among others, Benjamin Barber, Robert Bellah, William Bennett, Marshall Berman, Judith Butler, Noam Chomsky, Robert Dahl, Jean Bethke Elshtain, James Fishkin, Francis Fukuyama, William Galston, Lani Guinier, Amy Gutmann, bell hooks, Martha Nussbaum, Susan Okin, John Rawls, Richard Rorty, Michael Sandel, Michael Walzer, Cornel West, and George Will. Hannah Arendt was the leading political theorist of her generation, and her influence is still strong today. Her ability to engage many fields, periods, and literatures, to incorporate and challenge, to blend old with new, to be in and out of the game, and to be theoretical *and* political epitomizes the spirit of liberal arts. If anyone could be called *the* modern exemplar of liberal arts learning, it would be Arendt—and her lifelong association with political theory should not go unmentioned in that regard.[10]

If I sound boosterish, my tendentious talk may be due to a gnawing sense that political theory's virtues need some special championing today. For all the reasons that I see its compatibility with the liberal arts tradition, virtually the same criteria are frequently raised to discredit it within political science departments. Insufficiently wonkish or predictive or positivist, political theorists are derided for their tendency to address a political question from too many angles and to little real-world effect. Yet I might respond that political theory classes are well populated all across the country, whereas normal political science departments are losing numbers and majors. Graduate departments often fail to point out to would-be political scientists that almost half the jobs in the country are to be filled in undergraduate colleges, wherein the flash-bang, gee-whiz, number-crunching techniques of modern political science are not always celebrated with as much gusto as they might be in research circles.[11] Rather, the lingua franca of such undergraduate political science departments usually involves some working knowledge of political theory. Prestige and popularity in such venues accrue more to the person who knows her or his Aristotle and Locke than to the expert in regression analysis, formal modeling, and differential equations.

I am also not sure that my fellow political theorists, especially those situated for some time in large research departments, have fully embraced their own well-rounded liberality. Implicitly they might understand the field's default prerequisites for breadth, depth, and independence, but I am uncertain how many would openly associate those tendencies with the liberal arts tradition. Instead I detect occasional tendencies or undercover aspirations toward earnest professional standing as opposed to streetwise Socratic self-skepticism. A possible indicator of that opacity might be found in how many rising stars of the field have jumped ranks, when given the opportunity, from a small college position to a research university position. It is no surprise that a fair number of notable women theorists have enjoyed some measure of institutional mobility in recent years—if a position opens at the associate or senior rank, it may well be filled with a woman (and for good cause, I might add). But from my vantage, what that means, in effect, is that we see very few young women political theorists building lifelong careers as small college professors.[12] The ongoing attrition has become conspicuous over time.

Another indicator of widespread denial or oversight might be found in the main journal of the field, *Political Theory*. The journal has been in existence since 1973, and during the past twenty-nine years, the editorial board and advisory board members have numbered from between thirty-one to thirty-eight members. During the entire life of the journal, with all of those editorial slots coming and going, only *one* editorial member has, during the term of appointment, hailed from an American small college (the Oxford and Cambridge college affiliations are not really applicable). That person—George Kateb from Amherst College—is the subject of one of the chapters of this book. At the same time, by my quick count, more than 10 percent of the published articles appearing in this prestigious journal over the years have been written by persons who, at the time of publication, were writing from small liberal arts college posts. My political science colleagues tell me that that discrepancy between the editorial university-to-college affiliation ratio versus the authorial university-to-college affiliation ratio is statistically significant (not to mention that it also probably bears on issues of justice and representation).

Finally, I am not sure that my political theory colleagues writing from research departments are consistently mindful about the untapped potential for galvanizing an undergraduate reading audience, those students already interested in political theory and many more. Much of the published writing, even though political theory is implicitly liberal artsy, is inaccessible at the undergraduate level. When political theorists and their publishers do make a pitch for an undergraduate audience, all too often they produce anthologized textbooks that are appropriate only for large lecture courses at research universities. These edited anthologies do not fly, however, in a small liberal arts college classroom. Hence, we tend to assign "primary" source materials instead of contemporary commentary. It is true that political theory requires a great deal of preparation and background and involves high levels of abstraction and sophistication, but motivated liberal arts students are indeed capable of comprehending a great deal of material thrown their way, even before they have mastered the complete works of Hegel, Husserl, Heidegger, and Lacan. Top students, I have found, relish the chance to read the works of Hannah Arendt, and somehow her writings connect to undergraduate sensibilities without compromising the theory. Arendt's writing was both scholarly and imaginative, yet somehow, today, in much of our writing, the letter killeth the spirit. Some jazz saxophonists demonstrate tremendous technique, all sorts of scales and riffs and changes. But while you listen, duly impressed at their technical facility, you find that you just have not been tapping your toe to the music.

With some trepidation I propose the following chapters as melodies in an off key. First, I hope that they are *readable* and *interesting* to a wide undergraduate liberal arts audience. At the same time, I hope that my professional colleagues will find them engaging, for their own purposes and especially for the purposes of teaching. These pieces all, in various ways, circle back to issues of political theory and the liberal arts. My main reason for putting them forward for publication is that many of them have already been battle tested or focus grouped. Some of the chapters have been published before as separate articles, but now published together and according to the intersecting themes of political theory and the liberal arts, they reveal new angles and shadings. Some of the speeches that I delivered on various occasions, I can report without undue pomp and ostentation, actually produced tears, cheers, jeers, and even a few standing ovations. Over the years I have received numerous requests for reprints, and I suppose it makes sense to make them available to a wider audience beyond the Pomona College community. I also believe that the issues they address transcend the Pomona College context out of which they arose, so that any thoughtful reader can follow their train of presentation. I have added some explanatory notes, however, where necessary or helpful. In reading a speech, one must imagine for oneself the appropriate inflexions, phrasings, and pauses. No laugh track accompanies this book. Supply your own tomatoes.

Sometimes the connections to the theme of the book are stated and obvious, whereas other pieces are meant to be illustrative. On the whole I would like to be able to replicate the experience of classroom teaching, but that subject matter presents a moving target, one that is hard to arrest. If one tries to photograph it, the pictures turn out blank, as it were. Since we college teachers do not usually depend upon written lectures for our classroom interactions, I cannot simply publish a series of canned lecture notes. Much classroom chemistry depends on the class composition from year to year, and I am not sure how to bottle that. Videotaping is out of the question. So the occasional speeches presented here, delivered at the time for extracurricular purposes, provide an indirect peek at what goes on in a liberal arts classroom. But I do not pretend to be able to recreate the best moments of spontaneity, serendipity, laughter, and learning. The reader will just have to read *into* the works.

As someone who has published books before, I am not altogether obtuse about anticipating criticism and altering this or that in advance. But I really do not want to tinker with these chapters too much after the fact. I suppose that for the reader or reviewer who wants a sustained, book-length presentation, these pieces will provide thin or lumpy gruel. My response is that the organization of this book simply but deliberately, even perversely, pursues and exemplifies a different kind of *pedagogy*. Scholars usually are trained to beat a subject to death, so that all loose ends are fixed and tied. The systematic, exhaustive nature of such presentations typically invites (or coerces) the reader to defer to the authority of the text. I often admire such writings. Yet classroom teachers know that didactic, masterful accounts all too often preempt and thus ruin student participation in the material, especially an independent appropriation thereof. Such books can generate respect for their author but usually provoke little or no subsequent discussion. In teaching, saying less often is saying more. One plants seeds, one spins out ideas, but then to elaborate further, or too far, would be to patronize the student, which is to say, some scholarly writing presents a tacit insult to the would-be reader's intelligence, or at least showcases the author as scholar, as opposed to teacher. The following chapters may not satisfy, but they do not insult, at least not in the above respect. At best, I hope they spark additional debate, discussion, and disagreement. No self-respecting teacher wants mere concurrence.

The following chapters belong to particular times and places, and thus I want to provide a few program notes about their origins. Each has a story behind it, a few more worth telling than others. Some readers might object to such local color, and maybe the book as a whole, as overly parochial—life in a sandbox or fishbowl—but I see my task quite differently. Indeed, the larger significance of smallness; the importance of localism, regionalism, place, and context; the abiding pleasures of face-to-face encounters; the resonating virtues of institutionalized forbearance; the unspectacular ways of integrity and friendship; and the incalculable rewards of certain activities, especially education, pursued for their own sake: these themes recur throughout and provide nothing less than the stuff of this book. Many contemporary scholars argue these days for a heightened awareness of contingency, citationality, contextualization, pluralism, perspectivalism, particularism, and performativity—but they frequently continue to do so in abstract, impersonal, metatheoretical, crypto-universalist, do-as-I-say-not-as-I-do terms. I have invoked the first-person voice in many of these pieces, in contrast, in effect signaling the contingency of the account, not as a way of trying to grant privilege to an imperious subjectivity. If it grates or gets in the way, however, I apologize. I ultimately want to draw attention to the liberal arts, not to me. At the same time, by personalizing these accounts, I do mean to indicate, tip-of-the-iceberg-like, that there are numerous other individuals—a veritable legion of true-believing teachers, students, alumni, staff, and administrators—who continue to assert themselves passionately and steadfastly on behalf of liberal arts education, no matter what national educational and economic trends might come and go.

Chapter 1, "My Turn: A Great Bookish Tell-all," tells the story of my three-year stint as a Great Books instructor teaching in Stanford University's erstwhile Western Culture Program. That program constituted ground zero in the national culture wars at the time, and I was a grunt on the front lines. The program was Stanford University's attempt to instill some undergraduate liberal arts learning in the modern mega-versity, and the well-meaning efforts eventually were derailed by the debates over multiculturalism—which missed the point, I believe. That I, an upstart Ph.D. political theorist, should find myself teaching Great Books provided one of my first clues about the compatibility between political theory and the liberal arts. Indeed, four out of eight instructors in the Great Books track of Stanford's program were political theorists. Humanities professors had hired us at a time when deconstruction was all the rage in graduate literature departments. Theory in such departments—lit crit—evidently did not necessarily prepare one to teach honest-to-goodness literature. We political theorists, on the other hand, had already cut our teeth on Homer, Plato, Machiavelli, More—that is, most of the books of the course. It was an eye-opening experience in other ways. Our program was housed in the same building as Stanford's political science department. That department at the time had one (retiring) political theorist on board, and some political science faculty members were outspokenly boastful about the absence of traditional political theory in their operation. The philosophy track of the Western Culture Program had two other instructors trained in political theory, so altogether we had six instructors studying, discussing, and writing political theory as we went about our business teaching Great Books to undergraduates. Quite soon we realized that we had to conduct such activity on our collective own, since the political science department was not going to extend anything to the six of us but a cold shoulder.

One quickly learns one's place in academic pecking orders, so we shut our beaks, sealed our lips, bit our tongues, and found abundant consolation in our books, our classes, and each other. But after hearing so many national pundits discuss the Stanford Western Culture Program from afar and, worse, after hearing a few Stanford professors who had never taught in the program orate their uninformed opinions on the matter, I decided to go public with my insider's take on the program. I presented "My Turn" at the American Political Science Association meeting in August 1990 in San Francisco. The crowd was overflowing, in good part because a number of luminaries also were giving papers on the panel. As well, a buzz had already circulated about the fireworks to come. I had distributed my paper to the other panelists well in advance (big mistake), and one of them in turn drafted much of his paper in direct response to mine. I do not remember most of his rebuttal, except that he called me, in writing, a "leftist thug" and a "moral coward." Or maybe it was the other way around. Either way, I have been called worse. Since then, my paper has been cited a few times in books on education and political theory,[13] and it drew some other lingering interest. But mostly out of weariness, I left it unpublished until now. A fellow instructor in the program encouraged me to publish it, and instead we published a jointly authored piece along the same lines a few years later.[14] Still, this original version, more raw and provocative, cuts to the quick.

The piece also counted as my swan song to teaching at Stanford. I left before I had to, taking a one-year position down the coast at the University of California at Santa Cruz. Unlike Stanford in those days, Santa Cruz was a mecca for wide-ranging political theory, at both the undergraduate and graduate levels. I had the privilege of having students in common with Peter Euben, Jack Schaar, Bob Meister, David Thomas, Donna Haraway, Norman O. Brown, Hayden White, Teresa de Lauretis, and others. At the time, UC Santa Cruz still considered itself the sole member of the University of California consortium dedicated first and foremost to undergraduate teaching—but those days were waning. I spent a fair bit of time during that year with one of the founders of UC Santa Cruz, Page Smith, whose book, *Killing the Spirit*, written roughly during that period, tells about the university's changes from a liberal arts teaching place to yet another diploma mill.[15] In a similar way, I think the canon disputes at Stanford had the unintended effect of displacing the opportunities for intensive liberal arts teaching in a university setting. That may be an unfair swipe, but sometimes it is best not to mince words.

Chapter 2, "The Columbus Controversy as Confession," originated as a public talk that I delivered at Pomona College in February 1992—the quincentenary of Columbus's so-called discovery of America. By 1992, debates about multiculturalism were all the rage and raging. I was in my second year of teaching at Pomona College, and a colleague kept pressing me to give a talk in a Columbus series held that year. The dean of the college weighed in, asking me to use the occasion to introduce myself to a wider audience around the college. So I tried to connect some personal ramblings with a few political observations—and the audience seemed receptive to that kind of self-disclosing discourse.

Chapter 3, "George Kateb's Main Thing," has a checkered history. In the fall of 1992, I was back at Stanford, beginning a yearlong sabbatical at the Humanities Center, and I received an invitation to contribute to a celebratory volume, a *Festschrift*, in honor of my former Amherst College teacher, George Kateb, then newly affiliated with Princeton University. The

Festschrift would be filled with essays written by Kateb's former students, former Amherst colleagues, and other professional associates. I wrote the enclosed piece with a great deal of care and submitted it. The main editor of the volume called me and raved about it. I circulated the piece to others who knew Kateb, and I received nothing but glowing replies, one after another. Several college teachers, including Amherst professors, thanked me for giving them a "pep talk." I reveal these plaudits in order to say that I had been proud of the piece at the time I wrote it and found additional reason to extend my initial enthusiasm.

But years went by. The volume's editors had a hard time finding a press that would publish it. *Festschriften* had since fallen out of favor in publishing circles. Eventually the editors found a second-tier university press that would publish it in its entirety, but at the last moment, Princeton University Press accepted it as well. Then one day I received a call from the editor who had originally solicited my contribution. Princeton University Press had accepted the volume, he said, but with a few provisos. A few of the essays would need to be revised. But the Seery essay, he relayed, would not be acceptable in any form, it would not even be given a chance for revision. What was the problem, I asked? There was some stuttering and stammering about Princeton wanting to downplay the *festschriftlich* nature of the volume, and my piece apparently called too much attention to that genre. That explanation did not make sense to me. No one ever faulted the substance of the essay, so that it could not be tweaked and revised. I wrote a letter to the Princeton University Press editor, suggesting that to exclude the essay was to deny that an estimable point of view—that of Kateb's role as college teacher—should be given its due. In reply, I received a letter, signed by every member of the Princeton University Press editorial board, denying that their action amounted to censorship.

Readers can read that volume, now published, and judge for themselves.[16] None of the surviving essays discusses Kateb's career as a teacher at a small college and the implications of that period on his thinking. A number of the pieces are conspicuously personal and *festschriftlich*. I include the piece here, however, not to settle old scores, to open old wounds, or to embarrass the former Princeton editors or myself but to pay an insistent tribute to Kateb, precisely in keeping with the point of this book. What I had to say back then about Kateb the teacher still needs to be said, and I believe still ought to be heard.

Chapter 4, "What Teaching at Pomona College Means to Me," was originally presented as a public lecture that I gave in February 1994. Every year students in Mortar Board, the honor society at Pomona, uphold a tradition in which they vote for a professor to give a special public lecture as if it would be his or her last lecture ever given—hence, the title of the series, "Last Lecture." The stakes were high, and I am not sure I met them (nor am

I entirely sure that being asked to give a "last lecture" pays a compliment instead of revealing latent wish fulfillment). In any event, over the years, many Pomona students—and their parents—have asked for copies of the address, sometimes again calling it a much-needed "pep talk" about our small college ways.

An entire generation of political theorists has been enraptured with Jürgen Habermas's historical account of the postmedieval public sphere that is no more.[17] The space of the European salon or the coffeehouse offered the fleeting conditions, according to Habermas, for critical public discourse, eventually to give way to modern corporatist and consumerist co-optation. Yet Habermas and his American readers seem to overlook the contemporary space of the small college classroom that frequently offers a similar suspension of outside instrumentalist pressures. While sheltered from the public and nonetheless vulnerable to overriding statist or monied encroachments, the small liberal arts college classroom often conforms exceedingly well to Habermas's idealizing account of an erstwhile interactive discursive zone.

I first presented chapter 5, "Moral Perfectionism and Abortion Politics," as a conference paper in Utrecht in August 1996.[18] Immediately afterward, a Bulgarian physician approached and painfully confided that the talk addressed many of the issues that he was grappling with as someone who performs numerous abortions on a daily basis back home. Responses to the piece have continued to be dramatic, either positive or negative. Reviewers expressed great nervousness about it, with its volatile mix of politics and religion. The Los Angeles Times published an op-ed version of it,[19] which then was sent out for syndication across the country; some of the letters to the editors were laudatory, others downright nasty. An essay that grows out of classroom encounters, as this one did, can give one the confidence to take risks and to weather controversies. From experience, I knew that students did not want to talk about abortion politics without discussing, seriously and critically, metaphysics and religion—which occasionally requires that we challenge the fundamental terms of religion. I include the piece here hoping that fellow teachers might assign it to generate serious classroom discussions (I can almost guarantee that it will not be a conversation stopper).

Chapter 6, "Political Philosophy in the Twilight of an Idol," was originally an address that I delivered as the keynote speaker at a "Nietzsche and Modernity" conference sponsored by the philosophy department at the Pennsylvania State University in October 1997. The occasion was the publication of Nietzsche's Dangerous Game by Daniel W. Conway,[20] my former colleague and fellow traveler in Western Culture at Stanford University. I include the talk here, because that book expresses well (and itself enacts) a view of writing as a form of teaching. Conway attends to Nietzsche's acute sense of audience as a dance or dangerous game with one's interlocutors, images that also could serve parabolically for the risky dynamics of teaching. In fact, I await a book someday titled *Nietzsche as Teacher*.[21] My own liberal arts education as an undergraduate, doubling as an introduction to political theory, had much to do with reading Nietzsche, since Tracy Strong had an appointment at Amherst College coincidentally coinciding with my four years there.[22] Nietzsche's legacy lent itself readily to liberal arts learning: one had to read omnivorously, one had to think critically, and one struck up a respectfully testy relationship with one's mentors. I was enormously privileged to have Strong and Kateb as my undergraduate teachers, both living and breathing, walking and talking exemplars of liberal arts erudition that virtually compelled them, it seems in retrospect, to matters of political theory. Reprising and updating Socrates' cultural role, Nietzsche provided the Ur-model, and it should be no surprise that many of us branched out to take up the reading of Emerson, Weber, Heidegger, and Arendt. Conway's book is an excellent explanation of why Nietzsche's teaching methods snared so many of us. (In *Thus Spoke Zarathustra*, Nietzsche's title character encounters "inverse cripples," persons who have overdeveloped a single part of their existence while letting everything else atrophy—so that, for instance, a genius musician appears to Zarathustra as one huge ear attached to a small, thin stalk of a body.[23] One senses, in contrast, that Nietzsche would endorse a holistic approach to learning. Liberal arts education, in that regard, is more like full-body cross-training.)

Chapter 7, "Grant Wood's Political Gothic," which originally appeared in the on-line journal *Theory & Event* in January 1998,[24] was one of my forays into the field of art history. I include it here for many reasons, not the least of which is that it strikes me as the kind of cross-disciplinary research that can be best conducted, I believe, from a liberal arts college post, where poaching is permitted. My political theory background, untutored as it might be about aesthetic analysis, allowed me nonetheless to question some long-standing conventions of art history. Subsequently, I have given presentations about *American Gothic* at political theory conferences, in political science departments, at high schools, and in several college classes. Grant Wood's cunning and mischievous spirit connects with people, I have discovered, and his painting, with some prompting, generates a lot of discussion. In his own day he was closeted about many things, but he was outspoken about the virtues of the liberal arts. In his political manifesto, "Revolt Against the City," he called for a Jeffersonian resurgence of American democracy by way of new liberal arts centers across the country. The piece ends with a quote by his friend, Marvin Cone, the artist-in-residence at Coe College in its heyday. Today, Coe College is one of those teaching places facing tough times.

Chapter 8, "Do Media Studies Belong in a Liberal Arts Curriculum," originated as an address I gave at Pomona College in March 1998. Pomona College was the first college in the nation to feature a media studies major, due to the visionary efforts of the late English professor, Brian Stonehill. Brian died in 1997, and after his death some persons were starting to question (again) the propriety of such a nontraditional major in a liberal arts environment. Although I had never presented myself as any sort of media maven, I was asked to give the above talk and agreed to do so, deciding shamelessly to take the opportunity to pay a more general tribute to Brian. Haverford graduate, star teacher, prolific writer, daring administrator, and beloved colleague, Brian embodied the best in the liberal arts at a small college. We miss him. Small colleges, I want to say, are late-modern communities where individuals stand out and matter (absent fanfare). My insistence on keeping memories long and making them public here I hope will not be dismissed as a mere personal indulgence. The praise and dignity of individuals, I have come to believe, cannot be sung or effectively narrated through academic abstractions.

Chapter 9, "Unremembered Acts Remembered," was originally delivered on May 15, 1999, at Pomona College. Departing senior Pomona students voted me that year as their graduating speaker for "Class Day," an outdoor ceremony at which individual awards and honors are presented. I saw the event as an occasion to name names as a way of showcasing the kinds of accomplishments and relationships that thrive in a small college setting but fail to attract wider public regard. Were I to suppress this speech, choosing to withhold it from publication, I believe I would be complicit in upholding warped scholarly conventions of what counts as publicly important and transmissible knowledge. Yes, I may be making one kind of mistake in inviting the book-reading world to take a look at what goes on at little Pomona (and similar places), but at least I am avoiding committing other perpetual sins of oversight and omission.

Chapter 10, "Castles in the Air: An Essay on Political Foundations," first appeared in the journal *Political Theory* in the August 1999 issue.[25] Shortly after its publication, I started receiving letters and e-mails from colleagues in my field, most of whom I had never met before. The notes expressed unusual appreciation for the piece. Maybe other, more celebrated political theorists receive fan mail, but I had never received that kind of response—and I was taken aback. It was just a very different essay, many said. If true, I attribute that wayward quality to the fact that this piece grew autochthonously out of my teaching. Over the years I have developed a great love for teaching Virgil—*The Aeneid* never fails to provide a teaching highpoint for my academic year. One understands this oddity, I suspect, only by doing it. In reading and teaching Arendt for another course, I noticed that she seemed to express, late in her career, a special embrace of Virgil, and yet I could find no Arendt scholar who had ever mentioned anything about her crucial passages on Virgil. The canon dispute at Stanford had given me early exposure to the new English translation of Christine de Pizan's *City of Ladies*, and

I had been teaching that book for years in the same course in which I taught *The Aeneid*. Her Virgilian tendencies also became apparent only through teaching. I eventually put the two Virgilians together and, presto, an unconventional piece came together.

Chapter 11, "Political Theory in the Twentieth Century," first appeared as the opening chapter in a political theory anthology, *Contemporary Political Theories: A Reader and Guide*, edited by Alan Finlayson.[26] I accepted the invitation to write such a piece because the anthology, a mix of commentary and source material, was to be pitched widely to undergraduates. Once I started, however, I realized that I might have bitten off more than I could chew. Writing about political theory over an entire century, in a way appropriate for undergraduates, proved to be a challenge. Eventually I took refuge in Arendt's example, ending my chapter by taking a cue from her essay, "Understanding and Politics," where she issues a heartfelt plea that future works of political theorizing should attempt to appeal to the faculty of *imagination*.

This book closes with Chapter 12, "America Goes to College: A Manifesto of Sorts." The only piece written after the 1990s, it extends the discussion about what liberal-minded political theorists ought to be doing, a controversy fueled by Sheldon S. Wolin's recent jeremiad about the state of the profession. The chapter ends with a few definite policy recommendations, calling upon liberal arts learners to overcome their inhibitions and advocate for their cause.

In contrast, I shall close these introductory remarks on a more open-ended Arendtian note. Teachers, ever poised toward the future, have to be able to imagine possibilities that remain as yet undisclosed by the sum of worldly evidence. Thus good teaching, like Arendt's notion of good thinking, both of which attempt to fill in an existential gap between the present and the future,[27] must always remain something of a mystery to itself. Accordingly, good teaching can never be formulaic or programmatic. Sensing this, the liberal arts teacher seeks instead to educate broadly as a more auspicious way of pondering and confronting the seemingly inherent ambiguity, mystery, complexity, and chanciness of living, and living with others, at all.

1

My Turn: A Great Bookish Tell-all

I was there—a witness at the site of the most famous battleground in the civil war over the so-called "canon." I taught one of the Great Books courses full time for three years at Stanford University[1] in Stanford's infamous and now defunct Western Culture Program (the program has since been reconstituted into a new yearlong undergraduate requirement called "Cultures, Ideas, Values" [CIV]). My three years happened to coincide with the last three years of the program—1985–1988—a period, in other words, in which the program came under constant review and even became the focus of a national debate over core versus diversified curricula. From this insider's vantage, I have a story to tell. My remarks and anecdotes, I believe, can offer a new perspective on the debate, which even today remains heated and arouses strong feelings. Some of what I have to say is about the supercharged issue of race relations on American campuses and, relatedly, about the diversification issue, and I want to underscore at this outset that I profess to no great expertise in the field of race relations in America. I speak, rather, as a teacher in the classroom, one who especially during those three years had to think hard about the presentation of the canon in an increasingly multicultural setting.

My main claim is that from my on-the-ground view of the debate at Stanford, the Great Books course operated at Stanford in a very different fashion from the way it was debated, represented, and construed by the media and by the program's most outspoken critics and especially by its most

---

Presented at the American Political Science Association conference, August 31, 1990, San Francisco, CA.

outspoken defenders. In the following pages, I want to reconstruct some of the detail and texture of the course as it functioned at Stanford, and while these snapshots of the course will serve to localize the issue, I also propose that this reconsideration of the Stanford course contains a few general lessons about the current debate over education in America. But before I begin my narrative, I want to lay out my several subordinate theses in order to avoid confusion and to accommodate in advance my desire for a somewhat discursive presentation. These claims are:

1. I still want to affirm—provisionally—the value of reading and teaching the old die-hard classics even in a required setting, though I am no Straussian, nor some rearguard apologist for a declining white male military-industrial complex.

2. At Stanford, given its unique educational environment, the Great Books of Western Culture course functioned, in form and content, as a subversive course, which is the basis of my above affirmation.

3. The course was extraordinarily popular and successful according to its participants, including minority and women students. But the course operated differently for minority students at Stanford from the way it operated for majority students; more significant, the memory of the experience of this course, I submit, diverged for minority versus majority students.

4. The critics of the course criticized it for the wrong reasons, and their real agenda remained opaque, even to themselves.

5. The general move toward diversification of the curriculum, which I generally welcome, threatens, however, to crowd out a kind of education that I very much value and hate to see abandoned for the wrong reasons. The Stanford program, I concede, had to go, but I want to mourn its passing and remember its triumphs.

AN INSIDER'S GUIDE TO WESTERN CULTURE—
OR, MY STORY

Hired right out of Berkeley graduate school as a political theorist, I had no idea when I first accepted the job that this Stanford position would eventually prove to be so controversial. The job description sounded ideal: I was actually going to be paid to come in to talk about a different "great book" each week with small sections of extremely bright and energetic students, students from all over the country and from other countries as well. We would cover more than forty books in the year—from Homer and Plato to Galileo and Shakespeare to Marx and Freud. One of eight instructors, I discovered that my colleagues would be drawn from all sorts of disciplines in the humanities (Stanford professors in various fields also could volunteer to teach a section), so I would be learning as we went along. Moreover, it so happened that political theorists were highly valued in such a program, perhaps because the Great Books canon had much in common with a standard Plato-to-Nato, History of Political Thought sequence, and the result of this coincidence was that in my first year, four out of the eight instructors turned out to be political theorists—which meant that I would have disciplinary as well as interdisciplinary colleagues. Great students, interesting colleagues, no committee work—what could be better?

Teaching at the grunt level—which means that one teaches students face-to-face in a seminar situation, as opposed to blathering to a captive audience from behind a distant podium—immediately proved gratifying, for the Stanford students were extraordinarily industrious. But meanwhile the program, though historically a subject of some controversy, came under renewed and heightened attack. Minority students denounced the program as being ethnocentric at best and racist at worst. Feminists identified the canon as being sexist and phallocentric. Professional deconstructionists on the faculty claimed that the program privileged logocentric cultures, thus they recommended that popular issues and marginalized peoples be studied. In response to all of the criticism, Stanford administrators and faculty tinkered with and slightly reformed the program, now including works by Third World authors and women as well, but these reforms were then blasted by national celebrity conservatives such as Allan Bloom and then Secretary of Education William Bennett. Bloom and company charged that Stanford had pandered to the pressures of the mob and concomitantly had abandoned any claim to academic standards. Bloom and his book on such courses, *Closing of the American Mind* (as well as E. D. Hirsch's book, *Cultural Literacy*), galvanized a national debate over education in a declining America, and Stanford became a lightning rod for all sorts of charges and countercharges. The debate polarized sides, and practically everyone with an opinion jumped into the fray.[2]

Thus I found myself at the center of a national debate—a clip of one of my classes, for instance, appeared as file footage on the *NBC Nightly News with Tom Brokaw,* and friends across the country would call to ask whether I was the lackey oppressing students with Shakespeare and Dante. I went about my job, trying to put the best face on a difficult situation while letting the gods and goddesses decide the larger historical issues, but at times tensions would reach nearly the breaking point, for instance, when the Reverend Jesse Jackson came to Stanford and seemed to inspire a group of students to march around campus chanting, "Hey, hey, ho, ho, Western Culture's got to go!" Was I going to join the march or not? Did I support the proposed changes or not? What did I think about Bloom's book? Strangely, administrators and reformers did not solicit the views of instructors who would know what was actually going on in the program at the ground level, in the class-room. So, for the most part, it was pretty easy to keep quiet about my views, but inquiring minds, especially students, would sometimes ask for my opin-ions about Great Books programs, and Stanford's in particular. Still, I kept to myself.

I kept quiet in good part because I found myself—a Berkeley political theorist, no less—on the wrong side of the debate, that is, the nonprogressive or "politically incorrect" side: I found that I truly liked teaching Chaucer, Cervantes, and Wordsworth, and if pressed into answering the absurd ques-tion, "Which is more important for first year students, reading *Faust* or Alice Walker?" I ended up choosing the devil. And yet I refused to align with Bloom and Bennett, whose reasons for parading these works were vastly different from mine. The debate had gotten out of hand. I went under-ground, and I know that most of my colleagues did as well, largely because our perspectives did not fit the received political categories. I also did not know how I could convincingly reply to the charge that my position might be a rationalization of my privileged place and narrow perspective as a white male; such charges do not allow much room for counterargument. The par-ticular virtues of the course as it operated at Stanford issued from Stanford's unique context; hence, Stanford never should have been targeted as a na-tional test case. The national debate missed what was going on at Stanford. A few words about Stanford are in order, then, before I state my case.

Stanford is a peculiar place with particular needs, and its students may or may not be typical of students at other colleges and universities. The place itself is surreal. Massive stone buildings with uniform red tile roofs have been designed to give Stanford the extended look of a fake Spanish mission, with an occasional Romanesque colonnade that makes the breezeways all the more picturesque. The surrounding weather is always idyllic, sunny and yet cooled by ocean breezes. Palm trees, looking like overgrown potted houseplants, grow in strategic locations throughout the campus. People jog and bike all over the area's flat terrain. Roving bands of Hispanic and Afri-can-American laborers keep the yards well tended, and someone sees to it that the color of the flowers in the gardens is rotated on a regular basis. High-tech amenities help keep the flow of ideas flowing. Several classes are filmed and broadcast daily over a closed-circuit television network, by which they are piped into student dormitory rooms to be captured on personal VCRs and played back at one's leisure (of course). Professors can call up the library's reference catalogue on their office computers and order books by hitting the return key, and library personnel will fetch the books and deliver them directly to the busy reader, still at her or his desk. In general, Stanford drips with New World opulence, and people (especially white people) lead pretty much low-stress-level existences.

Stanford was a huge colossus, an overdetermined mega-multiversity that enjoyed a tremendous reputation, despite all. At the time, which was pre-earthquake, Stanford had surpassed Harvard in the *U.S. News and World Report* annual poll as the number one undergraduate university in the country, and droves of students applied for admission to the place. It could lure prospective students with grand and oh so lucrative visions of easy employ in neighboring Silicon Valley enterprises and other Northern California business.[3] Students attracted to Stanford traditionally came from mostly lily-white, Northern California, Waspish, nouveau riche or aspiring nouveau riche families. No blue bloods and old money here. Students were bright, but they flocked toward technical and engineering majors (good investments), which was Stanford's main area of expertise and comparative advantage. Lacking the tradition of liberal arts found at the old Eastern Ivy League universities, Stanford was really a trade school, though most of the country did not realize it. It was, and still is, more of a corporation than a college.

Stanford wanted to be more than a trade school, for it not so secretly emulated prestigious Eastern institutions (Yale Blue, Harvard Crimson, Stanford Cardinal—get it?). Several faculty members knew that the place was severely deficient in the humanities, and their expectations for transforming it were low and realistic. They merely wanted to get Stanford students to read some books before they marched off to corporate careers (though they aimed at achieving something a notch higher than cocktail-chatter proficiency). After rancorous debates, and starts and misstarts, the faculty eventually agreed to require all students to take a yearlong course in the humanities—the year was 1980. Thus the "Western Culture Program" was born. It should be emphasized that the original objectives of the course were extremely modest and, given Stanford's Silicon Valley corporate context, vaguely subversive. The leading advocate of the program was the vanguard campus radical, a Shakespeare scholar who was the person most responsible for later preventing the Reagan library from locating on Stanford grounds; the eventual program director was an eminent historian specializing in critical theory; the majority of the instructors were recruited out of Berkeley and the hills of Santa Cruz; and my political theorist colleagues were specialists in, respectively, Rousseau, Marx, and Merleau-Ponty.

One of the faculty compromises stipulated that the course not last more than a year, because engineering majors were already heavily burdened with course requirements; additional requirements would prevent a graduation in four years. What would be, then, the content of the new course, given these constraints? Hard choices would need to be made. Diverse faculty could not agree upon common themes, questions, priorities, and agenda; they could at the time, however, agree, or at least not disagree, upon authors. At the time, the names of Plato, Aristotle, Dante, Marx, and so on were ones that seemed sufficiently unobjectionable to most everyone in both the humanities and the sciences. The selection of these authors, a process that later would be called "canon formation," was hardly a concerted attempt to indoctrinate students into hegemonic practices (though I realize that authorial intentions may ultimately be beside the point). To repeat, in context, the course was intended to be subversive, at least from the humanities view of things, and it was largely staffed by those of us sympathetic to intellectual and cultural subversion. Though we never received explicit marching orders, the purposes and the ethos of the program were clear enough. Outsiders looking in had missed the point.

Allan Bloom thinks the Great Books are great because they embody and promote the higher concerns of the human "soul." In transcending the particular contexts in which they were written, in presenting answers to the "perennial" questions posed about the human condition, the Great Books attest to the best features of the West (if not to the West's greatness in general). Bloom holds out for higher truths and absolute standards, no matter how severely common opinion may discredit such projects. Cultural elitism is a dirty job, but someone has got to do it.

Once actually teaching these works, however, the lowly instructor soon realizes that the "Western tradition" consists not of a protracted pack of high-minded cultural elites (or those in effect promoting elitism) but rather encompasses an extraordinary series of cultural subversives, one right after the other, with Socrates and Jesus as the two most famous. How could this conspicuous feature be overlooked? The Stanford "canon" was filled with figures who wrote in the vernacular or popular tongue (Dante, Chaucer, Rabelais, Cervantes, Luther); with figures who turned their worlds inside out or upside down (Goethe, Hegel, Shakespeare, Galileo, Machiavelli, Darwin); with rebels, malcontents, and disaffected types (Pico, Luther, More, Rousseau, Locke, Descartes, Flaubert, Dostoyevsky); with tragedians (Homer, Sophocles, Aeschylus, Euripedes, Virgil, Goethe, Shakespeare); and with out and out cultural revolutionaries and blasphemers (Marx, Nietzsche, Freud). When Stanford initially tried to reform the canon (before throwing it out), it looked to include the voices of women and American blacks. Some feared tokenism, but actually it was an easy move to include the works of Sappho, Marie de France, Christine de Pizan, Mary Wollstonecraft, Mary Shelley, Virginia Woolf, Frederick Douglass, and Richard Wright, for these writers fit right into the Western tradition (as I have sketched it), and quite nicely.

I must say, after many hours of teaching these writers, that they work beautifully in the classroom. I saw it. Bloom is right, if for the wrong reasons. These books inspire good thinking. They inspire great papers and original ideas. They generate enthusiasm for learning and make learning—believe it or not—fun. They produce moments of magic in the classroom (and not every text does—let us not get carried away with lit crit theory). Why? My own pet theory is that at a place like Stanford, such works, advertised under the august banner of Greatness, perpetrated a certain irony upon the student mind, which prompted him or her toward greater participation in the texts of the course. Students arrived in the class suspecting that Stanford's sole required course would attempt to indoctrinate them into the cultural status quo, and instead these students became exposed to an onslaught of rebels and subversives. And even those authors in the course who were not outwardly subversive generally wrote in a way that disrupted dogmatic appropriations of their texts and instead invited or virtually required intensive exegesis. For students, all of this indirection was eventually liberating, if for a while bewildering—for their own readerly participation and even the possibility of harsh disputation were seemingly encouraged by the texts of the course, and thus they found themselves reassessing their initial anti-establishmentarian suspicions and even questioning their own anti-intellectual tendencies (a strain that runs deep, even among the best students). Was the course rebellious or not? Was it conservative or not? Sometimes they felt jerked around, but mostly the result was an engaging intellectual experience—because they had to judge works on their own, to judge the course on their own, to think on their own. Assumptions were called into question. Deeply personal issues were raised. Lives were occasionally transformed—or at least careers and career concerns interrupted for the time being.

If anything, the "Great Books" teach—explicitly and subtextually—moral and cultural self-questioning. Socrates is the star of such courses.[4] Bloom may be right in his suggestion that these books prompt us to examine our lives deeply, but he is wrong to suggest that Socrates (and even Plato) provides hard and fast "answers" to "perennial" questions. The beauty of these texts— the reason they stay alive year after year, the reason they continue to produce original student papers and brand new insights year after year—is precisely because they keep such *questioning* alive and going. Each generation can find something new in them, but this is because these texts do not present themselves as doctrinaire (whereas some texts, in certain contexts, do). Students feel the excitement of finding something for the first time, though a book may be centuries old, and they also know that they are not being force-fed a hidden agenda. They know when a professor or an author is being tendentious or rhetorical, and any successful teacher of "Great Books" soon learns to minimize his or her classroom presence, to get out of the way and let these books perform their spells upon students' minds.

Inside the confines of the classroom, teaching was marvelous at Stanford. Class morale was extremely high, and student ratings reflected this morale. Stanford students who were taking the course approved of it in overwhelming numbers (though not unanimously, of course); the statistics across the board were incredible, even though the course was a required one.[5] And based upon what I saw with my very own eyes and heard with my very own ears, the vast majority of minority students also loved the class while they were taking it. My very top students included African Americans, Latin Americans, Native Americans, and Asian Americans—no affirmative action needed here, thank-you. And women were superbly engaged with the course. Sure, in theory, I could be systematically fooled about many things, insensitive or oblivious or self-denying, but about this matter of student approval, minorities and women included, I am quite confident.

If what I am saying is true—that the Great Books of Western Culture Program at Stanford was by any measure an extraordinary success—then how did it get branded as elitist, racist, sexist, and so forth? If the course actually taught cultural subversion, how did it get construed as culturally conservative, if not reactionary? Why did minority students in particular evidently change their minds about the course as their Stanford careers progressed? Why did this curricular issue become the most explosive racial issue on campus, whereas there simply was not the same mobilization on, for instance, the issue of apartheid in South Africa or, closer to campus, there just was little opposition when the Stanford Business School built a big new building on land that encroached on sacred Native American grounds that had been protected in the original school charter?[6]

My encapsulated answer to this cluster of questions: the secret to the on-the-ground success of the Great Books program at Stanford was that these texts characteristically taught students to read between the lines, to distinguish between letter and spirit, to affect a critical distance that still implicates—in a word, they taught irony—and they generated enthusiasm for those who appreciated the opportunity to be ironical about texts, and to be ironical about being at Stanford in general.[7] Cultural subversion at a place like Stanford could be promoted only by way of irony, and one hoped that the cognitive dissonance that irony affords might inspire personal self-examination. (We instructors used to say that we hoped that every future Stanford engineer would read *Faust* in order to have a robust sense of modern tragedy.) The Western tradition is largely an ironic one; and the books in that tradition do not teach, after all, reverence for themselves but rather invite readers to question their books and eventually, one hopes, to question themselves and their world at large.

Here is the controversy: the Great Books did not work quite the same way for many minority students as they did for run-of-the-mill white Stanford students—though that difference was not one of abilities or levels of performance (for a great number of minority students fared splendidly in the program).[8] To repeat my claim, the Great Books taught, if anything, personal and cultural self-questioning. This critical stance was the lifeblood of such courses, but I imagine that many minority students had already "questioned themselves" before they came to Stanford and thus were perhaps less appreciative, over the long haul, of this particular aspect of the course. The white student—certainly not all but a great many—could more easily approach the possibility of entering the halls of sunny Stanford with straightforward, unadulterated pride; the function of the Western Culture Program, then, was to subject that pride to questioning. Though our secret hope was to instill a questioning attitude about what it meant to be at Stanford, what I think happened for most white students is that, once graduated from this freshman course in cultural subversion, such students did not, on the whole, become culture critics or revolutionaries but rather would look back upon their year-long experience as yet another test successfully completed, another triumph, another occasion for pride, and thus they looked back upon the course with an odd fondness, as a trying yet formative experience in their brilliant young careers.

What I suspect happened with many minority students is that they were more ambivalent, and not simply proud, about their initial decision to attend traditionally white Stanford.[9] Such students probably had subjected themselves to severe second-guessing when they initially agonized over the decision of whether to attend a formerly lily-white school built by railroad money and coolie labor. In the back of their minds, they may well have felt themselves vulnerable to the reproach that they had "sold out" to white corporate America, abandoning somehow their ethnic or class heritage. Such profound ambivalence, the feeling of being torn between past and future, is felt perhaps by any marginalized individual who attempts to forge a new future from within a dominant culture, but that tension was compounded by the extreme whiteness of sunny Stanford. Then, the minority student experienced a triple whammy upon entering Stanford, I imagine. She was already hypersensitive to personal and ethnic criticisms of her even being at Stanford, and then she soon discovered that the subtext to the one course required of her at Stanford beseeched her to "question herself and her moral foundations." At first, she enjoyed the whole classroom experience of criticizing these books and all that they outwardly represent—such an exercise was therapeutic, it allowed her to let off steam. It also was a bit like doing penance, absolving her for her decision to have come to Stanford (though it hardly allayed her anxieties). She excelled in such a course, for she was already versed in cultural self-criticism and motivated to continue (and her simpatico instructors exhorted her onward); but, by the same token, the course was not anything all that new for her, and she didn't hold on to the memory of it as being particularly distinctive or formative, as her white peers did. As she moved on in years at Stanford, becoming implicated herself in all that was Stanfordish, and overheard all of the standard lines about the course (racist, sexist, elitist), she was forced to repudiate the course. Though she may have inwardly remembered that once upon a time she actually enjoyed such a course, the marketplace criticism would now prove overwhelming, and thus she felt a strong need to fend off the hurtful charge that she might have once participated joyfully in an allegedly racist course. Besides, she might still feel a few pangs of guilt about being at Stanford (and for still enjoying it!). She was in no position to respond that the course was *not* inherently racist by design (are calculus classes that do not teach theorems by recent black mathematicians inherently racist by design?). By her senior year, she would sign a petition calling for the removal of the Western Culture requirement—in a successful act of psychological demonology—just before she went off, and deservedly so, to Yale Law School.

The national debate missed all of these social-psychological-situational undercurrents. The debate became politicized, Left versus Right. Bloom's insistence that the Western Great Books can be read not simply as a way of provoking self-examination but rather as an extended series of self-help manuals providing wisdom and truthful, universalistic answers to perennial questions provided the Stanford critics with a straw case that was easy to dismiss. Bloom failed to convince skeptics, and he mucked it up for the rest of us, putting us on the defensive and making it more difficult to get a fair hearing. The course was about irony, and Bloom was anything but ironical, but that was not the main reason for the program's demise; Bloom's contribution was only a distraction, a sideshow, a nuisance.

The Stanford faculty reformers lost nerve and went overboard, deconstructing everything about the program along the way. Their occasional silliness played right into Bloom's hands. One time it was proposed, for instance, that we begin to study "artifacts" systematically instead of books to embrace nonliterate peoples—in theory, this sounded promising, but then we instructors, the people who had to carry out such proposals, had to contemplate actually plunking a rock down on the seminar table and generating meaningful discussion.

What I fear is that the alternative course now essentially teaches affirmation, not criticism, even while it adopts an outwardly deflationary stance toward mainstream Western culture. Above all, it is celebratory of political pluralism, ethnic diversity, and cosmopolitan Otherness, but it is not, and by design cannot be, radically self-critical. What instructor would dare invite students to bash ethnic literatures in the same scathing ways that the Western tradition from Socrates to Christ to Marx and Nietzsche invites radical self-bashing? In short, I fear that the new course—or like courses and course curricula—good intentions to promote global awareness notwithstanding, no longer teaches *irony*. Hence, the new course may look more cosmopolitan, but "by design" it is actually less subversive (in context). It will be easier now for a student to look forward, qualm free, to engineering or law school, or to wear his or her ethnic or gender identity proudly as he or she walks into, say, the nearby Stanford shopping mall. (Stanford owns a large shopping mall right next door to the campus—so close, in fact, that it is sometimes hard to distinguish between the two). Whatever the particular virtues of the new course, I am troubled that an entire pedagogical approach, an entire trope, has gone by the wayside.

My own feeling is that a required Great Books program is not for everyone nor every college, nor should anyone pretend that an exclusive diet of Great Books will somehow lift educational standards across America, restoring discipline and civility and revitalizing the economy along the way. I do not think that these books contain panhuman lessons, nor do I think that they should necessarily be given priority in the general curriculum, and certainly not exclusivity. After following and participating in the many debates about "canon formation," I do think it is right and necessary to shake up the traditional reading lists, to awaken teachers from dogmatic slumbers and to lift generational blinders, and I find this trend on American campuses invigorating. We have expanded our perspectives, we have encouraged new and diverse ideas, we are reading new books, and we are respecting and listening carefully to once-excluded voices. It is an exciting time in academe to be reading, thinking, discovering, and challenging. Looking over the new Stanford CIV syllabi, I am envious of the people who have a chance to read and teach all of these non-Western books, and I do not for a minute think that the current crop of Stanford students will be deprived of a fine education.[10] (A hostile part of me is secretly thrilled that a bunch of white, upper-middle-class Stanford students are being required to read about exploited and neglected peoples; the new program is clearly a campaign to indoctrinate students into openness and liberality.) I am even a strong supporter of promoting curricular diversity through affirmative hiring practices, though I do not think that the best arguments for this action are always put forward (and as white male trash myself, I find myself a potential loser).[11]

Yet having made all of these admissions, confessions, and concessions, and knowing that I am making myself vulnerable to the all-too-easy reproach that I am clinging to a dead, white man's world, I will declare that I am still a supporter of the Great Books of Western Culture Program as it operated at Stanford. In fact, I deeply lament that the "Homer to Holocaust" trajectory of Western Books will no longer be emphasized as such at Stanford. What is taught at the textual level in a course is not always the same as what is taught at a subtextual level—and I am contending that the subtext to the Western Culture Program was not an oblique endorsement of the powers that be, and I am suggesting that the subtext of courses aiming to expand diversity may be other than it seems. I am willing to consider that this current generation of students may need more affirmation than self-critique, that historical forces are such that individual students need some remedial reassurance before deeply critical thinking may proceed, a pat on the back to say, "Hey, it's *okay* to be at Stanford." Maybe we are so culturally war-torn that multicultural and gender affirmation must be shoved to the forefront now, but I will go out on a limb and say that in the long run, I do not think that that approach will generate any great transformation in cultural affairs, and not much brilliantly original thinking, and finally, *very* few revolutionaries. Stanford now teaches cultural assimilation—openly and shamelessly, that is. Do not expect many cultural firebrands to be graduating from there soon.

To collect this train of thought: the particular character of the Stanford debate grew out of unique and contrived circumstances. The debate intensified, because artificial time constraints were imposed upon the Stanford curriculum. We were forced to agonize over the relative merits of Western versus non-Western texts, because the four-year engineering major was deemed sacred at Stanford, and thus we had but a year to work with. Reasonable people should never have been asked to decide between Dante and Confucius. The easy solution would be to avoid such debates, to sidestep such monumental cultural judgments. One option would be simply to assign *more books*, to expand the humanities curriculum (imposing constraints on engineering majors if need be), to require that students be exposed to a heavy dose of Western and non-Western texts, more of everything. Another option would be to abolish all core requirements, to return by default to an interest-driven, marketplace, liberal curriculum. Let 100 flowers bloom, and if some busy bees are too busy to read, so be it. Emile and Sophie should do what they want; none of that "forcing them to be free" paternalism. (An incidental benefit of the second option, by the way, is that self-selecting elective courses tend to produce higher student approval ratings; professors can preach to the already converted.) Of these two "solutions," I tend to favor the latter, if only because it has been my experience that requiring (Anglo) students to read, say, the Koran does not generate the hoped-for tolerance and understanding of Islamic peoples but rather all too often produces a knee-jerk chauvinism, a reactionary embrace of "Western" values. Still, I am not completely happy with the prospect of decentralizing all curricular operations, for such a move tends to undermine as well the above-described situational possibilities for self-referential irony.[12] One signs up for a course on, say, Narratives of Genital Mutilation in Somalia, and one gets in return pretty much what one expected. Everyone is happy, student and teacher are mutually and self-congratulatory, yet the course material usually is not subject to internal review as an integral, if a tacit, term of the course itself. In contrast, when one is required to study Marx or Nietzsche, one really has to examine and call into question the cultural conditions that make it possible, here and now, to study Marx and Nietzsche at all—which makes it more difficult to walk by those Hispanic and African-American gardeners as one scurries to class.

I am not entirely happy with the prevalent trend toward the complete liberalization of the curriculum, a trend that seems to be a correlate of diversification. I have a few nagging problems with the liberal model as applied to academe (here comes political theory). Though the Stanford Western Culture Program is dead and gone, and I see no chance for revival,

I would like to give a better sense of what went on in those small classrooms, what the course was about, and what I, for one, liked about it, though it was *required*. These vignettes will help build my case not against diversification in the general curriculum but rather against a liberalism that diffuses and eventually eliminates radical self-critique.

The Stanford Western Culture courses were designed especially as reading and discussion courses—goals certainly not exclusive to Western culture courses, but which I mention to help characterize the particular ethos of the Stanford program. We insisted upon reading primary source material, even after the distinction between primary and secondary writing had been thoroughly challenged by contemporary scholars who seemed to believe that their own critical commentary successfully obscured that distinction, as illustrated in their own near-literary prose. In practice, the distinction was pretty easy to respect, and the point of respecting it, even if ontologically untenable, was to convey to the student the need to rely upon his or her own faculties, to think, read, interpret, and judge for himself or herself. The students were forced to confront and plow through these texts largely by themselves, and the subliminal message was that they ought not rely upon external voices, secondhand reports, and ready-made authority figures who would do the thinking and reading for them. The point of *that* lesson, in turn, was not to instill an undue skepticism about human interdependence or to foster (male) autonomy but to convey the point that it was possible, indeed, enjoyable, to trust themselves, to become active readers of books rather than passive consumers of info-tainment.

Again, I must say that in practice this strategy worked well. Students read. We would, however, discourage them from reading the encyclopedia, crib notes, or secondary material when they were tussling with a text for the first time. We wanted their own naive but genuine readings. Although at first this practice would seem as if we were trying to draw blood from stones, soon enough students would discover that they *did* have ideas to contribute—and that became exciting. And we instructors studiously avoided lecturing about works and kept reminding ourselves about the need to refrain from lecturing, which sometimes required superhuman efforts at self-restraint on our parts. (We had all been to graduate school, after all.) Students picked up on these cues, namely, that they *could* read and think on their own, that they could and must participate in their own education, and that we would refuse to patronize them. (In contrast, the common academic practice of listing long bibliographies of "recommended reading" on course syllabi sends out the message: "There is more to this topic than you can possibly know [whereas I, the professor, know much]"—which serves little educational purpose than to make the student dependent upon the professor and to discredit in advance the possibility that a student can have anything new under the sun to say.) The virtues of the teacher are not always the same as the virtues of the

scholar, and we instructors in the program would continually remind ourselves that our mission in the classroom was not to show off how much we
knew but to encourage student participation—and the two often are at odds.
There were, of course, educational costs to such a strategy: the privileging of
text over historical context, a consequence of forsaking secondary sources
and lecture modes of presentation, would tend to make these works seem
disembodied, abstracted from their class, racial, and gender origins, and one's
historical sense would sometimes become fragmented if not skewed, but the
need to put student participation front and center in the program outweighed
these costs, we decided.

For similar reasons, we wanted this reading course to be populated by full
books, not selective snippets and cropped passages. Again, the point was to
throw the full burden of reading and interpretation upon the student and
emphasize the experience of reading and interpreting—whereas a survey of
snippets would serve one better on the game show *Jeopardy* or in a game of
Trivial Pursuit, but we wanted more than mere exposure to names, dates, and
places. This desire for student participation through readerly interpretation
probably was the reason the course tended toward works of imaginative
literature, as opposed to didactic works of analytic philosophy, history, sociology, and so forth. The course was largely a course in fiction (I have read
Nietzsche, so I know that this term is loaded), and thus some of those
professors who have a more social scientific or historical perspective upon
the Western tradition took exception with our overview and saw our presentation as limited or tendentious. But in practice, in the classroom, in the
trenches, the rule of thumb that students find fiction more accessible (non-
threatening, enlivening, fun, whatever), eliciting their active response more
often than nonfiction, is hard to ignore.

Moreover, the course was a seminar course, dedicated to discussion. We
insisted that a section be limited to sixteen or seventeen students—which
meant that Stanford had to commit to this labor-intensive policy, costly
especially since instructors were required to have Ph.D.s. The small scale was
meant to foster intimacy, conditions conducive to general participation.
Students became well acquainted with each other. Meeting for twelve hours
a week, in close confines, meant that one had to listen to and confront
others' views. In practice, these books routinely provoked a wide variety of
views. Throw Plato into a room of Stanford students and you are not going
to get sixteen similar reads—unless they first read the encyclopedia entry or
Bloom's essay. A seminar setting is a great way to prompt undergraduates to
learn to live with multiplicity, diversity, contestability, and ambiguity. (And
my own feeling is that Plato actually prompts this result more effectively
than reading Lao Tzu or Luce Irigaray, but I will not push that preference.)
With so many rival interpretations on the table, we soon learned that the

point was not to revere these books but simply to find some way to understand them and their seemingly protean ways.

Yet I cannot account for my appreciation of the Western Culture Great Books course at Stanford simply on the basis of these formal attributes—that the course was self-critical, participatory, readerly, interpretive, diverse, and open-ended. Many courses can teach the virtues of "critical thinking," and such lessons need not be confined to the West. Moreover, even within the bounds of Western literature, the Stanford course was quite limited and could never pass as an adequate survey of all things Western. The reasons I happened to enjoy the Stanford course, though, even in its limited, selective scope, did pertain to the content of the course. It did have an agenda of sorts. What did these books teach?

THE EPIC TRADITION

The Great Books course at Stanford was, to a great extent, a sustained survey of the epic tradition of heroic travelers in Western literature. This wandering theme was dominant among the texts of the course, and it provided an interesting hook to implicate the student reader: the notion of a linear plot, held together mainly from the perspective of a single protagonist, the individual wayfarer, invited the student to see a similar trajectory between the plotline and the experience of reading (this parallelism between poetry and pilgrimage sometimes is referred to as narrativity, sometimes as temporality). As the hero experiences various trials and tribulations, so goes the act of reading for the reader. Read one after another, these stories cumulatively suggested how the self is constructed in Western thought, and after reading so many individual odysseys and autobiographies, one gained a sweeping sense of how or why Western individualism developed as it did.

But an important aspect of the course was that it demonstrated that these stories indeed constitute a more or less continuous tradition. One became able to follow the intertextual references and allusions between and among the books and to appreciate the plays and variations upon the overall epic theme: from Homer to Plato to Virgil to Augustine to Dante to Christine de Pizan to Goethe to Descartes to Cervantes to Dostoyevsky to Nietzsche to Richard Wright. Note Virgil's reversal of the Homeric progression; watch Dante follow Virgil; ponder Nietzsche's parody of *Faust*. Against the greater backdrop of the notion of Western epic, Christian eschatology took on a new light, and then one could examine the works of Chaucer, Rabelais, Luther, and Goethe distinctly as commentaries upon the Christian narrative.

It is true that when a teacher puts a particular spin on a group of books, something else is lost or distorted. The above grouping of books into a story about the Western epic probably places undue emphasis on the individual (and by implication, the individual reader). Such a course needed an outside perspective upon itself, and to this end a dose of, say, Confucianism was called for.[13] But I also might note that these Western texts characteristically undermined themselves should they ever seem to be inviting straight identification and strict emulation. The moral exemplars in these texts usually were ambivalent about their projects; their stories usually called attention to the act of reading and the need for interpretation; and this epic tradition tended to announce itself as a tradition of fiction, at once epic and mock epic. Could Plato really be advocating the rule of philosopher-kings? Did Virgil really want to endorse Aeneas' brutality at the end? How could Goethe be offering a tragedy that also is a mock redemption? How were we to "follow" poor old Don Quixote's example, especially when he renounces his own quest at the very end of this strange book? Was not Zarathustra, fishing up in the hills, an odd teacher of virtue indeed? Was Emma Bovary a heroine or an anti-heroine?

Furthermore, this extended story about Western individualism, if that is what it was finally, was not, in the end, a triumphant tale. After a year of reading these texts and the progression they suggested, students were tempted to write term papers on "the rise and fall of Western coherence." About a third of the way into the course, Thomas Aquinas presented himself as the great scholastic unifier, the world made complete sense, faith and reason, past, present, and future were all reconciled, and the pagan and Christian worlds became one; Dante then extended this mind-expanding universe into the afterlife and collapsed the distinctions between temporal and eternal, sacred and secular, and art and life. Thereafter, the unity of the medieval world came crashing apart, and John Donne told his lament, and Shakespeare scandalized. But then the course picked up momentum in its successive efforts to decenter the Western self: Copernicus, Darwin, and Freud. By the end of the course, one had been exposed to almost all of the names in Nietzsche's *Genealogy of Morals*, and one could begin to appreciate Nietzsche's jokes. The course at its end announced its own denouement, and then it dropped the student off a moral cliff, providing no pat or summary answers and forcing departing students to fend for themselves thereafter.

A second prominent motif attended the theme of the wandering individual: death, by way of an imaginative excursion into a fictive underworld. These travelers, almost to a person, found it necessary at some critical point in their careers to descend into an underworld in order to gain moral insight into their affairs in the world above. If anything, this descent motif—which I have elsewhere called the Orphic-epic tradition—unified the cluster of books covered in the Great Books course at Stanford. Whereas many modern writers—Heidegger, Foucault, Derrida, and Richard Rorty—have contended that the Western tradition from Plato onward is a tradition of metaphysics, of transcendental yearnings, of rationalist impulses, of heavenward glances, the Stanford course presented a much different view of Western thought (it may be that the above modern writers overlooked the Western literary tradition and paid too much attention to religico-philosophical texts). Redemption was never the goal in descending downward. Rather, one belabored death in order to gain some insight into one's earthly attachments. Yet this whole exercise of imagining a world of the dead was conducted with such poetic good cheer! When Don Quixote, for instance, stumbles into the Cave of Montesinos (in a down-to-earth parody of our classical heroes' descents), falls asleep, and dreams the hellish thought that Dulcinea may be a disenchanted peasant girl after all, and we as readers begin to realize that the poor dolt has a deep psyche that knows he has been romanticizing the thought of Dulcinea all along, we then catch ourselves distinguishing between this fictive character's "real" versus "apparent" selves; after all that, we laugh. Not only do epic heroes renew themselves, reaffirm their worldly projects, as a result of descending downward, so too as readers do we find ourselves participating reflexively in the text, now reaffirming our project of reading after reading about death. A little work of fiction, we discover, can help withstand the defeatism that death might otherwise counsel. And to think we in the West have an entire tradition of writers, readers, and characters all confronting each other in the context of a fictive world of death, an extended community of dead poets speaking to one another beyond the grave by dropping creative references to Orpheus, all in service of celebrating the activity of reading little works of fiction, though all the while everyone involved in this protracted conspiracy knows that we all are subject to a literal death![14] Students were duly impressed.

When faced with the criticism, then, that the course was filled with "dead white boys," I had to cringe with the sense that the opponents who issued this charge did not realize how very profound their criticism was. Yet they did not give these dead white boys credit for acknowledging their own limitations (which was sometimes a needed lesson at Stanford, for some undergraduates and even many professors viewed themselves as walking immortals). The Stanford course was an elaborate meditation upon death; it grappled with the meaning of all attachments, all interpersonal ties in the face of death; it struggled with the meaning of conducting any mission, or reading any book, or taking any college course, or debating any curriculum, in view of human finitude. Far from effecting a tragic response to those open-ended issues, the course, by implication, affirmed the value of pursuing those issues, asking those questions, and trying to build those communities with the dead. Again Socrates led by example, for he was the person who knew that he knew nothing and was poignantly aware of his own mortality (he had been Delphicly reminded), and yet he persisted in striking up dialogues with other featherless bipeds around him. In light of self-confessed radical ignorance and in view of death, such activity was hardly rational, and we could make little sense of Socrates' activity by referring to some grand metaphysical scheme of things. We were tempted to believe, rather, that Socrates was led onward by his own sense of irony.

Another charge leveled against the course was that it systematically privileged a male point of view. The writers were male. The epic heroes were mostly male. Their individualizing tendencies probably had something to do with maleness. Their conquests were all too often brutally macho. The Orpheus tale repeatedly marginalized the female. Even the concern with death probably issued from a male anxiety.

Sadly, it was true that the course was far from equal opportunity in its selection of authors and themes. The male perspective was privileged, no doubt about it. That privileging, however, did not preclude a variety of contemporary feminist interactions with these texts. Depending upon the instructor and the class, the course could easily become preoccupied with "gender" concerns (read: the role of women). There was plenty to talk about. First, the course was full of women characters (though many of these women were abused, neglected, and trivialized): Utnapishtim's wife, Eurydice, Helen, Eve, Sarah, Antigone, Briseis, Clytemnestra, Cassandra, Camilla, Electra, Plato's philosophers, Aristotle's near-slaves, Lysistrata, Sappho, Dido, Monika, Isolde, Heloise, Marie de France, Christine and all her ladies, the wife of Bath, Beatrice, Gretchen, Emma Bovary, Mary Shelley, Mary Wollstonecraft, Mrs. Ramsay, Lily Briscoe, Dulcinea, Machiavelli's Fortune, Ophelia, Cordelia and her sisters, Dora. These texts presented opportunities to discuss all sorts of gender-related issues, which were hard to ignore, since were were reading them in a late-twentieth-century context. Certain questions jumped out, and certain silences were conspicuous by their absence. Does Western patriarchy stem from the Judaic notion of a male godhead? Why did Abraham not consult Sarah before he went off to kill Isaac? Why does Homer often shift to the perspective of women? What role do Aeschylus' furies play in establishment of the law court? Was Plato, given his misogynist culture, really serious in proposing that women be philosopher-guardians? How could Aristotle, as a student of Plato, dismiss women so? Why were so many people through the ages threatened by Sappho's success? Do the Tristan stories suggest that romantic love itself is but a story? Did Augustine have a problem with his mother, or what? Why were Dante and Goethe attempting to re-write Christianity from the perspective of a "woman-principle"? What, after all, was Chaucer's view of his vampy wife of Bath figure? Why was Shakespeare constantly confusing gender roles? How could Rousseau espouse equality and artfully explain the difference between natural and civil inequality and then be so blind to women's plight? Was Emma Bovary a female Faust, or a female Quixote, or both? What, if anything, did Mary Shelley's modern Prometheus, her tale of postpartum monstrosity, have to do with her dead mother's politics? Was Virginia Woolf advocating, through the character of Lily Briscoe, a stance of moral androgyny? How would Nietzsche, who claimed that Socrates married only to prove the point that philosophers do not marry, respond to Christine de Pizan's assertion that Xanthippe had to be a pretty incredible woman to put up with that penurious mouthpiece (who did not even consult her before he drank the hemlock)?

I can report that the instructors at Stanford placed great importance on feminist issues (more so than on class or race concerns, it so happened), though there was much debate about what the best strategy would be for treating these issues. Some felt that the Western Culture Program presented far too many depressing, debilitating images of women, and that it was necessary as an antidote to include stories of strong women characters, such as Medea, and to include as positive role models important but slighted women writers. Others felt that the course was a study in patriarchy, pure and simple, the study of which, however, could be militarily justified as a tactic "to know the enemy." Still others felt that feminist demands were particularly Western, that Aristotle and Rousseau, for instance, might have been misogynists, but that later claims for women were nonetheless based upon some of their original notions, hence, reading them was necessary and unavoidable. Yet another group felt that a feminist stance could be maintained even while the content of the course might not convey that everything is right in Western culture gender relations. Some of us (myself included) were skeptical of the revisionist attempt to search for excluded women's voices from within the Western tradition, the point of which seemed to be to convey that women have been transhistorically capable of writing and thinking (a pathetic, low self-esteem premise, to my mind). I felt it was more impressive to let the sad historical record speak for itself, to show itself as an overwhelmingly male-dominated enterprise for thousands of years. By the end of the course, we need not feel crushed by that history but rather would get a sense of how very much is left to be done. If anything, modernist writers, those writers toward the end of the course—Machiavelli, Rousseau, Marx, Nietzsche, Freud—taught that Western culture is all of a piece and, as such, is contingent, a construct, a long story, the product of reading books and of reading practices and thus could be changed and changed radically. Such a call *should* leave one disturbed about the course that one has just completed, and that is well and good. It is not true that the immediate subject matter of a course (or the authors of the books of a course) has to agree with or reflect one's own politics or one's hopes for the politics that the course might prompt. What I feared about revisionist feminist history was that at Stanford it served an undergraduate complacency (even among women) about feminist issues: Let us just throw in a few women authors and get on with our business, let us feel basically good about being included (co-opted) in the Western world.

All of what I have said so far presents a rambling case for offering a Western-Culture-Epic-Tradition-Great-Books course somewhere in the curriculum, but I want to make a stronger claim: I still want to defend the Stanford course as a required one (though I am not advocating a revival, because I no longer see such a course as feasible). Again, I appreciated the particular virtues of the course—as required—in the peculiar context of Stanford, but I also want to propose that this Stanford experience indicates the occasional need for required courses elsewhere, and thus I want to extract a few general lessons from this ordeal (and I qualify my remarks, because I am unsure how far the Stanford model can in fact apply—that remains an empirical, ad hoc matter finally).

First, the course functioned well as a required course. A required course can fail, of course; the requirement can provoke resentment and frustration, for no one wants to be held captive, force-fed wisdom and knowledge. But when required courses work, it usually is because certain things can be done more effectively in such a setting, certain themes can emerge under those auspices. The mere notion of a requirement can put a certain slant upon course material, raising the stakes and thus concentrating minds.

At Stanford, a school that had been actively attempting to diversify its studentry and had been relatively successful in that effort in recent years, the Western Culture requirement served as a social laboratory and quite possibly as an exercise in social engineering. Students from a variety of backgrounds would be thrown into these small rooms together. The result would be a hodgepodge, a mix of pre-majors, races, and parental income levels. They would be defined by no prior interest, no self-selecting criteria.[15] The only things they would necessarily have in common were the facts that they were at Stanford and that they all were reading Plato.

A required setting is superb for discussing "taboo" topics. It was an eye-opener, for believers and nonbelievers alike, to be able to read and discuss Judaic and Christian religious texts together in a nonreligious setting. (Reading the Koran after reading the Hebrew and Christian bibles helps give one a sense of Islam's claim to succession, which would be an argument for a required comparative religious studies course at particular universities.) Reading Marx in such a setting allowed for a semi-disinterested perspective on the material (which was hard to achieve at Stanford, where the resident Hoover Institute maintains a $48 million endowment with the express purpose "to expose the evils of the doctrines of Karl Marx"). Since everyone had been thrown in the same boat together, the situation was as if everyone could let down his or her societal guard a bit, as if everyone were on a vacation cruise, taking a step out of time and away from business as usual. Things were said that might never be said otherwise. Women would confront men, and vice versa. Races would clash, or try to come to terms. Students on financial aid might point out what it means to work or to go deeply in debt in order to gain an education. Gay and lesbian students might talk about what it means to live in a compulsory heterosexual society. This *required* seminar setting created a supercharged classroom atmosphere. Students paid attention to each other. They *talked*. They would sometimes end these lengthy two-hour sessions perspiring, or laughing.

The notion of "Western Culture" originally was meant, I believe, not as a particularly telling rubric but as a diffusely comprehensive term. (We now view it differently, as Western *as opposed to* non-Western; the original name was more unwitting than arrogant.) The intent of this term, as the title given to Stanford's sole required undergraduate course, was to imply that the course material somehow related to you, the individual student (and it was on these grounds that some minority students, women, gay students, and others later insisted that the course did not in fact include or relate to them). As asserted above, students in the course soon discovered that the course subjected them, albeit through a soft-sell strategy, to constant self-scrutiny and examination. It turned out to be a *critique* of Western Culture, and the point of *requiring* that critique was that students were to take this critique to heart—this was no time or place to distance oneself intellectually. For the duration of the course, as I have contended, this exercise worked extremely well, and students took these books seriously and read with avidity. As Stanford students, they were apt to identify with these pilgrims and heroes (it probably had something to do with having traveled to the West Coast). I was sympathetic to the person of non-European extraction who said in retrospect that he or she just could not "get into" reading Shakespeare, because Shakespeare's plays were set in white settings, and those white concerns just did not connect to nonwhite lives. But in my view of the point and purpose of the Stanford course, I read this appeal at Stanford as a roundabout bid for exemption from radical self-critique. The course held up a moral mirror to its participants, and all were implicated, as a function of being at Stanford, like it or not. Critics had seized upon the terminology of the title, but that was a red herring. If the course had been celebrating Western culture, and such was the privileged status of these privileged works, then I could see that the outside criticism would apply. But these were works that for the most part damned and scolded their privileged readers—in effect, for being at Stanford—and claiming exemption on the grounds of ethnicity or gender was a dodge. The course, even with its cavalier title, was required in order to suggest that all students now at Stanford participate in a similar history in the sense that they all share the present, and that all are implicated, as a function of being associated with Stanford. That premise of basic inclusion was a performative claim, issued to make the charges stick, and it was somewhat beside the point whether that particular version of history was distorted or narrow or elaborately mythological. Whatever the terminology, the point was to implicate *all* students as a setup for self-examination. We tried. Maybe we missed the mark. Maybe we went too far.

In contrast, self-selecting theme courses and the new, more cosmopolitan Stanford course drop this good intention of trying to effect comprehensive self-critique. Theme or disciplinary or boutique courses just do not in practice attract as diverse a group of students as required courses can and do, and the sales contract between teacher and student implicit in elective courses makes it harder to present a course whose material ends up teaching lessons substantively contrary to advertised expectations (I suppose you could offer courses in "cultural guilt-tripping," but I would expect that only students predisposed to that agenda would enroll). The new CIV course, although required, drops the presumption that the course material necessarily applies to all students (the title is pluralistic), hence, if self-critique is its aim, I think it might be easier for some students to dismiss or bracket particular charges. The Western course succeeded, because it started out on the premise that this material applies to you (or so you should think) and to everyone in the class. The problem in looking to other cultures as a noble experiment in global anthropology, or as a domestic lesson in pluralism, is that such an act already announces lines of division, the Other *as* Other. Latin American novels contain important, creative critiques of Western imperialism, but I also think the *act* of reading a Latin American novel *as* a Latin American novel can undercut the force of the criticism. I fear that Stanford students generally will not read themselves into the story line. They will be all too conscious that they are reading a non-Western work as a sampler. If the point of the new course is to present new information, histories, voices as voices, samplings, and exotica, then that is well and fine, but it should be noted that such a course presents another kind of education altogether, not just an expanded, better version of the old, and I grant that such lessons may be needed at this juncture in our history and may be just as valuable, everything considered, as the old ways. But I am worried, frankly, about what the change indicates, and I do not want the old ways to fall into desuetude for the wrong reasons.

But back to the Stanford course (my nostalgia creeps into this chapter). An outsider might think that this little social experiment was bound to explode and fly apart, that diverse students would yell at each other for a while but eventually would stop interacting, or that many students would become bored or distracted, along for the ride only. But that portent simply did not happen, time and again (and I have taught enough classes elsewhere that did not click to know the difference). The Stanford course consistently produced wonderful classroom experiences, intense discussions, extremely ambitious papers, and—perhaps most important—integrative, cohesive classes, which coalesced out of all of these different peoples. I can report that I witnessed many friendships, unexpected friendships, formed in front of my own eyes. And classes, even after a quarter's worth of animosity, would plead that they all be allowed to stick together from one quarter to another (they

would present petitions to the registrar). Students would meet outside of the
class, and they would hold mini-reunions in successive years after the course.
Seniors would stop by my office and allege—and there was no gainful motive
to do so—that they never had a class match their first-year Great Books'
experience. Call me crazy (friends can testify that I normally walk around
jaded), but these little classes were the closest thing I have seen to successful
liberal communities in practice—little educational utopias (to borrow Hannah
Arendt's notion). J. S. Mill would be ecstatic. They worked. Firsthand I saw
them work twenty-seven times in my time at Stanford, and I could take little
or no credit, as much as I would like to receive plaudits. Colleagues reported
similar findings, students said the same, and comparative student statistics
reflected this approval. My experience is that not every seminar (very few in
fact) creates a special chemistry among class members. It is a crapshoot
determining in advance whether a particular political theory theme course
will produce memorable moments, but the Stanford course presented a sure
bet, class after class, year after year. I lost interest only when teaching became too predictable.

Why were these classes so successful? I am not entirely sure. Maybe the
love and death themes enticed, or maybe the taboo subjects titillated, maybe
Stanford students were naturally drawn to adventures in epic self-criticism
because they were narcissistic masochists. But I am tempted to supply another answer. The required setting, the initially forced liberalism, created in
turn a true liberal community, a genuinely educational experience, that
countered the false liberalism and instrumentalism of the rest of the Stanford
multiversity. In practice, the course had no real agenda behind it—the concept of "Western Culture" was too diffuse to provide a defining focus, and
these books were too elusive to pin down one theme or central purpose.
Even the notion of an "epic tradition" was not evident as an overarching
theme until well into the course, and certainly this theme did not provide
a sufficient reason to get excited about the course. It became clear that the
point of the course was not to confirm or deny the "greatness" of these Great
Books. Rather, it was simply to read and to try to make sense of these books.
That minimalist project somehow created a community of readers, of ques-
tioners, of Socratic seekers. Students drew together in this common project
and discovered that it was enjoyable to think together. These texts, I have
claimed, were such that they fostered reading communities.

The classic problem of liberalism and liberal theory is that liberalism begs
questions of justification. Plain and simple, it is not clear why anyone *should*
respect and listen to and interact with others, especially others different from
oneself. Mill enjoyed modeling society after a debating club, but that inclina-
tion toward lively discussion probably was related to his odd upbringing and
peculiar psychobiography, and thus it is hard to generalize beyond his personal
example. These Stanford reading communities initially were fashioned under

contrived circumstances—they were required of every student—but once underway (and you will just have to grant me this observation and trust it for the sake of argument), they picked up their own momentum and provided, as it were, their own internal justification. Students were very aware that such a course would probably not help them in their chosen majors, and they knew that most of these books would serve them ill in landing a job after graduation. There was, in short, no good reason to get so involved with these texts, to read so damn much, to get so involved with their peers, and yet they did. Given the fact (or the students' pervasive and well-founded sense) that a Stanford diploma provided a ticket to almost any coveted position in America, reading great books at Stanford was a great waste of time—and they knew it.

Reading for the sake of reading is useless, according to most definitions of usefulness. The ethos of the program was thus wayward and perverse, given the normal calculatingly careerist, eagerly upwardly mobile, get-ahead climate at Stanford. In such a setting, it does not make sense to pay extremely close attention to texts, to pore over them like a medieval monk. One probably will not be recognized or rewarded for one's reading efforts, nor should one pretend that reading produces marketable skills, and that this is what one is doing when one reads. Maybe this eudaimonaic aspect of the Stanford course was what made it so attractive: one read for no (consequentialist) purpose whatsoever. The course thus liberated students for a time each week from the pressures of having to be concerned about eventually producing tangible returns on their parents' educational dollar. It conformed to a fairy-tale notion they might have once entertained, a distant rumor they once overheard, namely, that the college years were supposed to be a time for the free pursuit of ideas, a period of repose, a reverie of the mind, a preparation for life, before all of the hustle and bustle sets in. Yes, this was a truly subversive course. We got away with something. It was fun, anyway, while it lasted.

In the context of Stanford, the Great Books course functioned as a sub rosa, off-the-shelf covert operation. This guerilla movement succeeded in the limited space of the classroom, because there it provided a critical commentary upon, a living foil to, the failed liberalism of the larger Stanford community. But then everyone who participated in the canon debates sensed that the debate was really about America at large, and that Stanford was really an idealized America, or an America in microcosm. (A Stanford student was elected Miss America the year after I left.) Maybe there are, finally, certain lessons or insights about the lingering "Johnny can't read" problem to be drawn from the Stanford episode.

Another bit of reportage: the most vocal group to oppose the Western Culture Program at Stanford was the Black Student Union. Mightily displeased students decried the Western Culture Program as being inherently racist, and they wanted no more of it. Requiring students to read Plato may not seem on its face an act of racism, they argued, but racism is a despicable villain, willing to assume many underhanded disguises. They were probably right. Stanford had privileged Plato over non-Western, non-European literatures without paying sufficient attention to issues of race. To be sure, there could still be good reasons to require and give a privileged place to Plato, and maybe one would want to conclude finally that race should have little bearing on the selection of such material (and that it might be possible to exempt race as a criteria without lapsing into a false neutrality), but first the issue must be put on the table, and Stanford had yet to do that.

The Black Student Union wanted more, however, than curricular soul searching. They wanted black authors to be included in the yearlong syllabus (Augustine did not count). In what was meant as a good-faith response to their demands, we in the Western Culture Program assigned Frantz Fanon's *The Wretched of the Earth* as the first book, with the explicit aim of broaching issues of minority identity. In the book, Fanon declares that a worldwide process of "colonization" and Europe's history of imperialism have robbed ethnic persons of their native traditions. "Negroes" (his term for all Third World peoples) do not know who they are, but for Fanon, the possibility of returning to one's roots in an attempt to recover a lost identity no longer exists. There is no going back. Nor is assimilation of any form an acceptable option. Fanon's solution, for which the book is famous, is to advocate the violent overthrow of the whole of Western Culture (i.e., white, European culture). After such a violent revolution, Third World peoples can begin anew to construct positive, independent forms of identity in which all vestigial tendencies toward imperialism and cultural domination might eventually wither away.

The Black Student Union at Stanford requested that Fanon not be taught, that he would not count as an acceptable black author. They claimed that Fanon was an extremist and thus was not representative, and they specified that they wanted an *American* black author instead.[16] (For a while we experimented with African slave narratives, such as *Equiano's Travels*, but that was a complete bust in the classroom, and Equiano turned out to be an embarrassment to everyone, a black Candide.) Eventually we suggested Richard Wright or Toni Morrison, and those choices were fine (though they did not save the program).

I found this incident revealing: Richard Wright, not Frantz Fanon. My read of the incident was that Fanon's rejection of Western culture went too far in that direction for some Stanford blacks; Wright was safer, even if he had been a member of the American Communist Party for a time. What is more, he was American, a potential role model, a positive role model, the story of an exceptional black person. His story, *Black Boy*, was really an ambivalent (if in the end a victorious) odyssey of personal liberation: how can one be oppositional *and* successful in America and yet retain one's ethnic sensibility? My take on the affair was that Wright's story was indeed closer to the experience of many Stanford blacks: how can one be black and yet justify (especially to oneself) one's presence at Stanford? The answer, in short, was that one could earn one's ethnic credentials by publicly denouncing the Western Culture Program, even though it was a program that now included Richard Wright. But no way could one read Fanon and believe that arguing about course curricula at Stanford would profoundly advance the general cause of one's race.

When all of us had graduated from textual tokenism, the next step was to propose an entirely new track dedicated to addressing directly issues of race, imperialism, colonization, and exclusion. Yet instead of developing a truly cosmopolitan course, the designers came up with a course called "Europe and the Americas" (the precursors were called "Western Culture: An Alternative View," "Conflict and Change," and "Western Culture and its Victims"). Such a course would examine European exploitation of Native Americans, Africans in America, Andean and Mexican cultures, and Latin America generally. I read this move similarly: the original call for cosmopolitanism in the curriculum was not really a call for cosmopolitanism and global awareness but rather concealed (barely) a plea for a forum on America itself, on American pluralism, on American liberalism, on American society. Something was indeed amiss at Stanford, but it was just an index of a larger frustration, a greater begging of the questions of our politics and of our educational goals.

The Stanford Western Culture course had been singled out at Stanford as a test case for diversification in the academy, and that test case soon became one for such trends nationwide. The critics won, and the course is dead. But as an insider to the program, I saw, I knew, that the charges were misplaced, that they did not ring true to the actual course I taught in the setting where I taught it. But how could I, at the time, with so many people personally, anxiously invested in this particular issue, come forth and contend publicly that the criticism was not really critical of Stanford at all but rather was symptomatic of a deeply ambivalent desire for inclusion into everything that Stanford represents? As a member of an underground of teachers whose pedagogy depends upon indirection, I decided that it was best to lay low and wait for another time to speak forth.

What interests me in retrospect about this whole affair is that the usual lines of political opposition became blurred during the debate—and it was hard to find the right language in time to discuss these new tensions. For instance, some extremely talented, ambitious, and enterprising Stanford minority seniors, already driving BMWs and now admitted to the top business, law, and medical schools in the country, would call us lowly, exploited but dedicated teachers of Great Books—who had been recruited out of Berkeley and the hills of Santa Cruz and who once upon a time had taught these students Marx, Nietzsche, and Freud—these students would now call *us* the neoconservatives of the world—and all they had to do was wave Bloom's book in our faces in order to convince themselves of that (they bought the hard-cover edition). They were reassured with their new goals in life, but we instructors felt betrayed. And the faculty critics of the program, the professional deconstructors, were not the fanatical leftist academics that they rhetorically hoped themselves to be and that their conservative critics as well hoped them to be. Rather, we instructors in the Stanford program read their campus agenda not as subversive but as an attempt to legitimize their boutique courses by having them included in and officially recognized as part of a new, expanded Stanford canon.

The practical issues of inclusion are complex, and the needs of many minority students attempting to enter the halls of great, white universities are probably not the same as the needs of most middle-class white students, and if we as educators are serious about educating the students who come or who are brought to us, then we must think long and hard about how and whether course material relates to all students—treating them simply as "individuals" ignores many important issues. We must also think about who is doing the educating, whether one's person does and/or should bear upon the presentation. But these concerns, very real concerns, informed the Stanford debate only as rhetoric and embroidery; the actual situation had little to do with the greater debate about curricular diversification, and distinctions could have been drawn. The course did not deserve the anger that was directed toward it. My worry was that its merits would be run over roughshod, and that the move toward complete diversification in all nooks and crannies of the academy was tending to entail the sacrifice of a certain kind of educational experience, one in which the student, as an active party to the proceedings, suspends his or her instrumentalist concerns for a spell. One reads for no apparent purpose, and under such precious, ivory tower conditions, the prerequisite demand for affirming ethnic or gender identities can play little or no part (if such identities are affirmed as an indirect, unintended consequence of a course, then that is great, but not as the point and purpose from the outset of every course). My own ulterior motive in promoting such quaint educational ideals—please do not respond that mine is yet another defense of white male impersonality—is that I think they offered the best chance, at a place like Stanford, for getting a foot in the door to introduce cultural self-criticism, participation, and community among students—rickety goals that are sometimes overlooked in the rush toward diversity. I refuse as yet to yield to the contention that such goals, educational and political, are a white male luxury, and if a luxury they be, then I want to find ways of extending that luxury to nonwhites and marginalized women.[17] Diversifying the university is desperately needed and long overdue, but I do not want the virtues of inclusion simply to be presumed along the way.

More, my insupportable but firm sense is that the academy must be in good part buffered from the pressures of the marketplace in order to function freely on its own terms—as vulnerable as that notion is to the charge that such a policy ensures stagnation and the loss of external accountability. Of course, I believe that university officials and educators may respond to outside exigencies for which they have chosen to take responsibility, and that we academics must always subject to internal review the delicate issues of town-gown relations; but we also must remember, whatever our politics and our grander institutional visions, that for the student, as an educational strategy for his or her sake, the question "Why should I study?" is one that *should* remain provocatively unanswered at the college level. Or to put it in trickle-down terms: If Johnny can not or will not read across the country, that national malaise may well be related to the fact that Johnny has been told in so many words that the reason he *should* read is to get ahead, to get a job, to reap the benefits, to feel good about himself—and little Johnny already knows better, and his instinct is that American education has been debased somewhere along the way and is no longer worthy of his best efforts.

2

The Columbus
Controversy
as Confession

S everal months ago I was approached by a colleague of mine serving on
the esteemed public affairs committee and was asked to give a Blue
Room lunch series talk on Columbus,[1] and so here I am. But I must tell
you that I was, and still am, more than a little unsure about giving such a
talk. First, I don't know much about Columbus, I haven't read the spate of
books that have come out on Columbus, frankly I am no Columbus expert,
and I'm unclear about my status as a speaker, about my right to say much of
anything on the whole Columbus controversy. Besides, the topic in this year,
1992, is loaded, full of controversy and dangerous pitfalls, and it would be
easy to offend many people and almost impossible to please everyone. Nonetheless, I am here, and I can see that an audience has indeed gathered, so
I must go ahead with this talk. My friend on the public affairs committee
tried to allay some of my anxieties by telling me that this talk would afford
an opportunity for others to get to know me, so I've decided to take that
mission seriously and literally, and somehow I'm going to talk about Christopher Columbus and John Seery in the same talk. (Those of you who may
want to leave at this point, please feel free.)

A good part of my reservation about speaking here on this topic is
that I am a white male—I am not a person of color, and to the extent
that the debate over Columbus is a debate about contemporary America
and in particular about America as a multiracial society, then I cannot

---

Talk delivered at Pomona College, February 18, 1992.

speak experientially from the vantage of the silenced, the victimized, the outcast in America. Oh, I suppose I could try to present myself to you nonetheless as a man of the people. Or I could try to dazzle you with a postmodernist theoretical apparatus that would challenge the existential primacy of racial, ethnic, and gendered perspectives; but all of those strategic moves are too clever at this point. I can't fool you, I am a white male. If this Columbus issue tends to divide us into conqueror and conquered, colonist or native, then I am the oppressor, plain and simple. Before I get on with my talk, then, I want to admit that stance, I know that I'll be marginalizing the Other, my words will be unduly self-centering and self-indulgent, I'll be privileging my point of view, so I want to issue this disclaimer in advance—1992 is probably not the year in which white males should enjoy a forum such as this one, and yet here I stand.

I was politely encouraged to change the title that I originally proposed for this talk—namely, White Boy Speaks. In lieu of that theme, I have chosen to speak on the idea of confession. Hence, I am, to be sure, a bit pretentiously modeling this talk after St. Augustine and Rousseau, both of whom tied the act of autobiographical confession to issues of politics, and I will attempt to do something similar today (I want to say at this point, forgive me for I know not what I am doing). The act of confession, for those of you who have never publicly flagellated yourself, is a strange act—it is at once self-denigrating and self-aggrandizing, both intensely private and exhibitionist, a mix of humility and arrogance, an act which focuses relentlessly and agonizingly on the self, all the while of which one imagines oneself to be both depraved and yet somehow exemplary. Freud might have said that confession is a time in which the ego tries to engage the id and superego in dialogue. Michel Foucault might have said that confession is deliberate self-surveillance, a witting search for, a desire to subject oneself to, internalized mechanisms of discipline and control and guilt.

It strikes me that much of 1992, many talks in this quincentenary year, will be cast in the confessional mode, and that may be well and good and therapeutic and revealing. We as a nation will be discovering and admitting the dark secrets and sins of our past; some of us may ask for atonement of sorts, others not, defiantly not. What amazes me about the whole affair is that it has taken 500 years for this issue to be addressed in a public way. Let us be clear about what is at stake in the Columbus controversy: it is nothing less than the meaning of America as a nation. The stakes are high. The Columbus controversy is not just an antiquarian dispute among academic historians, nor is it just a matter to relegate to the distant past. We don't know how to portray Columbus in our elementary textbooks: "In 1492 Columbus sailed the ocean blue"—that line just won't work anymore. We don't know what to teach our children, we don't know what to tell each other and ourselves about our pasts. The Columbus event, the story of this guy inadvertently bumping into the Bahamas, thinking or hoping that he was near China or else the islands off India, calling those darkish peoples he encountered India Indians (they all look alike), and then proclaiming that he had discovered this new world, an act which would bring both gold and glory to Christendom—this story has reached a mythic, murky, legendary status in our collective memory. It has become an origin story for our nation, to be narrated alongside other origin stories with slightly different registers over the founding and meaning of America. America as a concept, as a story, has always been a site of contestation for European storytellers. America was the Promised Land, the New Jerusalem, where Puritans—and later Mormons and others—could imagine themselves as the legatees of ancient Hebraic prophesy. It was also a return to the garden, a wild untamed place, where Lockeans could mix their labor with land and produce property, now imagining the appropriation of property as a sacred act, divinely ordained, protected and justified. For many Europeans, America as this New World represented the superiority of Western, and particularly Christian, ways (whether Catholic or Puritan). It held the promise of heaven on earth, a land of milk and honey; the religiosity to this story put a nice spin on mercantile, trade, and gold-and-silver mining activities. No matter that much of Christianity up to that point had taught poverty, that you couldn't serve God and mammon at the same time. In this New World, Americans would have it all. Redemption was at hand, was palpable, was real.

Now we have a bunch of naysayers trying to subvert this fairy-tale-ish story, this grand national mythology, these not so seamlessly interlocking stories of wealth, religion, and racism. Columbus stands at the intersection of these stories, and much will depend on how we view him. America is once again up for grabs, a site of contestation. Some people today want to retain the upbeat, triumphant story. Who cares, they say, if Columbus was a hapless explorer, a terrible governor, a brutal slave trader, an ignominious schmuck after all? He was brave, he was faithful, he was daring, he was an entrepreneur. Some of these Columbus admirers want to repress or at least dismiss the new information coming out about Columbus. The past is past, they say, let's let bygones be bygones; in any event, what can you do about it? I think that that attitude—viewing the past as truly past—will only continue the repression, maybe even the oppression, that has gone on in America for 500 years.

Those who have examined the record report that it's pretty clear that Columbus was a murderous slimeball, and it's hard today to see him embodying foundational heroic qualities except in some primitive Virgilian sense. The question, then, is what do you do when you discover that your past is murderous, and that you are implicated, or at least you enjoy, by extension, the bounty from murderous expropriations?

One answer in the available literature is that you must simply grow up and harden your heart to the realities of national realpolitik. If we listen to some of the best minds on political foundings, we will discover that almost every great national foundation story has been soaked in blood. We hear that in Thomas Hobbes, who in a sense tells us to leave behind our violent past and to attend rationally and soberly to the civil order in which we now find ourselves. Or we might listen to René Girard at Stanford, who tells us in a brilliant pyrotechnic display of structuralist erudition that every nation is founded on an act of violent scapegoating, a primal episode in which the perpetrators try to sacralize their act of violence, reinterpreting it and re-describing it as heroic and necessary.[2] Greatness is always tainted, always compromised, always murderous—that's precisely why greatness is great, don't be naive—such minds inform us.

In more popular form, there are people who will advise you in so many words not to contest the main Columbus story because America today is working, more or less. Nabobs of multiracial negativism should try to assimi-late like other good Americans instead of belaboring their ethnic differences. This is the melting pot, after all, so melt. Get with the program. Don't try to recover a lost identity, because to be in America, to be an American, is to participate in a great experiment, namely, an experiment of trying to live peaceably with and alongside of diverse peoples, all of whom have come from somewhere else (except the natives, of course, but they are on reservations).

But I am here today to tell you that the myth of the white American melting pot is maybe mistaken. Here I can speak from experience. I hail originally from Middle America; I'm about as American as you can get. I was born and raised in the heartland, Iowa, where corn is king and pigs outnum-ber humans 5 to 1 (in the movie *Field of Dreams* there is a line, "Is this heaven?" and Kevin Costner replies, "No, it's Iowa"). My parents both grew up on farms; mine was the first generation to leave the farm and to be college educated. I was the first in my family as well to leave the Midwest; I was the first to become landless in my native state, having witnessed the family farms broken up and sold to corporate bidders for the price of beads and trinkets. I'm from Cedar Rapids, Iowa, the home of Quaker Oats (a company that proves that breakfast cereals can be religious and nonviolent). Cedar Rapids is a place where smells of feedlots and corn processing plants fill the air if the wind blows the wrong way, and often it does (the city motto is Cedar Rapids, city of five seasons—but the city joke is that it is Cedar Rapids, city of five smells). I grew up so "American" that it's embarrassing. A few years ago my hometown replaced Peoria, Illinois, as the city that advertisers use for na-tional test marketing purposes, so now the correct phrase is, "Will it play in Cedar Rapids?" The national news media for many years has been dominated by one consulting firm that operates out of a suburb of Cedar Rapids—the major trends in national news reporting are largely created by this one firm. And one trucking firm in my hometown transports most of the steel across America. And once upon a time (before the deindustrialization of America)

Cedar Rapidians built all of the heavy cranes and street sweepers for America. A cousin of mine operated the largest crane towering over this crane manufacturing plant. My hometown is where Grant Wood grew up, the artist of the "American Gothic"—and I swear that the couple in that picture looks just like, the spitting image of, a bunch of my relatives, pitchforks and all. I could go on and on.

But I can report the Midwest isn't populated by well-adjusted, all-American, salt-of-the-earth type individuals. Rather, it was founded and is still characterized by pocket communities that have persisted throughout numerous generations. These pocket communities are still intact, and they hardly teach their individual members to assimilate and integrate into an amorphous mainstream. Furthermore, these pocket communities are at war, subtly and sometimes openly, with one another. The Midwest looks like a quilt of communitarian experiments, a bunch of sectarian landlocked immigrants who for many, many generations retained their ethnic and religious identities and enforced them through strict internal codes (and because most people were white, these internal codes were probably stricter and more severe for purposes of differentiation than the codes that you find in coastal, multiracial cities). My mother came from nine generations of pureblood Norwegian Americans, and my father came from five generations of pureblood Irish Americans. Her family was staunchly Lutheran, his was devoutly Catholic. Somehow my Norwegian Lutheran mother, Mildred Jean Knudsvig, and my Irish Catholic father, Francis Thomas Seery, broke with their ranks and started dating each other, over the angry objections of their respective family clans. What brought them together? They both came from large farm families; she had four brothers and one sister, he had four sisters and one brother. Both aspired to attend college, both had an opportunity at one point to attend college, and both had these aspirations dashed and the opportunities lost. My mother had won the state high school Latin contest—the study of Latin in those days still meant respectability, and she desperately yearned for respectability, since she felt great pangs of humiliation from being the daughter of an unsuccessful Lutheran alcoholic farmer father (as a little kid I always asked why my grandfather's shoes curled up in the end—no one would tell me that he had lost his toes due to frostbite after having fallen down drunk in the snow and then falling asleep). My father, his forearms thick and strong from carrying buckets of corn, became the most highly touted high school baseball pitcher in the state. Baseball and sports became for him an allegory of redemption of sorts—he evidently suffered from certain male anxieties—he stood only 5' 7", and always thought his name Francis, while saintly, was also sissy. Anyway, their college hopes—she through Latin, he through sports—were dashed when the war broke out, and they had to stay home to help on their family farms. But on weekends they would leave the damn family farms, which now represented their life's confinement, and they would venture into the big city—Cedar Rapids—where they would attend big band dances. But an Irish-Catholic dancing with a Norwegian-Lutheran—it was unheard of, unthinkable, scandalous. But they had Latin in common—hers was academic, his was religious; you see, perhaps more than anyone, Christopher Columbus, that instigator of cross-cultural contact in the name of the Latin Church, was responsible for bringing my parents together. My father was impressed because my mother could actually understand what the priests were saying in Mass, and she no doubt was impressed with his strong fatherly maleness. Besides, they both hated the farms, they both had frustrated dreams. Over the objections of their families, they married, and they honeymooned on a Caribbean island once utilized by Columbus—Cuba (though Columbus never knew that Cuba was an island). The Catholic and male and farm tendencies in the marriage produced a large family—five kids, five overachieving kids, five kids who would be taught sports, who would be taught languages, who would be taught music. My mother would read constantly to us, and I remember her running around the house always conjugating Latin verbs. Here was a woman who spent a good many years of her life changing baby diapers, and muttering Latin while changing diapers was about the only thing that kept her sane. As Flaubert writes in *Madame Bovary* about the upbringing of Charles Bovary: "His mother always kept him near her, she cut out cardboard pictures for him, told him tales, entertained him with monologues full of melancholy gaiety, chatting and fondling in endless baby-talk. In her life's isolation she transferred on the child's head all her scattered, broken little vanities."[3]

Alas, this Seery family was not to live happily ever after. Religious tensions surfaced, old family ghosts appeared. Sibling rivalries grew fierce between the blue-eyeds and the brown-eyeds in the family. As the kids excelled, these parents, especially my mother, became very jealous of their successes. She was ambivalent about her new family now, which held her further captive. She blamed the Catholic religion for so many children. He was now unsuccessful in business, mainly because he went into partnership with less-motivated, and semi-corrupt Catholic relatives who, she felt, gave too much money to the Church. Family relations became more than strained, they were awful. Religion became the main source of controversy. My mother kept us out of Catholic schools, unlike all of my other Irish relatives, but my father saw to it that we would attend catechism classes. The sexist division of labor in those days required, however, that my mother be the person to drive us to these classes whose theological lessons she increasingly despised (for me, the Protestant Reformation was not a sixteenth-century phenomenon). My memories are of a mother crying as she reluctantly drove us to catechism classes, where we would learn about Hell and damnation. Talk about a double-bind and a double dose of guilt! These kids grew up eventually hating their mother, fearing their father, hating religion, hating business, and in the contemporary psychobabble jargon we would call such a family "dysfunctional."

We kids developed a coping strategy by achieving success on the outside and forsaking family life altogether. It was awful at home, and we would seek support and sociability with others. What made me who I am—and I don't claim that this narrative is particularly interesting or unique, nor am I suggesting that it holds profound parabolic implications—is that I became my father's and mother's son, replicating their coping strategy, seeking relief in the hidden diversity of Midwestern life.

First, I befriended a good number of Jewish kids my age. They seemed to have a distanced perspective on Christianity, and they could relate to my guilt. Jews in the Midwest, you say? Of course. From the 1860s onward a fair number of Jewish immigrants settled in Iowa, and many postwar Jews evidently didn't want to resettle in coastal Jewish ghettoes and chose the Midwest instead. I remember that several of the parents of my friends still had their identification numbers tattooed on their arms.

My closest friends in this postwar period, besides several Jewish kids, happened to be a German kid named Schmidt and the son of a transplanted Japanese family named Owara. Here we were: myself, a Jew, a Jap, and a German innocently playing G. I. Joe together. I learned how to use chopsticks at a very early age. I took German classes in high school, because German instruction was excellent in my school—in good part because Cedar Rapids was right next door to the Amana Colonies, where half of the population to this day still speak their original German dialect (the Amana Colonies were formed in the mid-1800s by a group of Germans—the Society of True Inspirationalists—who believed that the Lutheran Church had become too worldly, and they founded a commune of true believers which eventually became prosperous and which later would be inspired to manufacture refrigerators and air conditioners—that's where Amana refrigerators and so forth are still made). There was also an Amish community nearby, and a Dutch community as well. As I kid I had a pair of wooden shoes from Pella, Iowa.

The largest Czech community outside of Czechoslovakia happened to be in Cedar Rapids. I grew up eating a Czech pastry called kolaches, and not until I landed in Berkeley in grad school did I think that the word *bohemian* referred to an eccentric character type rather than an East European ethnicity. These "bohemies," as we called them in my hometown, were great musicians, especially in jazz. I received excellent musical instruction in the public schools; in fact, I remember visiting Prague before the Gorbachev era, and in a little jazz bar I told a scared Czech group that I hailed from Cedar Rapids, and the whole group broke out in tears. There were also sizable Armenian, Hungarian, Danish, Swedish, French, Greek, and Italian groups in my town. The oldest Islamic mosque built in North America, the Mother Mosque of America, is located in Cedar Rapids, founded in 1934 by Arab immigrants attracted to an Islamic community that first settled in the city in the 1880s. And there was a notable African-American community. In my own passion for sports, I ventured into the "black" neighborhood and year after year became one of two white boys in all-black basketball leagues. And I grew up playing saxophone in bands, yes, many big bands, that were disproportionately black according to Midwest norms (I now have several Czech and black friends from my hometown who are professional musicians in L. A.).

Now my personal relation to Native Americans is more checkered. I grew up speaking, surrounded by Indian names and didn't even know them as such—Decorah, Haiwaitha, Poweshiek, Keokuk, Wapsipinican, Oskaloosa, Wappello, Maquoketa, Mesquakie—and Iowa (which is a Frenchified pronunciation of an ancient Indian name). The famous fifth season of my city of five seasons was a period called Indian Summer. Cedar Rapids was located fairly close to an Indian reservation, and as a kid if you wanted a headdress made of real feathers, it was readily available.

But who wanted to play the part of Indians? We watched those spaghetti westerns and wanted to shoot up the Injuns. One of the happiest days of my childhood was when I received the Roy Rogers autographed model gun and holster set for Christmas. Years later, after an uncle passed away, I inherited a real Remington six shooter that had been in the family for generations. (By the way, Michael Rogin at Berkeley claims that cold war middle Americans such as Ronald Reagan simply transferred their wild western aggressive fantasies from Indians to Communists—red Indian, red Communist, get it, you shoot them both, because both were a threat to white American property ownership.[4]) I learned several years ago that my middle name, Evan, came from the Norwegian side of my family, from a guy named Evan Tinderholt, whose claim to fame was that he helped found Fort Atkinson in Iowa, which was the only fort ever built by the U. S. government to protect Indians from other Indians. The U. S. government had forced the Winnebago tribe to resettle from what is now Wisconsin to some neutral hunting territory in western Iowa, but this move encroached on the territory of the Sioux and the Sac and the Fox tribes, so the Winnebagos feared for their lives and needed protection. Later, Fort Atkinson soldiers would force the Winnebagos into Minnesota, to make room for more white settlers (and yes, it is a sad fact that the Winnebago motor home is named after this reluctantly mobile tribe, and those motor homes are indeed manufactured in western Iowa).

I also remember, since we're on this Columbus discovery theme, that many of the arguments between my father and mother were over his desire to join a Catholic men's club named the Knights of Columbus. Well, I left the Midwest, applying to a school in the East that I had never visited, Amherst College, and upon arrival I learned that the school totem, the mascot, the founding father, was Lord Jeffrey Amherst, who had been a British officer whose sole claim to fame was that he ingeniously laced a bunch of blankets with smallpox before distributing them to thankful Indians, and this act earned him much glory and gratitude, and they eventually named a college after him. Eventually I ended up teaching at Stanford, a place where the architecture is fake Spanish missionary, a place that was built with railroad money extracted from coolie labor, a place that features a very odd museum displaying the bizarre Indian artifacts personally collected by Leland Stanford Jr., a place where they changed the totemic name from the Stanford Indians to the Stanford Cardinal, a place where, during my tenure there, the Stanford Business School built a big new building on sacred Native American territory that had been protected in the original school charter. Well, I then left Stanford to become a banana slug, then a Jumbo elephant, and now I'm happy to be a chicken of sorts.[5]

As for the Midwest, I visit regularly, but I don't like going back. The class divisions, the ethnic and religious hostilities, the repressions, still rage on. Entire cities there stand in need of therapy. Entire lives are lived in clouds of confusion. The place really could explode one day.

But I go back to see my parents. I have forgiven them, they have forgiven me, I have forgiven myself for the guilt over hating your parents. But it's not easy. I am still ambivalent, I still must work through my past, though it's now less of a preoccupation and a burden. But it is hard to feel profoundly ambivalent toward your parents, to feel extremes of love and hate; and once in a while I'll tell students that in some cases they can avoid years of professional therapy if they accept that it's okay and normal to feel both love and hate toward your parents. You never get over it, there is no easy psychological resolution; your relations toward such parents will always be complex, and, at times, you hope, less intense, less dramatic, less interesting. You tell your stories, you put a self-servingly triumphant spin on them, but the pain and the regrets continue. I knew all too well, at too early an age, what Hegel meant when he claimed that the ultimate purpose, the telos of the family, was to disintegrate, to bring about its own dissolution.

What has this to do with the Columbus controversy and the so-called discovery of America? I am intrigued by the idea that acts of confession and forgiveness could take place on a national level. We Americans aren't very adept at dealing with our pasts, with our memories, of thinking of ourselves in historical terms, of dealing with each other as complex beings. I'm thinking here that a national day of forgiveness, an official holiday, could help define who we are as a people, using the past performatively to create a new future. There are certain real precedents for such an idea. Abraham Lincoln called for a national day of humiliation and atonement.[6] He viewed the Civil War in religious terms, believing that it was America's penance for committing the sin of slavery. And to heal, to bring the nation back together as a nation, he thought that we must come to terms with our sorry past, for neither the war nor all the emancipation proclamations in the world would repair the wounds that the nation had suffered due to slavery. Hannah Arendt, the twentieth-century political philosopher, a Jewish woman who fled Germany and adopted America as her new home, speaks of forgiveness as a performative act that can help forge ties between past and future.[7] But how do you cope with a past, a history that includes genocide and unspeakable atrocities (and Arendt was well aware that she was substituting one genocidal nation for another)? Arendt thought some consolation could be found and won in the idea of the nation, of a collective identity that endures over time, but she thought America's constitution was flawed and needed reworking to make modern democracy more meaningful and participatory. Sheldon Wolin extends this Arendtian idea in a book partly edited by my colleague, Fred Krinsky, in which Wolin contends that Americans need to learn that politicalness, being political, has an inescapably historical dimension.[8] The main impediment to confronting our political past, thinks Wolin, is our national political mythology of contracturalism as the allegedly consensual basis of our democracy. Social contract theory attempts to relieve the individual of the burden of the past by erasing the ambiguities bequeathed to us by our forebears; it pretends that we can claim a fresh start and an innocence about what has gone on before us. Let me read from Wolin:

> The sacrament of innocence brings absolution from the foolishness of our fathers and mothers. It soothes us with the knowledge that we were not there when blacks were treated as a species of property; when Indians were massacred and deprived of their ancestral lands; when the early strikes of workers were broken by the combined force of government and business corporations; when the liberal government of FDR refused to admit refugees from Hitler's Germany; or when the bomb was dropped, not once, but twice. As president (Reagan) remarked in his inaugural address, "We, the present-day Americans, are not given to looking backward. In this blessed land, there is always a better tomorrow."[9]

Against this conception, Wolin writes, we might set the words of Richard Hooker, an English theologian of four centuries ago:

> Wherefore as any man's deed past is good as long as he himself continueth; so the act of a public society of men done five hundred years sithence standeth as theirs who presently are of the same societies, because corporations are immortal; we were then alive in our predecessors, they in their successors do live still.[10]

Clearly, says Wolin, we can never renounce our past without rendering the idea of a political community incoherent.

I see certain precedents, glimpses of hope, in our neighbor Canada's recent return of vast land rights to its natives, and I see hope in Nelson Mandela telling Americans when he visited here that we must confront seriously our own Indian apartheid zones, the reservations—that is the most important issue for Americans today, Mandela told us. We must rethink radically the idea of property rights (don't laugh, if rethinking property rights can be done in the former Soviet Union and the Eastern Bloc countries and Nicaragua and elsewhere, it can be done here as well). John Locke, looking at America, told the world that property is created when human labor is mixed with land, but he included an escape clause to exempt the Native American from the right to property ownership. There are precedents for such belated reconsiderations even in these United States. For instance, the Indians of Iowa sold all their land to the U. S. government between 1825 and 1851 (in 1825, by the way, the southeastern corner of the state was set aside as property for the children of white fathers and Indian women). The average price paid to the Indians for their land in Iowa was about twelve cents an acre, which was far below market value at the time. In the late 1950s, the U. S. government announced that it was willing to pay more to the tribes who sold land in Iowa from 1833 onward. It was estimated that the actual value of the land in 1833 was about eighty cents an acre, and for a while it looked as if the deal would go through. At any rate I am encouraged that at one point our Congress was willing to make amends to the descendents of the Iowa Indians, albeit more than 120 years after the fact.

I am also intrigued by our neighbor Mexico's tradition of conquest dances. These festival days attempt to forge a unity between conqueror and conquered (they are very different in spirit from one-sided celebrations of indigenous peoples), and I could see a similar day being proclaimed to good effect here in the United States. I am also emboldened by the advances in legal circles forwarding serious theories of reparations, which were spurred on by the reparations paid to interred Japanese Americans. Such an official act is good for both oppressor and victimized parties. It allows a perpetrator, or extended beneficiaries of perpetration, to say that we made a mistake, and we want to make amends as a nation, we want to be the sort of people who attempt to make amends, though it is hard, if not impossible, if not sometimes undesirable, to try to restore relations to some perfect, natural state. That is a key insight of both Augustine and Rousseau—confession doesn't completely repair, doesn't redeem, doesn't save, doesn't make whole again. The sin still persists (the Pelagians were wrong in their view of perfectibility).

What I am saying, what I am calling for in calling for a national day of let's call it multicultural forgiveness, a day not simply of self-flagellation and finger-pointing, but a celebration in *common* of our differences, of the American experiment in multiculturalism, is that such a day would not make everything right again. We would still have our problems, we would still have our ghettoes and reservations, but at least we would be coming together as a people, which is a starting point for eventually redressing in material terms certain past wrongs. For then we become a people, a nation, and not just a plurality, an aggregation, of interest groups. The act of mutual recognition and forgiveness transforms us—we become a people whose way it is to engage in such attempts at reconciliation, who make more than merely symbolic gestures in that direction. In short, and I don't want to sound grandiose, but I think we need to change our notions of what it means to be an American, and I am suggesting that we need to incorporate *ambivalence* into our self-image. The nation, the people, isn't a concept, but an act, an ongoing act, an event, an event that needs to be renewed and reviewed, in which the past doesn't just haunt us or embitter us but becomes the basis, the site, for a new kind of common identity. We become the kind of nation that attempts to work through its murderous past, and not simply forget and repress those horrible moments. Why do I think such national identities are important—especially at a time that we have been warned against Procrustean schemes of unification? My fear is that interest group politics, the politics of pluralism, the politics of power, the language of rights and respect, will not solve our worst multicultural nightmares. Interest group politics will not clean the ghettoes (don't hold your breath for that one), nor will they ever deal with our official apartheid zones. To be sure, multicultural groups need to ask for recognition of their particularity, need to demand that their local identities be respected in their specificity, but such an overdetermined, hyperreal version of Madisonian politics will not, I fear, solve our problems, nor bring us together. The problems, I've tried to suggest, run much deeper than skin color, and they are problems that persist all across America. All Americans have committed, psychologically speaking, an act of murder and aggression in their past; all have sundered ties from mothers and mother-lands, all attempted to leave an old world for this new world. The two ethnic exceptions to this scenario of a murderous, complicit America are the Native Americans and the African Americans, neither of whom by and large chose to come here from elsewhere. Native Americans and African Americans might have committed their own atrocities, but they weren't complicit in the official American story. Still, our histories and their histories now converge, like it or not. Columbus didn't really discover America, but he went looking for something *cross-cultural* to discover, and like it or not, all of us must now deal with his presumptuous quest that forced separate worlds and different peoples together. But would we, Native and African Americans included, would we, even knowing what we know now and have discovered about America, would we really want to live in a country that wasn't multiracial? There is no return to the garden, my friends, there's no going back to nature, there's no easy solution to this Columbus thing, there's no way to put the story to rest, no way to achieve happy closure, no comfortable end to the maddening contestability of the whole affair. But maybe we can start asking for, and sometimes granting, forgiveness to each other a bit more.

Well, I fear I've said too much, that I've made a spectacle of myself. The worst that can come of this is that the Public Affairs Committee won't ever ask me to give another Columbus talk, but do forgive me for rambling on and subjecting you to all of my stories. In the words of both my mother and father, mea culpa, mea culpa, mea maxima culpa. Thank you very much.

A coda and an update, or as Paul Harvey says, page 2: my parents, in retirement and still together after forty long years, are happier now. My iron-willed mother, after all of her kids left the nest, fulfilled her life's dream of going to college, and in her late fifties she received her bachelor's degree in English from Coe College in Cedar Rapids; and my father, after his mother died, at a time therefore when he felt he could finally be candid with himself and his male needs, legally changed his name from Francis to Frank; it was about that point that his eldest son became a student of irony. And now you know the rest of the story.

3

George Kateb's Main Thing

—the main thing being the average, the bodily, the concrete, the democratic, the popular, on which all the superstructures of the future are to permanently rest.

—Walt Whitman, *Democratic Vistas*

This chapter is about George Kateb's commitment to liberal arts education. I wish to insist on associating George Kateb with Amherst College, the place where he taught for thirty years, from 1957 to 1987, before leaving for Princeton. It is hard for me, as a former student of his at Amherst, to think of Kateb except as a teacher at this small liberal arts college—even though I well know that Kateb is an outspoken champion of a theory of individuality that resists any identification with group or institutional alliances. I admire enormously Kateb's writings in political theory, but what I want to tell the world about Kateb, upon prompting, cannot be confined to his scholarly texts. My memories are too vivid. Thus this chapter requires that I throw off my academic garb for a while and turn personal and anecdotal. Realize that I do not do so easily. I fear that I might be violating confidences, betraying friendships, crossing some all-too-real threshold between private and public. One worries about writing about a close friend and teacher. Such writing can be too intimate and gossipy. I do not want to sound as if I am passing judgment or slaying a father or eulogizing at a funeral. I do have a point, an end in sight, and it goes beyond idle reminiscing. Let me say that I am writing what I am writing because, to borrow recklessly from Whitman, something like a democratic spirit urges me on.

I would like to dwell upon the fact that George Kateb taught for thirty years at a liberal arts college. Indeed, I dare say that his reputation in the field of political theory owes more to his animated, generous, and feisty presence as a teacher and conferee than to his texts (which is not to slight his work at all); surely it was a reputation, well-deserved, that preceded him to Princeton and has been only heightened ever since landing there. Thus we might ask: how is it that a classroom teacher, associated for thirty years with a liberal arts college—as opposed to a research university—might today be commemorated in a *Festschrift?* There is no Kateb school of thought, no cult of Kateb, no *Katebkreise*. His students and readers are not disciples. A trickling of grad students is beginning to seep out of Princeton, but it is probably safe to predict that there will never be a deluge of "Katebians" flooding the job market. George is no guru.[1]

At annual American Political Science Association conferences, Kateb characteristically steals the show (in my humble opinion, if I need to qualify the statement). He provokes and stirs and gets people talking and thinking. In these moments his political theory colleagues catch a glimpse of the consummate teacher at work. But such displays, even a cumulative career's worth, would hardly seem to warrant a *Festschrift* in the conventional course of academic events.

To be sure, Kateb's defense of liberalism attracts attention. It is odd. Liberalism seems, on its face, to be such a sadly compromised moral-political stance in life, and to find such an ardent and eloquent and unapologetic defender of the cause raises eyebrows. Kateb does not just spin out arguments for a liberal position, he sings them. He has studied the Muses, he has read Homer and Virgil, he has taken seriously Whitman's call for an American poet of democracy. Even those of us who occasionally put up feeble resistance to the inevitabilities of contemporary liberalism welcome, if secretly, his efforts. We are all closet liberals, fighting our own demons, and Kateb, in waging a mock battle against us, offers us consolation against part of ourselves. We can find gems of affirmation and hope in his words, but one need not even value Kateb's political liberalism in order to enjoy his company. His friends and colleagues include Foucauldians, Freudians, and feminists. He clearly loves a good debate, and he brings out the best in his opponents. It is a well-known but seldom-mentioned curiosity among political theorists that the resident liberal at almost all of the major research universities across the country is typically mean-spirited and defensive in his or her defense of liberalism, and more often than not, he or she is caustic if not nasty in his or her personal demeanors as well (give me a passive-aggressive Straussian any day). Kateb, however, breaks rank with his ill-tempered, ill-liberal liberal allies. He enacts the tolerance that he preaches.

Still, all of this springs from and harks back to little Amherst (which is not to forward some marxoid theory of material conditioning). Kateb's theories—and practices—of democratic individuality were forged during his years at Amherst. I cannot imagine a theory of liberalism so polished and so nurtured except in a liberal arts setting. Since I happened to be present as a witness on the scene during several of those critical years, I would like to reconstruct a bit of the texture of life at Amherst College in the following pages. Inquiring minds would probably like to know: what went on, what goes on, in those little classrooms?

First, professors teaching at a liberal arts college are very aware that they are not working at a research university—especially those at Northeastern liberal arts colleges so proximate to Cambridge, the holy hub of academic research. Although one attempts to write in the nooks and crannies of the academic year, on weekends or in the wee hours of the night, most research and writing must be deferred until the summer months or until sabbatical semesters. Teaching takes precedence at all other times. Amherst, like most liberal arts colleges, refuses as a matter of policy to hire teaching assistants of any sort, thus professors do all of the teaching, paper grading, and advising. Teaching loads, moreover, are on paper and in practice much more onerous than at research universities. One simply teaches more. A liberal arts professor usually must teach several general education courses in one's field, as opposed to boutique courses; seldom can one offer a seminar on a narrow specialty topic or on one's particular research, as one might do in a graduate seminar, en route to one's next book. In reality, the two ways of life, liberal arts teaching and university teaching, are not comparable.

But I sketch this quick comparison not in order to suggest that teaching undergraduates is without its great joys and gratifications. Quite to the contrary, the pleasures are many, meaningful, and lasting. In such a small setting, one gets to know one's students (and one's colleagues, if all goes well) very well; students are not simply faces facing the lectern. Looking after another's intellectual development takes time, and care, which takes energy, emotional and intellectual. One takes the time to talk with others, to reflect upon the day's events, to read and to pore over passages. The liberal arts colleges in America are pockets of educational freedom and engagement, the notion of the ivory tower at its best, if only because the instrumentalist pressures for careerist advancement are somewhat abated, and teaching is given its due. Real talk, real debate, and real research should go on at the research universities, pure research for research's sake, but many have instead become trade schools, havens for the kind of specialized scholarship that would make the likes of Goethe and Weber turn over in their graves. Pettiness often prevails, and self-importance passes for normality. Teaching graduate students, to be sure, potentially brings the thrill of higher sophistication and greater appreciation, but graduate students by the time they are graduate students have already made their big decisions in life, and thus at that level, ideas are but ideas, theory but theory, and jargon but jargon. Nietzsche quips, in *Twilight of the Idols*, "*From a doctoral examination.* 'What is the task

of all higher education?' To turn men into machines. 'What are the means?'
Man must learn to be bored."[2]

Undergraduate students who are attracted to and attend liberal arts
colleges usually know why they are there, instead of attending a major university—if only because they have deliberately avoided the pomp and fanfare. At Amherst, a few students evidently bumbled their way into the place,
without giving it much forethought; a few saw it as an easy extension of prep
school life; some had acted upon a questionable calculation that Amherst's
supposedly elite networks would better launch them into medical school,
business school, or law school. But the main reason most students were there
was that they valued, above all, close interaction with their professors and
with their fellow students, and they knew about and believed in the liberal
arts ethic. Amherst in particular also boasted, at the time, about the diversity
of its students, well before diversity became a buzzword throughout the country. In my years, Amherst sought to matriculate a cross-section of students
representing geographic, economic, and public versus private school diversity
(race and gender were just starting to become pressing concerns). As a financially
well-endowed institution, Amherst could afford to admit students on a need-
blind basis. But it also sent its emissaries out across America to recruit geographi-
cally wayward students, even though it had no shortage of well-heeled, capable
students nearby who were already applying. This is where I enter the picture.

As a son of the Midwest, the third out of five children, with parents who
never attended college and were struggling to make ends meet, I never dreamed
of attending Amherst. Frankly, I had never heard of the place. I learned
about Amherst only after its director of admissions had given a talk in a
town near mine, and he assured me that, if admitted, sufficient financial aid
would be forthcoming. The sales pitch about four colleges and a university
all residing in one happy valley sounded promising, and I liked the idea of
a diverse studentry living and eating and studying together in close confines.
I left my home state, a big deal in those days, and found my way to this
strange place. My story is not one of complete triumph and self-made-manism,
but I will say that I found myself in unusual circumstances: a working-class
stiff who, overnight, was rubbing elbows with true-to-life sons of kings and
U. S. Supreme Court justices and captains of industry. Parading celebrity
students was not, however, what Amherst was all about. Amherst was one of
the few schools in the country that would grant generous financial aid, and
without publicity, to worthy foreign students (usually foreign students are a
source of income for most institutions). My close friend at Amherst, and my
dear friend to this day, was a Jesuit-educated Cameroonian who came to
Amherst literally out of the jungles. I also belonged to the first fully coed
class at Amherst, which had shocked its old-boy alums by finally admitting
women (but these liberally educated types eventually came around, as could
be expected).

Here we were, from Cameroon, Monaco, Dallas, Maryland, and Iowa, boy and girl, black and white, rich and poor, gay and straight, all thrown into little classrooms together. We were told to read, to discuss, and to think. The agenda was vague but therefore expansive. We were to ponder the universe, to pursue differential equations, to question everything. And Amherst had but one dining hall, thus we would all eat with each other and talk over food. Kind people looked after every detail of our existence; they treated us as if we held great promise and possibility, and they asked for little in return. In this setting, the phrase "the life of the mind" would be ritually invoked in hushed tones as a kind of mantra, and there were seventy-six beautifully manicured tennis courts should one desire bodily sport as well.

In my first year I signed up for a course in constitutional law with Earl Latham, a professor of some distinction since, for one reason, he reportedly had been offered a U. S. Supreme Court appointment years before by then-President Kennedy. Many Amherst students were taking the class, since the word spread that Latham, who was getting up in age, would either retire shortly or die. It turned out that he indeed passed away toward the end of the semester, having assigned and graded only one batch of class papers. Kateb assumed the administration of the final days of the class. The paper I had written evidently caught Latham's eye, for he had made a notation in his grade book about it. Kateb discreetly mentioned the notation to me when I first met him.

For the next several years, Kateb was to teach specially funded classes— the Kenan seminars—which would allow him to team teach small classes with other Amherst faculty members. Tracy Strong left the University of Pittsburgh to come to Amherst to teach Kateb's regular political theory courses for three years. That next year, my sophomore year, Kateb would be teaching a Kenan Seminar with Barry O'Connell, an American Studies and English professor who had a reputation as a firebrand of sorts (left over from his student days as president of the Harvard chapter of the Students for a Democratic Society). Liberal meets lefty, and fireworks would fly. The class would be limited to fifteen students, demand was high, and seniors would be given priority. Kateb made an exception in my case, traceable in good part to that notation in Latham's grade book (a tribute not to me, but to his former colleague).

Kateb made us sweat in that seminar. "I want your best sentences!" he demanded as his charge to us before the first paper assignment. He pushed us, he prodded us, he queried. My head would spin at night—that little bespectacled guy drove me crazy at times—but nothing else in the world seemed to matter except the controversies that that class raised.

One time, in connection with our reading of Whitman's *Leaves of Grass*, the class was arguing about which American writer was the appropriate modern heir to Whitman. Members of the class were suggesting various names, and Kateb was rejecting their suggestions with unusual bruskness. "Robert

Frost?" ventured one voice. "No," replied Kateb. "Norman Mailer?" "Absolutely not," said he. "Saul Bellow?" "No, not at all." "Allen Ginsberg?" "No, no, no!" "Bob Dylan?" "Certainly not!" The class then turned on Kateb. One older fellow put the question to Kateb: "Well, Professor Kateb, then who do *you* think is the modern heir to Whitman?" There was a long pause, and Kateb said—plainly and matter-of-factly, after long reflection, as if the answer had occurred to him for the first time right at that moment—"I am. I am the modern heir to Whitman. Not in anything I've yet written. But I am. I am the modern heir to Whitman."

We were stunned, if only because this admission, forced out of Kateb through our collective schoolboyish candor, seemed so out of character. It was not like Kateb to be self-aggrandizing, so we knew immediately that there must be truth or at least utter sincerity in his statement. Imagine what we reported back to our friends that night in the dining hall!

Thereafter I collected many more such memorable episodes, always with Kateb at the center. He would seldom fail to baffle or befuddle me, yet increasingly I found myself growing suspicious of his way of thinking. Whatever our disagreements, he always found time in his busy schedule to meet with me (and many others). We continued to have many contentious conversations—"exchanges," as we would call them—and along with a good number of my peers from those George Kateb/Tracy Strong years, I chose to continue studying political theory in my after-Amherst life. But not until many years later, after several of his essays had been published, did I begin to understand what Kateb meant by naming himself (quietly, unpublicly) as an heir to Whitman. The question, however, still lingers and haunts me: how could this genteel, tweed-jacketed man, a scholar-teacher at an insular liberal arts institution, proclaim himself an heir to Whitman? Whitman embraced all of America, he knew its people in all walks of life, from coast to coast. Kateb, for God's sake, had never visited Mount Rushmore in the Black Hills of South Dakota (I was particularly sensitive to lacunae in Midwestern lore). How dare he?

The answer, unexpected and perhaps unsatisfying, is to be found in the liberal arts environs of Amherst College. This quaint college, with its limousine liberalism, its commitment to diversity and education for the sake of education, had attracted into its halls a virtual microcosm of America. Kateb, just by sitting attentively in class, on his perch, in his place of garret, could effectively keep his pulse on the rhythms of America. Sir James George Frazer, we learned in our anthropology class, had conducted his many investigations without ever leaving his armchair. Political theory, we have known from Plato to More to Rousseau to Donna Haraway, is largely an exercise in travel literature, yet many of these road trips can be taken imaginatively, and sometimes the imagination produces better political theory than those who actually and patronizingly go out to visit the natives. But Amherst College brought the natives to Kateb, collecting specimens of the best and the brightest as well as the common and the many. And then Amherst College asked all of these strange beasts to talk with one another. Aliens looking down on us from other planets would think that we were nuts.

Liberal arts colleges are precious experiments in liberalism, even if conducted under contrived circumstances. Perhaps these pocket communities, as islands of civility and diversity that actively promote the free exchange of ideas, are the only places in America where liberal theory is explicitly promoted and, for the most part, successfully practiced. John Stuart Mill would be thrilled. Amherst College ripped persons away from their social contexts, told them to talk with one another, dine with one another, and then repair to the library cubicle or dorm cell late at night to digest the day's events. It was odd, but it worked. Our young Amherst heads burned for ideas—we read book after book after book, we debated ideas as ideas and as if they had consequences, and we all wrote senior honors theses 300 or 400 pages long on abstruse but important topics. Kateb was in fact thrilled, or so he seemed.

But alas, Kateb left Amherst. How does one account for this monumental loss? My own view is that he wanted to export the liberal revolution that he helped spark at Amherst. It was time to write about the lessons of Amherst, from afar, without naming the place as such (call it America instead). Princeton had its academic attractions, I am certain, but it could never match the understated integrity that fostered Amherst's liberal ways. Being close to cagey New York City would have to do, as a substitute for youthful diversity. But can one, even someone with Kateb's restorative powers, really sing, à la Whitman, about New York, especially the grubby and greedy New York from 1987 onward? Could New York ever serve as a stimulus if not a background model for American liberalism in Kateb's buoyant sense? I fear that Kateb's exuberant idealism, his theory of democratic individuality, is today vulnerable to a growing shift in emphasis, and I already detect a change in his outlook.[3]

In his best paragraphs of writing, paragraphs that are indeed better poetry than prose, Kateb's democratic individualist theory reaches out to potentially anyone in America. It is pluralist and inclusive, even if Kateb confines his purview, a bit artificially, to the idea of America as a New World experiment. Who else, though, better recovers the Emersonian heart of democracy than when Kateb whispers that democracy teaches, because it presupposes, the "moral identity" of all of its citizens.[4] Everyone counts, and the full impact of that official declaration has yet to be felt. The sheer idea of democracy has not quite settled in. But there is more. For Kateb, this moral equality entails the recognition that individuals are diverse; in fact, moral equality requires the full expression of diversity, plurality, and multiplicity, in one's self and in others. At a time when other theorists are either deconstructing the subject or else clinging to its ascriptive attributes, Kateb sketches a story about the individual who is paradoxical. The self is indefinite and elusive, he teaches, instead of being well defined and self-possessed. Whereas other liberal theorists indulge in a fantasy of the self as master of its own house, beholden only to internally compelling interests and desires, Kateb speaks of the liberal self's instability and inessentiality. Such a self "wonders at existence" and ponders the precarious mysteries of being.[5] Individuality, moreover, is pursued through a kind of detachment from the self, a self-alienation; it is a restlessness, an uneasiness about being at home in the world. Kateb shocks and unsettles, as when he writes, following Heidegger, that perhaps the time one is most alive, most attached to this fragile, indefinite, contingent, mysterious existence of ours, is when one fully confronts and contemplates the fact of human mortality. One is most alive, then, when one is a bit dead while alive.[6] He continues to astonish, when, at the very end of a piece extolling the virtues of democratic individuality, Kateb adds—an "admission" he calls it—that the life of democratic individuality "is probably not a life of happiness, and the pains eventually outweigh the pleasures."[7] Disconcerting, almost unendurable, ideas, but the cadence of Kateb's sentences reveals absolutely no hint of disingenuousness. He means what he says.

Even as the whirl of ideas constituting his liberal self might discomfort, Kateb welcomes us back to ourselves and thus offers partial solace. Yet his individualist theory is no apologia for selfishness or self-interest, commonly understood. His political theory does not amount to a rationalization of the liberal status quo. Far from it, for Kateb's liberalism provides a trenchant critique of many current political and governmental practices and produces a rationale for resistance. While he expresses his aversion to "statism" at every turn, Kateb reserves his strongest condemnation for policies that have served the interests of most self-anointed liberals. Throughout the 1980s Kateb refused, for instance, to subscribe to the nuclear policy of mutually assured destruction. I suspect that he will never forget, nor forgive, the evils of a policy that threatened to kill others (read: other individuals, including other non-American individuals[8]), even though such a policy is now widely credited with having won the Cold War, for bringing about the end of history, and for assuring that limited-government liberalism will be globally ascendant.

Yet even as he complicates and subverts a caricatured version of the liberal self, Kateb's complication, the task of revealing the self as various and protean turns invidiously on a notion of community that is surprisingly flat. Kateb has always been a broker in binaries: utopia versus anti-utopia, individual versus group, private versus public, Old World versus New World. Such thinking has yielded rich results, a deepening in our understanding of self-reliant individuality. The cost, however, is that Kateb has had to ridicule communitarian thinking along the way, often by distortion and inflammatory rhetoric. The notion that a participatory politics, or any informed ties to a group, might strengthen a democratic, rights-based individualism, or intensify one's individual reverie, seems to have been lost in the shuffle. He has brutally and relentlessly parodied the concept of community.

Although many notions of community probably deserved his rebuke, it may well be time to reexamine that entire effort, divested now of some of the gratuitous hostility. For Kateb, group membership necessarily means a loss of individuality, a zero-sum trade-off, an engulfment of the self by the herd. Membership in the herd is but a second-order existence, an abstraction, a grammatical fiction, whereas individual existence, while indefinite and fleeting, is for Kateb more real, an experiential given, closer to the ground (even if more enigmatic). At times Kateb reveals that he considers group thinking "shallow," and that shallowness not only degrades but also potentially endangers. Shallowness, to unpack his terms, means that one's thinking is not "inward."[9] The key to Kateb's equivalencies is that the best thinking is somehow projected "inward," inwardness is deep and complicated, and deep, complicated thinking takes place by oneself, alone. One grapples with the spectacle of existence not in concourse and intercourse with others but by oneself, evidently in one's study. One confronts human finitude in solitude. "We perish, each alone," teaches Mr. Ramsey in Virginia Woolf's *To the Lighthouse*—a "philosopher" who thinks that "loneliness" is "the truth about things," and whose wife at one point guesses that Mr. Ramsey secretly believes that "he would have written better books if he had not married."[10]

But let us ask: is this true? Do friendship, companionship, love, and community necessarily entail a loss of individuality (rightly understood)? Is Kateb's either/or a telling dichotomy? I might suggest that he has clarified our minds about individuality only by putting the choice between individuality and connectedness in terms too loaded and too stark. His generalizations about community do not ring true. He should not be quite so dismissive, or self-assured.

I once blurted out to Kateb, in one of my frustrated moments, that he clearly had never played in a band (I do not know whether that is true). My thinking was about jazz improvisation in particular. One studies and practices chords and techniques on one's own, but these efforts do not reach fruition until one plays and plays with others. Reading music, even composing music, is not the same, and is not as good (to my mind) as playing it. In jazz improv, one is not simply rehearsing in public what one has internalized in private. One actively communicates with other members of the band, one listens, one tries this or tries that, musical risks are taken, there is playfulness, there is spontaneity, there is interpretation, and there is a broad range of emotions and ideas that can be attempted in and through this medium. The left and right hemispheres of the brain must be in dialogue. Intense concentration and discipline are coupled with relaxation and fluidity. Brilliance sometimes surfaces, yet group brilliance—hitting a groove—is more meaningful than individual displays of virtuosity ("it don't mean a thing if it ain't got that swing"). The point of it all is not to confirm Schiller's or Lukács' theory of aesthetics—the point is to play.

Another example comes to my mind: basketball (or similar team sports). As a mathematics buff, I love the beauty of numerical theories and the pleasures of calculation, but I learn much more about the geometric complexities of the body and the brain while on the basketball court. Running, stopping, leaping off balance—then in a split second the mind-body calculates the appropriate parabola required to project the ball into the eighteen-inch diameter hoop fourteen feet away—and this information transmitted supersonically to the tips of the fingers. Swoosh (if all goes well). But that act is not as exhilarating as calculating and predicting the movements of fellow teammates—all in moving 3-D Technicolor. There is no better experience in the world, reading Habermas included, as successfully executing a give-and-go with one's teammate. Here is a sphere of discourse, a form of lived communication, enacted through mutual understandings, a subterranean stream of exchanged information, that is all the more exciting because it need not be put into words. The thrill of playing basketball has to do with the fact that it is a collective exercise in communicative understatement. Reading texts, in comparison, is a poor substitute for reading humans on the run (unless, as I have argued elsewhere, one has a wry sense of reading texts as an exercise in irony).

Kateb has warned me that I should not view aesthetics or sports as models for participatory politics. I think such a warning issues from an inadequate understanding of what it means, as an individual, to play in a band or on a team. Bands or teams are groups that accentuate individuality precisely through participation in the group activity. Such groups need not engulf the self; they can allow it to flourish and to be more complicated. There need be no loss of self, no shallowness, no retreat from inwardness, no march toward order. In fact, to my mind, reading, studying, and contemplating in the cubicle compromise far too many ways of thinking, eclipse too many sentiments and emotions, for such activity to suffice as a model of the highest human existence possible. When I am engaging in such (admittedly) playful activities, I begin to understand what Hannah Arendt, Kateb's frequent foe, meant when she looked to the ancient Greeks and to other moments in history to find, in and through public life, a sense of lived *eudaimonia*. One engages in the activity for, as it were, its own sake. Time freezes for a bit. The activity, to use other words, seems to provide its own justification. It seems to be the time when one is most alive, when one is most free, most attached to existence as such. Arendt states boldly (about Jefferson's America) that "no one could be called happy without his share in public happiness, that no one could be called free without his experience in public freedom, and that no one could be called either happy or free without participating, and having a share, in public power."[11]

Playing basketball and playing jazz also strike me as being very "American" activities—activities that proudly display individuality and equality simultaneously. Across the United States, I have played on all sorts of courts and on all sorts of stages, and in both activities I have played with African Americans, Native Americans, Hispanics, Asian Americans, Jews, Wasps, Muslims, gays and straights, rich and poor, male and female, and short and tall. These were great equalizing activities (despite the advantages of height in basketball), as all kinds of people were brought together; and yet, the court and the stage allowed one's individual talents and techniques to be fully exhibited. Such moments have allowed me some glimpse of insight into Arendt's insistence that the American founding was indeed an exercise in republicanism—participatory, albeit constitutional self-government—on a scale never before attempted. All across America there are bands and teams, and these groups comprise thinking, performing individuals, not mindless herds and tribalist mini-mobs.

The other activity that for me limns a living example of what Arendt meant by invoking Aristotle's notion of the well-constructed life, the *eudaimoniac* life, is to be found in the liberal arts classroom, where one supposedly learns and talks for the sake of learning and talking. Such learning is necessarily interactive and participatory and, yes, it gestures toward greater political applications, perhaps in America in particular. But I fear that Kateb has taken that spark of intellectual electricity, ignited in the classroom, and has attributed it to the cubicle, to thinking as such. In what sense can he possibly mean that the solitary life is the best life? In what sense is he or is anyone ever truly solitary? Physical solitude cannot be the issue here. Even confined in one's cubicle, in periods of repose, there is hardly such a thing as solitude. Although physically alone, one is occupied and animated by all kinds of voices. Ghosts routinely fly in and out the door. Dialogues, real and imaginary, continue in front of the computer screen. Is one ever alone, especially as a reader and as a writer, as an academic? Books are merely ways for the dead to speak to us from beyond the grave. I simply do not understand why Kateb must insist on solitude, especially since I resist the notion that some special plumbing of the thoughtful depths occurs when my friends happen to leave the room. Rereading Nietzsche or Emerson will not do. Soaring appeals to quasimystical, silent bouts of reverential rhapsody (even if impious) will not vindicate solitude either.

I fear that lately Kateb has mistaken the freedom to write (a freedom from distraction) for the truly liberal freedom of the classroom, a freedom that is positive and participatory and potentially political. Maybe the classroom was inevitably too precious to serve as a platform for political theory, and it was high time to move on, but the idea of liberal arts remains. I worry that Kateb has shifted from a freedom that is democratic, an individuality that is expansive, to a notion of freedom that is singular, and an individuality to which few can aspire (which does not mean that it is best or highest in any sense). Whitman knew that democracy must perform a juggling act:

> First, let us see what we can make out of a brief, general, sentimental consideration of political democracy, and whence it has arisen, with regard to some of its current features, as an aggregate, and as the basic structure of our future literature and authorship. We shall, it is true, quickly and continually find the origin-idea of the singleness of man, individualism, asserting itself, and cropping forth, even from the opposite ideas. But the mass, or lump character, for imperative reasons, is to be ever carefully weigh'd, borne in mind, and provided for. Only from it, and from its proper regulation and potency, comes the other, comes the chance of individualism. The two are contradictory, but our task is to reconcile them.[12]

More:

> This idea of perfect individualism it is indeed that deepest tinges and gives character to the idea of the aggregate. For it is mainly or altogether to serve independent separatism that we favor a strong generalization, consolidation. As it is to give the best vitality and freedom to the rights of the States (every bit as important as the right of nationality, the union,) that we insist on the identity of the Union at all hazards.[13]

And still more:

> Political democracy, as it exists and practically works in America, with all its threatening evils, supplies a training-school for making first-class men. It is life's gymnasium, not of good only, but of all.[14]

Although Whitman, in his famous essay, looks to literature, then to religion, then to law, and finally to history as a source of glue for American political democracy, he focuses upon a decidedly economic concern: "The true gravitation-hold of liberalism in the United States will be a more universal ownership of property, general homesteads, general comfort—a vast, intertwining reticulation of wealth."[15] He confronts the economic preconditions for liberalism in the states, upon which, he says, he raises "the edifice design'd in these Vistas." Liberal democracy must address its own nervousness about poverty: "So that, from another point of view, ungracious as it may sound, and a paradox after what we have been saying, democracy looks with suspicious, ill-satisfied eye upon the very poor, the ignorant, and on those out of business."[16] The genius of poetic inclusion inheres in the attempt to extend democracy, into the culture, into the workplace—"democracy 'in all public and private life' "[17]—which means that democracy goes well beyond official pronouncements and the formal process of voting. Note as well that Whitman tells in his essay of "mutterings" about a "revolution" that "must be heeded" concerning the coming inclusion of women in American political culture.[18]

"The average man of a land at last only is important."[19] Compare these democratic words of Whitman's with those of the late Judith Shklar in her charitable attempt to explain Emerson's notion of (allegedly) democratic solitude: "There is, to begin with, far less inequality between individuals than we pretend, so we may not need to reform each other . . . [t]here were simply two immovable propositions from which he [Emerson] never departed. The first was that the approach to truth could be made only in complete solitude. If it is unspoken, it is, after all, beyond doubt and dogma. The second was that if there is a moral law, it was democratic. He might choose to be alone, but he would not look down on the ploughboy."[20] How very big of Emerson! Should the ploughboy be flattered? (My gentle advice to Emersonians: you probably should not tell the ploughboy about your attitude toward him.) If this is a wedge we can drive between Whitman and Emerson, then I vastly prefer Whitman.[21]

Liberal theories almost always look pretty on paper; the trouble is, liberalism, as a practice, all too often fails to live up to its beautiful designs, fails in actuality to extend its aspirations and benefits to people at large (how often must we rehearse this commonplace criticism?). Today in America, regrettably, far too many people count in theory only, in the barest of senses, and the notion of "moral identity" has been reduced to a sham, a hollow ideal, mere words. We are living at a time when the discrepancies between rich and poor have become obscene—and one need not resort to a pinko analysis to take simple heed of the many indignities suffered by the disenfranchised—call it "economic" disenfranchisement, if one must split analytic hairs. (Symptomatic of the state of American liberalism is that Amherst College, one of the last bastions, lately has considered abandoning its need-blind admissions policy.) Arendt, no Marxist she, courageously called for a reexamination of the relationship between political freedom and economic liberty in the America of her day. A treasure had been forgotten, perhaps lost. Do we really need to elaborate on the current shortcomings of political liberalism, a liberalism that coyly claims indifference about its own economic underpinnings? The contemporary ploughboy, the migrant worker, in addition to strenuous physical burdens, must labor under the cruel national mythology that he is as free and as equal as any other citizen in America. He, however, happens to be running along a different track of freedom, but free he supposedly is, no wage-slave, morally identical with each and all. At least the theorists of the ancient Greek polis, in good faith, called a slave a slave.

Can one be a "communitarian" without being a communist, an authoritarian, a conservative, a statist, an order freak, a patriarch, a member of the herd? Certainly, but those are the limited options that Kateb often has forced us to accept. Along the way I think he has given up too soon on the vision of a vital and viable American republic. Liberalism can do better. I gather from some of his opponents, those pesky "communitarian" theorists, that they share an informed hunch that a participatory politics, a return to some mythic republicanism, might actively address some of the ills that a stilted liberalism would deem "social" and thus out-of-bounds. Such theorists point to political participation and democratic inclusion not in order to affirm a new metaphysics of selfhood or to smuggle in a tendency toward crypto-fascism, rather, they see an inkling of possibility in the idea that a participatory politics might create a culture that remedies, as a way of life and not just as a matter of welfare policy, the instrumentalism and atomization that now surround us. They believe in human dignity. They are not averse to a rights-based liberalism. They have a tendency to believe that some of the abuses and horrors of modernity—classism, racism, sexism, substance abuse, gangland crime, murderous militarism, pointless profiteering—can be linked to a creed of rampant individualism.[22] Their theoretical scapegoat, individualism, may not be the same as Kateb's glowing individuality, but give these critics their due. Maybe, just maybe, atomization is a worse problem in America today, a greater threat to democracy, than is any widespread retreat from solitude, however considered. I hear Whitman proposing similar solutions, amidst and despite his reservations about democratic politics, in a paragraph that follows immediately his most exalted words on solitude:

> To practically enter into politics is an important part of American personalism. To every young man, north and south, earnestly studying these things, I should here, as an offset to what I have said in former pages, now also say, that may-be to views of very largest scope, after all, perhaps the political (perhaps the literary and sociological) America goes best about its development its own way—sometimes, to temporary sight, appalling enough. It is the fashion among dilettantes and fops (perhaps I myself am not guiltless) to decry the whole formulations of the active politics of America, as beyond redemption, and to be carefully kept away from. See you that you do not fall into this error. . . . It is the dilettantes, and all who shirk their duty, who are not doing well. As for you, I advise you to enter more strongly yet into politics. I advise every

young man to do so. Always inform yourself; always do the best you can; always vote.[23]

I well realize that Kateb has been thoroughly acquainted, if not pre-occupied, with the democratic dilemmas that I have outlined and alluded to above.[24] His fascination for reconciling democracy and thoughtfulness runs throughout his book on Arendt, a thinker who interrogated the boundaries between the *vita activa* and the *vita contemplativa*, and that motif becomes explicit in the appendix to his book, where Kateb examines Arendt's "accusation" of thinking, her "indictment" of philosophers who withdraw too far from the world of appearances.[25] That same tension largely informs his nuclear project of attempting to rectify the "anti-democratic" strains of Heidegger's and Nietzsche's individualist doctrines with the democratic tendencies of Emerson and Whitman. I am not tell-ing Kateb anything that he does not already know in telling him that transcendentalism can be a tad too tempting. In *Utopia and Its Enemies*, many years ago, Kateb wrote:

> We have already said that on the face of it, it seems absurd that there are those who would advocate that we turn our backs on what we have always said we wanted, just as we are coming to feel that we can have it, at least in theory, after all. It could be said, in reply to this charge of apparent absurdity, that all through time there has been no real agreement on what we have wanted, that fantasies of the most amazing divergence from each other have abounded, that scheme has followed upon scheme, that each age has furnished paradise in a different mode, that there has been, in short, no uniform view on the ultimately desirable social condition of man. Add to that, that there has been not only a great variety of dreams and visions, but also, obvi-ously, abundant opposition to almost any dream or vision one would care to cite. Why, to take just one example, criticism of Plato's Repub-lic is nearly as old as *The Republic* itself. Plato was answered by Aristotle; and Aristotle went on, in turn, to devise his own "ideal commonwealth."[26]

Somehow, Aristotle, the supposedly pluralist critic of Plato and Platonism, becomes, over time, an advocate of his own ideal commonwealth, which upon inspection reduces to a fantasy about the individual "best" life, namely, philosophic contemplation. The best polity is that which allows thinkers to think thought. Kateb's newfound utopia seems to fall into the same trap: solitude, not democracy. Emerson, not Whitman. Princeton, not Amherst. These are not fine or merely academic distinctions. I offer my reminding words as no reproach, but rather as a way of insisting upon and adhering to my unforgotten connection to Kateb, by way of an institution that we both once loved.

> Did you, too, O friend, suppose democracy was only for elections, for politics, and for a party name? I say democracy is only of use there that it may pass on and come to its flower and fruits in manners, in the highest forms of interaction between men, and their beliefs—in religion, literature, colleges, and schools.[27]

4

What Teaching at Pomona College Means to Me

I think that a purpose of this last lecture series is to reveal a secret or two. We all keep secrets. One of mine is that if I were to be somebody else in life, I would be a trumpet player. Playing the trumpet is a primal experience, human lips pressed next to cold brass, no need for a quivering reed in-between, and somehow flesh and metal together produce a sound at the other end that is clear, clarion, bold, the call that heralds angels. Playing the trumpet combines aesthetics with athleticism. It is the height of macho. Chops, cheeks, breath control, tight stomach, tight butt, erect posture, flexed biceps, spit. And now I will tell you a dirty little secret. One of my favorite trumpet players is a guy named Maynard Ferguson. I was once a member of the Maynard Ferguson fan club. This is a dirty secret, because Maynard would never be the choice of self-respecting jazz aficionados, and I'm afraid that naming him as one of my guilty pleasures will probably discredit me among my music colleagues here. Most trumpet players start out in a low register and work up to higher notes; good ones go only so far upwards, because they don't want to blow out their lips straining for higher notes. Maynard was born a freak of nature. He is known as a screech trumpeter. He started out on high notes and worked his way down. He played lead trumpet in Stan Kenton's big band in the fifties, so he's not exactly a musical slouch, but he was never known for his subtlety and sophistication either. In the last twenty-five years he's had his own band, produced his own records, and

Talk delivered at Pomona College, February, 18, 1994.

every, every Maynard song features Maynard working up to and eventually hitting a high G above triple C. When he gets there, it is a sonic spectacle to behold. The audience roars in approval, and Maynard milks the applause for all it is worth. Usually Maynard appears in concerts in an orange full-body jumpsuit with a scarf around his neck, and he jumps to center stage displaying an innovation that he introduced into the musical world which he calls the pelvic thrust. When Maynard hits his high note, simultaneously he arches his back and juts out his pelvis, presenting it to the audience as a visual gift of sorts. Maynard is a man's man. A Maynard Ferguson record will feature screech renditions of songs such as the theme from *Shaft*, the theme from *Rocky*, and, of course, *Hey Jude*. Maynard surrounds himself with bright young musicians right out of school who tour with him for a year and then leave, maybe out of embarrassment. Just before I left Boston for Pomona four years ago, I had the once-in-a-lifetime pleasure of hearing Maynard play with a full band accompaniment in a little bar, Johnny D's in Somerville. Maynard was about to take his band out on the road, and he wanted to try out some material in a small venue before he hit the concert scene. I told my friends about this rare opportunity, and we all stood about five feet away from Maynard as he thrust his pelvis at us and blasted away. I lost part of my hearing that night, but I also thought I saw God around the second chorus from the theme from *Star Trek*. Glory, glory Hallelujah. Maynard Ferguson—he has a great name, a perfect name for celebrity, like Shaquille O'Neill. Maynard holds clinics in high schools all across this country, and every drum and bugle corp member in every small town shows up. They buy his mouthpieces and records, and he is almost single-handedly responsible for keeping together many music programs in America for the last twenty-five years. Maynard is a living idol in some small-town circles, even if he isn't a household name in Hollywood. Yes, there's a part of me that would like to be Maynard, a flamboyant, good-guy, screech trumpeter.

But alas, I was fated to be a saxophone player. Sax players aren't bold, brassy, and macho but rather are purveyors of subtlety, sensitivity, and sophistication. They're erotic, but their eroticism is unisexual. They convey complex moods. They play a lot of notes, and it is not always clear where all these notes are heading. As a listener to sax music, you must concentrate along the way to catch special riffs, cute and coy in's and out's, quick cascades—and these notes don't all culminate in a dramatic G above triple C. Sometimes they just peter out, in a decrescendo.

I'm afraid I've organized this talk as a saxophone piece, not as a Maynard Ferguson trumpet solo. There will be no triple C's, no orange jumpsuits, no pelvic thrusts. I don't expect roaring approval, and at best there will be a fadeout that may make you brood, or scratch your heads. But at least you won't lose your hearing.

The idea of a last lecture puzzles me. I don't know quite what to say that could possibly live up to the occasion. I don't have something valedictory to say to you, a gem of wisdom that you might take away with you and then from time to time pull out of your back pocket to see how it keeps on shining. Besides, I don't believe in using an academic podium to push political programs and personal agenda. Max Weber, the German sociologist, was asked to give two last lectures, which he gave on the lives of scholarship and on politics as vocations, respectively. In his "Scholarship as a Vocation" lecture, he deliberately refrained from telling students how they should live their lives.

> Fellow students! You come to our lectures and demand from us the qualities of leadership, and you fail to realize in advance that of a hundred professors at least ninety-nine do not and must not claim to be football masters in the vital problems of life, or even to be "leaders" in matters of conduct. Please, consider that a person's value does not depend on whether or not he has leadership qualities. And in any case, the qualities that make a person an excellent scholar and academic teacher are not the qualities that make him a leader to give directions in practical life or, more specifically, in politics. It is pure accident if a teacher also possesses this quality, and it is a critical situation if every teacher on the platform feels himself confronted with the students' expectation that the teacher should claim this quality. It is still more critical if it is left to every academic teacher to set himself up as a leader in the lecture-room. For those who most frequently think of themselves as leaders often qualify least as leaders. But irrespective of whether they are or are not, the platform situation simply offers no possibility of *proving* themselves to be leaders. The professor who feels called upon to act as a counselor of youth and enjoys their trust may prove himself a man (*Mensch*) in personal human relations with them. And if he feels called upon to intervene in the struggles of world views and party opinions, he may do so outside, in the market place, in the press, in meetings, in associations, wherever he wishes. But after all, it is somewhat too convenient to demonstrate one's courage in taking a stand where the audience and possible opponents are condemned to silence.[1]

We academics love to be righteous and indignant; we love to get up on a soapbox and preach, especially to the already converted, but I must tell you that I'm not a cleric or a prophet, and I can't give you that kind of talk today. But I am aware that neither do you want me to present my latest academic findings regarding Plato, Pico, or Bataille. You want *something* revelatory, I imagine. Two years ago I gave a Blue Room lecture in which I confessed all the sordid details of my own past—so I can't really do that again. In thinking about this talk, I reread Emerson's famous lecture, "The American Scholar," but I found that woefully pretentious.[2]

What I've decided to do is to draw again on my own past, to tell you about two more heroes of mine of sorts—heroes if not exactly role models. I do so in order to underscore my profound ambivalence about being here today, speaking to you about what it means to be teaching at Pomona College. I must tell you, twenty-one years ago I never would have expected that I would be giving a talk such as this. I tell you that not as a way of introducing a longer tale of odyssey and triumphant overcoming. America is full of self-made men and women stories, rags to riches recollections, tales of wandering and discovery, stories about captivity and deliverance. The redemption genre, the prophetic tradition, usually features an extraordinary hero who leaves or escapes the past, only to find that the past is somehow still with him or her. The ultimate redemptive moment, American style, is then to give up a bit on the dream of redemption, the dream of beginning anew all over again, of getting a second chance in life, and finally to accept one's surroundings, one's homecoming, with a new found good cheer.[3] I'm not going to do that, however.

My story is that twenty-one years ago I wasn't quite yet poised to become eventually a professor at a small liberal arts college; it wasn't fated that I should be here. At the time I found myself rather thrown into the role, occupying the very real life, of being a Teamster truck driver. I had an idea that I wanted to attend college, though my parents hadn't attended college, and mine would be the first generation in the family ever to do so. But we kids knew that we'd have to pay for it ourselves. The task seemed insurmountable. I had a paper route from fifth grade on, and I hated that paper route, because it took me away from friends every day after school, but those solitary walks every day made me meditate upon this and that, it made my legs strong, and I can still fold and fling a newspaper faster than about anyone.

But I also needed more money. I eventually got a job putting away hardware at a retail lumberyard. One day they asked me to deliver some hardware to a job site. I didn't know how to drive very well, and I didn't know how to drive a stick shift at all, but the other drivers didn't care. They laughed at the stupid young kid. There was a lot of bucking and kicking in the pickup on that first trip, but the damn hardware got delivered. Soon I was graduated to big, full-size lumber trucks. Double axle, long-bed, flatbed trucks, ten gears forward, two backwards. When I started driving such trucks, at fifteen, I couldn't legally drive them, nor could I belong to the union. I was so scared every day that I'd be pulled out of the cab either by a cop or by a union guy. But at sixteen, the next summer, I got my chauffeur's license and my union card. I was now an official member of Teamster Local 238, and

I remained an active member for eight years, driving every summer and during vacations.

In this context I worked closely with two guys who are the subjects of my talk today, the yard foreman, a guy named Ronnie Nath, and the head truck driver, Dennis Winkie. They were characters, spirited personalities. I don't mean to romanticize working-class stiffs, that isn't the point of my talk, nor is it to parade my own working-class credentials; these guys were just special characters, and I happened to spend a lot of time with them. They were always effusive and gregarious, always had a joke or special story to tell; they had a gritty zest for life that was built around other people. People came into the alleyway of the yard just to shoot the breeze with Ronnie and Denny for a spell, and I was an observer of these many conversations.

Ron was a gruff, scruffy, bearlike guy. He had a big barrel chest and a weathered, ruddy face that showed the strains of divorce and eight kids, eight daughters, and far too much Jack Daniels and Wild Turkey. He had a belly that merged with his chest and hung over his belt. He smoked Mores, those long, thin, brown cigarettes. Ron was a tough guy. He slept only three hours every night and then worked all day. He had no teeth in his head. They had rotted out, and he just told the dentist to yank the rest all out, never to be replaced. But he could eat anything, steak, whatever, gnawing and gumming at it. The only thing he couldn't eat were peanuts. If you wanted to piss Ronnie off, that is, to see him get pissed off in a mock-macho sort of way, chuckling after he had called you some names, then offer him a few peanuts. (And of course I often did.) It was a good ritual.

Denny was younger, a farm boy and Vietnam vet. Denny was good look-ing, dashingly handsome, really, a ladies' man, with a great smile and bulging muscles, but not because he ever pumped iron in any gym. He smoked Camels without filters. Both Ronnie and Denny wore the same outfit every day—blue jeans, a buttoned cotton shirt with rolled up sleeves in summer, a flannel shirt in winter, cowboy boots. It was a look, a proud look. The two of them worked together like a team—Ronnie would load his forklift with a load of lumber fit to the specifications of the job. He'd band it with a steel band, and then load the bundle and other pallets onto Denny's truck. Denny would tie it all down, add some materials to the order, and then he'd haul off to the job site, dump the load, and return.

And then I became the third special character, the kid. We were a threesome. Although there were other drivers and yard workers, Ronnie and Denny took me under their wings. We developed a camaraderie that went beyond a working relationship. Ron was the ringleader. He was the center of attention. He was a master storyteller. He told stories every day, every ten-minute break; every lunch period was filled with a story, a joke, a quip, an urban legend, *talk* in general. He dazzled me with tales about people and their lives, stories he heard last night at the bar, stories from his checkered past, stories from ingoing and outgoing customers. His storytelling had a cadence and a special vocabulary, mostly filled with expletives, but the rhythm and the lyricism were undeniable. Some people disgusted him, some were the butt of his jokes, some were exalted as exemplary individuals. These stories filled my head at a young age and provided the emotional stuff of my summer existences. Life, every day during these summers, was an adventure. I looked forward to coming to work every day. The days were filled with stories, were filled with action, with drama, with special sights and sounds and smells— lumber, sawdust, forklift exhaust. Ronnie and Denny would go inside the lumberyard, into the offices, and sometimes tease and provoke and cheer up the secretaries, clerks, and office personnel. But those people had indoor jobs, behind a desk or a counter, and Ronnie and Denny looked with contempt and some pity upon such people. Who would want to work indoors when you could work outdoors? Why would you want to work indoors where it is cramped and stuffy? Outdoors the sun would shine, or maybe not. Outdoors, when we had to pee, we went inside a shed and peed on the ground. And when we worked, we worked hard, physically hard, and it felt great. During the summers it was so hot and humid, and we'd work up a sweat, and then break time would come, and we'd down Pepsis and donuts. I loved that combination, I loved that combination, hot weather, hard work, cold Pepsi, donuts, cigs, and stories.

I learned a lot about life from these guys. First, they were always intense, alert, inquisitive about all matters around them. Nothing would escape their scrutiny. They had a fully three-dimensional sensibility, employing all senses, not just one side of their brains. I had to learn, for instance, how to follow their directions taking me through the country roads of Iowa, directions that were very different from the map-reading skills taught in school. "Go three-quarters of a mile down the road until the bend to the right, where old man Higgins went off into the ditch that time, loop around until you get to the mile marker, there's a rusted bailer lying in the field there, and take the second dirt road near the stump." Their directions were always right on target—they had memorized the entire world, every street and stump, in this fashion—and I learned that I could trust such directions entirely.

Next, Ronnie and Denny were simply damn good at what they did. Ronnie was an artist with a forklift. That forklift seat was his throne. Sitting up there, he could maneuver that machine, fully loaded, through the tightest places; he could pile units of lumber higher than anyone I've ever seen. Operating the forklift was second nature, it was a gift. Denny exuded a more quiet competence. He tied down his loads with a variety of intricate knots; he knew the physics of conveying lumber on a flatbed truck; he also had certain interpersonal qualities that enabled him to mix with any potentially contentious contractor on any job site. He could diffuse any hostile situation with a quip and a disarming smile. "Hey, I'm a lover, not a fighter," he'd tell an angry carpenter. Moreover, nothing ever seemed to bother Denny, at least outwardly; his disposition was always upbeat. He just got the job done, day in, day out. He could ripsaw with the best of them, though Ronnie was master of the saw as well. Both of these guys had extraordinary minds, fascinating minds. Ronnie especially prided himself on being able to load a pad of lumber in a way that the carpenters could unload it off the top just as they needed, and the task was to deliver just enough lumber so that the carpenters at the job site never needed any more or any less. Reading but a job order, Ronnie and Denny could calculate the dimensions and material needs of an entire house. And then, years later, they could recall, with virtually total recall, I swear, everything that they had loaded and delivered to a particular house. It was an astonishing display of human ingenuity, and I got to witness it every day. They had an almost telepathic communication with various carpenters and crews; they knew and adjusted for the different eccentricities and work habits of different crews. Carpenters would come in grateful and admiring of their talents—this on-the-ground understanding was something about which managers, developers, real estate agents, and architects were completely oblivious. I, too, aspired to learn how to load the perfect load such that there'd be little waste. It was a challenge, an intellectual jigsaw puzzle—imagine, how would you plan to deliver all the materials for an entire house and in the proper order, the bolts, the nails, the two by fours, the two by tens, the plywood, CDX and AD, the sheetrock, the trusses, the windows, the doors, the felt paper, the shingles, the trim, and so on?

Once the truck was loaded, I got to deliver these cargoes. Let me tell you about that. The truck would normally hold three or four pads of lumber, but Ronnie could squeeze on (illegally) as many as eight. And then we'd put a couple of steel i beams on top—that was a load! I'd drive to the job site, downshifting much of the way, making sure not to accelerate or stop too quickly. You'd get to the job site, find out where the carpenters wanted the load dumped. The truck had a hydraulic hoist underneath it, which raised up the front end of the bed. I can't fully describe how exciting the process of dumping lumber was. As the hoist started to rise up, one end of the lumber, banded together, would fall to the ground off the end of the truck, and then, as the hydraulic piston kept pushing up the front end of the truck bed, you'd drive the truck out from under the pile, letting all the lumber crash to the ground. The trick then was to drive away quickly so that the lumber wouldn't catch the end of the truck as the hoist retracted. It was precarious, because when the hoist was fully extended, the weight of the lumber might twist it. The entire truck was usually sitting on mud, imperfectly balanced, and there was always the chance that the truck might tip over, or that the entire steel piston might just snap. But oh, what a feeling of accomplishment when you heard that crash of lumber, and then the second crash of the bed back onto the truck. You knew then that all was well, you could pull out, wave to the carpenters, go back to the yard, get a little windshield time in. It was exciting, orgasmic. The reward for a successful dump was to go a coffee shop on your way home, sit for a moment, and reflect.

After a few summers, I told the guys I would be going to college. They started calling me, even back then, Professor Squeery. But that was okay. They suspected that I wouldn't be a truck driver all my life. "Kid, you've got the world by the tail on a downhill pull," Ronnie would tell me. One summer, respecting my academic skills, they assigned me a bunch of background reading about vasectomies, because they all decided to get them (the summer before they had all gotten divorces, and I had helped with their divorce papers). There was a competition about who could return to work the soonest after the operation. Of course, Ronnie won. He came back to work that same day. But his balls swelled up, and his entire groin area turned black and blue. "I'm shooting blanks," he told everyone.

These guys were tough, the work was tough. We never wore gloves handling and loading the wood, because gloves, even leather gloves, would wear out in less than a week. Your hands became callused, they became packed full of splinters, but soon enough you learned to ignore the splinters. Besides, as Ronnie remarked, the splinters eventually fester out anyway. (Most of the guys were missing a finger, a digit, or a nail, claimed by the saw.) It was also one of my jobs to cut glass and repair windows, so my hands became all cut up, splintered, callused, swollen, and festering during the summers. During the summers I couldn't play the saxophone—my mangled hands became a joke among my nonlumber yard friends (not to mention a romantic turnoff). I didn't really care—I was learning too much. About priorities, for instance. Since Ronnie slept only three hours per night—there was too much life to live to waste it sleeping—he had to know how to pace himself on the job. "Hurry up with that load," I'd yell to Ronnie, "I've got to get on the road by eleven." "Kid, there were two bulls, an old bull and a young bull, standing on a hilltop, overlooking a valley, and they spotted a herd of cows down below. Hey, says the young bull, let's run down there and fuck one of them cows. The old bull replies, let's walk down there and fuck 'em all." The lesson I learned from that joke, by the way, was *not* that rape and violence against women are okay if only you plan ahead and trivialize women as cows.

In the first of several jarring life transformations, I found myself, between summers, attending a liberal arts college on the East Coast, Amherst College. At Amherst I didn't like the prissy, rich frat boys whose idea of male bravado was to guzzle down beer. One of the reasons I like being at Pomona College is that there are very few preppy assholes here (that's a strictly technical term, by the way, preppy asshole), and you all should fall on your knees and thank the goddess every day that you attend a private liberal arts school that has avoided somehow, miraculously, the preppy element, or at least the conspicuous display thereof. I'll tell you, as a freshman I myself bought a pair of preppy-like brown khaki pants, so much in fashion then, but soon enough I became alienated from that whole scene. These people were not people I wanted to emulate. I started wearing again my flannel shirts, work boots, blue jeans, even overalls—and it amuses me to no end today to see that my natural grunge look has become fashionable. One of my preppy roommates always introduced me with some patronizing glee as the working-class hero. Gilbert Hecker, Gib Hecker, son of Margaret Cox, a member of the Mayflower Society, a daughter of the American Revolution, Gilbert Cox Hecker—I would get back at Gib by telling people who met him, say his name three times real fast—(Gilbert Cox Hecker, Gilbert Coxhecker, Gilbert Coxhecker). Gib. He wore brown khaki pants, topsider shoes, a white shirt, and a very natty red plaid vest; the only social life Gib had known before attending college was to escort debutantes. Despite our class differences, I loved Gib. Word was that Gib committed suicide last year, which I still can't understand or accept, and I'm angry about it. How could anyone, in good health, squander a life? Such a person, Ronnie would say, could fuck up a free lunch.

Anyway, there *were* some high points in my college days also. Two guys from California approached me about starting a big band, since the snooty Amherst music department didn't feature any jazz, except for a pretty boy a cappella singing group called the Zumbyes. I hated the Zumbyes. Ronnie and Denny would have hated the Zumbyes. One of those two California guys hailed from Los Angeles. He looked just like the singer Lou Rawls, he talked, he had a voice just like Lou Rawls, his last name was Rawls, but he didn't know who his father was, it was rumored, and he was from L.A. And musically he was talented. That guy played a beautiful trumpet. The three of us got together about twenty student musicians, we found some sheet music, we borrowed some music, we started playing some paying gigs and then could buy some more charts. Soon enough we were put on a twin bill with the damn Zumbyes, and I'm happy to report that we blew them off the stage. Russ Rawls' trumpet solo, his rendition of Maynard Ferguson's version of *MacArthur Park*, stole the show. By the end of the year, Clive Barnes wrote a piece about us in the *New York Times*. One of our trombone players, a woman from Seattle of all places, diplomatically suggested that I should start wearing something else to the concerts besides blue jeans and shit-kicker boots. I got the message.

What does it mean to me to be teaching now at Pomona College? It is a blessing, but, given my background, a mixed blessing. A few years back, Ronnie was fired at the lumberyard. I admit, to persons in authority he was a troublemaker, he had a chip on his shoulder, and the boss finally had enough of it. Part of the reason for Ronnie's demise is that Denny had left a few years earlier. He married a woman named Brandi who already had five kids and wanted Denny to leave Iowa for Texas. "Show me a happily married man," Ronnie groused, "and I'll show you a fool." Denny split up the tandem, broke those male bonds. But then we heard that Brandi had left Denny for another man in Texas, and now Denny was supporting eight kids, three by an earlier marriage. And then, just about a year ago, I heard that Denny had moved back to Iowa, and that he hired on at the same truss-construction company where Ronnie was now the yard foreman. But I haven't had the heart to go back and see them. My hands are prissy again, I've forgotten how to tie my knots to secure a load, hell I haven't operated a forklift or a radial arm saw with a tungsten steel tipped, sixteen-inch blade or a flatbed double-axle truck in years. I used to be so proud of the fact that I could reach into a nail bin and pull out the exact weight of nails that a customer requested. And I don't wear blue jeans anymore (this is sounding like a bad Neil Diamond song). I just don't have the guts to tell Ronnie and Denny that I've taken an indoors job in life. As Robert Reich has remarked, some of us get paid to pour concrete, and some of us academics get paid to analyze symbols. That bodily divide doesn't fill me with a sense of guilt now but rather one of unremembered loss.

But this isn't a downer talk. The compensatory joys of being at Pomona have been abundant. I don't want to be mawkish here, but there is a particular character about the Pomona studentry that I like and in an odd way reminds me of the Ronnies and Dennys of the world. I like the intellectual energy and the undiscriminating curiosity that attend a liberal arts environment. I like the inquisitiveness here, the hard work, the talk and debate, and the fact that there are a myriad of stories, lives, and memories in the making. There is something else I like about being here in particular, and I'll tell you another secret. Appearances often can be deceiving about people, in fact, they can be inversely related to a hidden truth of a situation. Some of my well-meaning but possibly myopic friends in academe might take one look at Ronnie and Denny and all they would see are a couple of crude, rude, sexist, redneck jerks on whose offensive language they would want to put restrictions; having spent time with these guys, I knew that they weren't angels—far from it—but I also know that they were two of the most expansively democratic individuals I have ever encountered. They could talk with anyone, and they wanted to talk with everyone. They were interested in building houses, as opposed to tearing them down—perhaps in part as a result of their own broken marriages. "You can win the argument," I was told, "but you'll lose the customer"—which, by the way, was *not* a statement about how to sell more 2 x 4s, and it also confounded Carol Gilligan's understanding of gender differences. Those textbook labels we throw around to classify people—homophobe, misogynist, male, labor—don't capture who Ronnie and Denny were in particular.

There is something similar about the Pomona students, a situation wherein appearances belie reality. Pomona students, on the whole, I've found, don't know how good they are, and accordingly they don't know how good each other, their own peers, are—sometimes this leads to a morale problem. Somehow Pomona students seem to think that the center of academic activity exits elsewhere, say at Stanford or Amherst, and that they, Pomona students, must be therefore a bit reserved or even apologetic about attending this liberal arts college of ours—Ponoma, Poboba, Posoba, Cal Poly. Since I spent four years at Amherst and four years at Stanford, methinks that you've got the best of all undergraduate worlds here—but you're probably not in a position to realize that. Amherst, to an obscene degree, doesn't attract kind students, generous and friendly students; Pomona students, by contrast, don't feel a need to puff themselves up, don't feel a need to wear their intelligence on their sleeves; they—you—carry your virtues more lightly. Stanford is a superb trade school and country club, but it is an abysmal place for the liberal arts. You don't read books at Stanford, you jog—and last year I was really astounded to hear how many Stanford seniors didn't know any professors at all from whom they could ask for a letter of recommendation. There's a good part of me that doesn't want to blow the cover on this little public relations misconception; there's a part of me that doesn't want Pomona to be ranked number one or two on those U. S. Snooze and World Distort polls. If that happened, you'd start attracting students here for the wrong reasons; you'd start to get a larger asshole element. I'd rather that Pomona remain a secret; sometimes I'm even glad that there is a smog cover here, so the place remains relatively hidden to the untrained eye, and that we continue to attract students who come here not really knowing how or why they ended up here. Pomona students seem to come here a bit tentatively, a little unsure of who they are in the national scheme of things, but along the way, because of that ill-defined identity, they retain, I think, I hope, a spirit of inquiry and self-questioning, a sense of the provisional nature of things. If I had my way, I would legislate somehow that our ill-defined collective identity continue to characterize our inquiries and our relations here with one another. If what Emerson, in his lecture "The American Scholar," was doing was to declare that students at Harvard need not have an inferiority complex vis-à-vis the Europeans, what I want to say to you, a bit less grandiosely, is that Pomona's West Coast inferiority, a Southern California/Los Angeles inferiority, an occasional crisis of confidence or self-doubt, or rather, to put it another way, less backhandedly, the unassuming integrity of our students, a kindness mixed with competence, is precisely why I like it here. Let's keep it that way. Weber ends his lecture by noting that if communities are to flourish today, they must be understated communities, communities fashioned by indirection.

The fate of our times is characterized by rationalization and intellectualization and, above all, by the "disenchantment of the world." Precisely the ultimate and most sublime values have retreated from public life either into the transcendental realm of mystic life or into the brotherliness of direct and personal human relations. It is not accidental that our greatest art is intimate and not monumental, nor is it accidental that today within the smallest and intimate circles, in personal human situations, in *pianissimo*, that something is pulsating that corresponds to the prophetic pneuma, which in former times swept through the great communities like a firebrand, welding them together. If we attempt to force and to "invent" a monumental style in art, such miserable monstrosities are produced as the rnany monuments of the last twenty years. If one tries intellectually to construe new religions without a new and genuine prophecy, then, in an inner sense, something similar will result, but with still worse effects. And academic prophecy, finally, will create only fanatical groups but never a genuine community.[4]

Here at Pomona, I haven't talked about the joys of teaching in the classroom. As serious as I believe that activity to be, I am also aware that students have lives and concerns that extend beyond the classroom. And I like the idea that the spirit of liberal arts is to encourage you to try your hand at a range of activities. There is a time to be bookish, a time as well to play a part in a theatre production, a time to take a class that won't simply lead to a job, a time to make friends. For my part, I don't get to drive a truck anymore, but I have my hands back to play saxophone again, though not enough time to play it very well. Still, I get to play in the band here, which is an utter joy after a fifteen-year hiatus. I'm not in charge of the band, so I get to sit back in my chair during rehearsals and watch the students perform and, altogether, produce music. I get to participate just a bit in their lives. I sit behind the flute section—they are a very giddy bunch but strike me as the most intelligent and hirsute section in the band. We have a wisecracking minister from town in the band who plays a beautiful baritone; Professor Alma Zook conducts research on the physics of music while she blows a mean oboe. There's an old guy in the band, an alumnus of Pomona College from the class of 1948, who plays trumpet after all these years—imagine, playing the trumpet at age seventy with really nice college kids at your alma mater—hey, that's my idea of getting a glimpse of heaven on earth. I get to sit next to fellow sax players Pam Rino and Amy Schmeider, and we crack jokes, and I will miss them greatly when they are gone next year. And I will remember them and will keep their places warm after they leave. Presiding over this motley crew of personalities and musical aptitudes is our conductor, Graydon Beeks, at whose indefatigable patience and goodwill I continuously marvel. Somehow he keeps this all-voluntary group going, and in good spirits. I might remind you that the band, like so many organizations on this small campus, is your band as well. Having reminded you of that, I'd like to put in a plug. The Pomona College Concert band will be playing at little Bridges, Saturday, April 30, at 1:30 P.M. We have been working especially on our pianissimos and decrescendos. I invite you all to attend. Thank-you.

5

Moral Perfectionism
and Abortion Politics

T his chapter explores a line of interdisciplinary speculation that suggests
the possibility, if remote, that a pro-abortion political stance (often referred to in minimalist and somewhat euphemistic terms as "pro-choice"[1])
might be intellectually reconcilable with a variant of moral perfectionism.[2]
In brief, the case to follow argues that some of Georges Bataille's reflections on
religion and political economy can be applied to Christian theology, so that
the result, now sufficiently modified, yields a perfectionist teleology that can
productively serve contemporary liberalism with respect to abortion politics.

The political background to the following experiment is well known:
abortion continues to be a divisive issue in American politics today and at
times threatens to disrupt the relative tranquility of constitutional liberalism.
Abortion clinics have been bombed, medical practitioners and educators
intimidated and harassed, and murders committed through ostensibly well-
coordinated conspiratorial acts of domestic terrorism. One's public stance on
abortion can serve as a litmus test, a wedge issue, for presidential politics,
judicial appointments, and even local school board elections. "Pro-life" and
"pro-choice" movements have squared off in repeated electoral and extra-
legal contests, to the point that neither side now expresses much hope of
striking common discursive ground for adjudicating differences amicably.
Escalating, embittering, and uncivil confrontations seem to be in store for
the foreseeable future—or, as a calm before the next storm of protest, "stealth"
candidates and behind-the-scene movements go underground, lying in wait
for the opportune time to strike out in public.

Landmark U.S. Supreme Court rulings—*Roe v. Wade, Griswald v. Connecti-
cut, Eisenstadt v. Baird*—have not, time and again, laid the issue of abortion to

rest. One side may lose a particular battle over this court case or that judicial nominee, but both sides now brace for a protracted civil war of sorts that will last beyond any particular election or even the lifetime appointments of current Court personnel.[3] There are reasons for such commitment. Pro-choice advocates argue on behalf of women's autonomy, while working to avoid the pain, suffering, and deaths of women that are always attendant to the criminalization of abortion. Opponents of abortion often claim that the moral issues involved in abortion transcend legal procedures and remedies. Killing the fetus is tantamount to murder, and all of the U. S. Supreme Court or legislative declarations in the world cannot excuse murder. Murder, even if legally permissible and democratically sanctioned, must be steadfastly opposed— by any means necessary. Especially with abortion, morality trumps politics.[4]

The issue strikes at the heart of liberal democratic theory. According to an only occasionally contested commonplace of liberal theory, the liberal state enjoys relative autonomy from the demands of various interest groups and civil associations, because it gives procedural priority to "rights" over substantive "goods." The liberal state is not supposed to promote an overarching principle of human excellence or cultural mission but rather negotiates between and among conflicting claims.[5] The neutral liberal state may choose to try to maximize overall happiness or distribute goods justly, but the raison d'être of the liberal state qua state is not to promote the cultivation of great individuals, great works, or great deeds. Perfectionism, as John Rawls resolutely asserts in A Theory of Justice, is "denied as a political principle."[6] Parties in Rawls's original position, in view of their disparate aims and their attendant embrace of the principle of equal liberty, do not agree to an overarching principle of perfection.[7] Although persons in the original position know that they have "certain moral and religious interests and other cultural ends which they cannot put in jeopardy" and are "committed to different conceptions of the good and . . . think that they are entitled to press their claims on one another to further their separate aims," they nonetheless recognize that even their "spiritual ends" will be better served by preferring equal liberty over perfectionism.[8]

Rawls's critics have been many over the years, but only recently has his nonperfectionist liberalism been challenged by the abortion debate.[9] Michael Sandel, in Democracy's Discontents, cites the abortion debate as an example of liberal reluctance (read: Rawlsian reluctance) to discuss public matters in "substantive" ways.[10] Liberals often attempt to steer the debate away from the moral-religious dimensions of abortion, he claims, but focusing on the "procedural" issue of women's choice will not capture the hearts and minds of Americans generally. We must confront the life-or-death stakes of the matter instead of pretending that the abortion controversy can be adjudicated by laying fair ground rules for decision making. The pro-choice position simply cannot engage the convictions of someone who truly believes that abortion is murder. Murder is murder, and a society cannot allow even the most thoughtfully agonizing women to choose murder. Religious conceptions of the good must not be "bracketed" from the discussion, maintains Sandel.

Although Sandel himself avoids a substantive religious discussion even as he calls for it, other liberal writers have been attempting in recent years to try their own hand at bringing religious language into a public debate about abortion. Feminist author Naomi Wolf, for instance, broke with some pro-choice ranks by arguing that "the death of the fetus is a real death,"[11] pardonable only by reference to "great religious traditions" of atonement.[12] Helen Alvare, representing the Catholic bishops, responded approvingly, thus, "Usually when I debate on this topic, I feel like I'm behind a podium speaking French and the other person is behind a podium speaking Finnish. There's no common ground. But Naomi Wolf allows a conversation to begin."[13]

Wolf caught the attention of the Religious Right by insisting that the choice to abort the fetus is not one between a woman and her doctor but "between a woman and God." The choice, she adds, is not simply personal: it is a profoundly moral issue about "life and death, right and wrong." Liberal legal theorist Ronald Dworkin committed a similar apostasy in writing that abortion should be viewed not primarily as a matter of legal entitlements and privacy rights but, rather, that it belongs to the dominion of what counts as "sacred" in life.[14] Dworkin does not condemn all abortion in light of life's sanctity, but he thinks that legal language is inadequate in addressing the deeper issues involved. In an unacknowledged reversal of Rawlsian originalism, Dworkin reasons that the unborn have no prior interest in a life that they never achieve: only from the retrospective position of the living can such an interest be articulated. He denies that abortion should be viewed from the perspective that the fetus is a rights-bearing person whose rights must be weighed against the rights of women; rather, the "detached" principle of the sanctity and inviolability of life should hold sway, a principle that "has a secular as well as a religious basis."[15] Legal and feminist theorist Drucilla Cornell chastises Dworkin for abandoning a rights-based defense of abortion, but she insists that her rejection of Dworkin's abortion argument is not because she disagrees with him that "the debate over abortion has an important religious dimension."[16]

Hence, liberals, even pro-choice liberals, seem to be finding religion as they talk about abortion in public.[17] Part of this new deployment of religious rhetoric may be merely strategic: the Religious Right has pursued both constitutional and extraconstitutional means of fighting legal abortion, and its resolve seems unwavering, thus it may be prudent to head them off at the pass, to preempt their own terms. Yet Sandel, Dworkin, Wolf, Cornell, and others seem to be making sincere concessions to the view that religious conceptions of the good should be brought to the bargaining table of politics[18]—they seem to be calling for greater political respect for moral perfectionism in a way that Rawlsian originalism cannot accommodate.[19]

Part of the problem may be that Rawlsian originalism simply cannot accommodate the particular perfectionist claims of abortion opponents, because Rawls apparently never considers the abortion issue as a question of justice.[20] The problem may be endemic to the original position: Rawls never gives a good motivational theory about why parties would want to leave the original position, whereas earlier, state-of-nature contractarians provided such narratives and thereby issued commentaries and judgments about the relative benefits of the civil versus natural worlds. But by retreating from such naturalism into a constructivist account, Rawls cannot issue an overarching principle about the benefit of post–originary living as such, especially for those whose existence is politically at issue. He does not count sheer existence among the most primary of goods, whereas the pro-life position wants an originary testimonial to the excellence of human life that would envelope even Kantian regard for the intrinsic value of those already living. Rawls assumes that parties to the original position will in fact be born (though they do not know when), which reveals a lacunae in Rawls's intuitionist purview: the lives of these parties are never in theoretical jeopardy, and thus never taken into political account. Rawls has not considered potentially aborted fetuses as contractors, and thus his contractarianism, situated between perfectionism and utilitarianism, begs or erases the question of consent for parties that may or may not wish to be born.

Dworkin does not think that consensual or contractual accounts illuminate the abortion debate at all: "We cannot explain our concern about future humanity, of course, as a concern for the rights and interests of particular people. . . . It is absurd to argue that we would then have done terrible injury or injustice to people who would otherwise have lived, unless we think that in some very crowded mystical space people are waiting to be conceived and born. We sometimes talk that way, and may even fall into ways of thinking that would make sense only if there were such mystical worlds of possible people with a right to exist. But in fact our worries about humanity in centuries to come make sense only if we suppose that it is intrinsically important that the human race continue even though it is not important to the interests of particular people."[21] Rawls, in fact, is irrelevant: "Our concern for future generations is not a matter of justice at all but of our instinctive sense that human flourishing as well as human survival is a matter of sacred importance."[22] Dworkin tries to explain what is meant by "the sacred," and essentially he asserts that many conceptions of the sacred issue from a respect for creativity, whether divine, natural, or artistic.[23] Respect for life as sacred and inviolable can be secular as well as religious, he insists. But in the end he does not push the explanation too far,[24] except to say that the sacred (however construed) must be given its due in any debate about abortion, and that giving such due may serve common cause:

> Seeing the abortion controversy in the fresh light I described will not, of course, end our disagreements about the morality of abortion, because these disagreements are deep and may be perpetual. But if that fresh light helps us to identify those disagreements as at bottom *spiritual*, that should help bring us together, because we have grown used to the idea, as I said, that real community is possible across deep religious divisions. We might hope for even more—not just for greater tolerance but for a more positive and healing realization: that what we share—our common commitment to the sanctity of life—is itself precious, a unifying ideal we can rescue from the decades of hate.[25]

Whereas Rawls rejoined that his theory was political, not metaphysical, Dworkin wishes to recenter the abortion debate as spiritual, not political.

We might take a step back and view these recent liberal overtures toward religiosity as admirable in intent: such writers are trying to understand and appeal to their pro-life opponents; they resist conventional liberalism, perhaps Rawlsian contractarianism in particular, in the name of convictions seemingly more compelling than liberal accommodation; they want to speak truth to human values that seem elided by rational-analytic philosophic approaches. Yet I might suggest that while attempting to give voice to religiosity, such writers might be too deferential, too uncritical, and too narrow in their overtures toward and acceptance of such religious viewpoints. Dworkin, in particular, seems too eager to respect the unquestioning respect performatively invoked by appeals to "sacred" notions. As William E. Connolly suggests, the interrogation of the sacred/secular distinction needs to travel in both directions:

> Tocqueville recognized the profound interdependence in America between the Christian experience of the *sacred* and *secular* presentations of nature, reason, and morality. Subterranean connections between these two contending cultural forces persist today. But today we may be on the verge of a movement to reconfigure that relationship, a movement of drawing sustenance from recent drives to pluralization in the domains of gender, sexuality, immigration, dying, and privacy. The hope is to *pluralize the contemporary sacred/secular duopoly control over the cultural currency of morality*.[26]

In abortion politics, such a fruitful pluralization of the religious language of the sacred would require secular scrutiny of certain propositions drawn from Christian theology. In the remainder of this chapter I explore a way in which Christianity in particular might be challenged and reconfigured so that a new strain of Christian perfectionism might be compatible with a pro-choice political stance. This experiment attempts as well to remain situated within a Rawlsian framework of liberal constructivism, although resistance to Rawlsianism will necessitate modifications to the original designs. Rawls understands his earlier principles of justice as serving "as part of a doctrine of political economy."[27] Georges Bataille also announces his major work, *The Accursed Share*, as a book on political economy,[28] but he relates the language of political economy intimately to the language of ethics and religion, Christianity in particular—a connection that Rawls refuses to draw. I propose taking a few insights from Bataille and applying them to the religious language often invoked in the abortion debate, so that a modified Rawlsian scheme might be better able to address abortion discussions.[29]

Bataille proposes viewing global forces in economic terms, albeit from the greatest macroscopic perspective possible: the material basis of the world depends on the production and consumption of *energy*, thus one studies its overall interdependence and interaction, the circulation and flow of energy. While economists routinely analyze patterns of circulation, characteristically they focus on energy production, seeing value only in creative labor, and characteristically they see resources as limited. Moreover, they tend to see consumption of excess resources as wasteful and thus nonuseful. But Bataille wants to reposition the importance of apparently nonuseful consumption—expenditure—as being crucial to the overall flow of energy.[30] Living organisms frequently encounter more energy resources than are required for their brute survival, and human beings often display a desire to consume excess energy resources (call that wealth) beyond need. They often spend lavishly. They squander resources, they give exuberantly, and they consume pointlessly. Classical economics, which proceeds from the labor theory of value, fails to recognize this destruction of energy as anything but destruction: Bataille calls that limited economic outlook "restricted." A "general" economic outlook sees excessive consumption and extravagant destruction as being crucial to the overall circulation of energy resources.[31] From the vantage of general economics, even death can be creative.[32]

Bataille relates his economics to a theory of religion, but before we rehearse that connection, let us return briefly to Dworkin. In Bataille's terms, Dworkin's understanding of "the sacred" proceeds from a theology of restricted economics: what is sacred is sacred, because it has been created, whether by divine, natural, or artistic intervention. That creation is to be respected and protected, presumably because it holds value as a limited resource of sorts. The labor theory of value largely informs Dworkin's notion of sanctity, with God as the ultimate creationist force. Typically, Dworkin can understand death only in noncreative terms: "Abortion is a waste of the start of human life."[33]

For Bataille, the sense of the sacred is related to the festivity of sacrifice, and all sacrifice involves destruction.[34] The Christian religion posits a duality of sacred and profane worlds and, thus, from a general outlook, Christian theology confronts a logistical problem of conceiving energy transfers (as it were) from one world to another. This theological problem is compounded, because Christianity posits an eternal, continuous soul that must be connected somehow to a finite, discontinuous sensual body: "... how to adjust the sacred world of continuity to the world of discontinuity which persists. The divine world has to descend among the world of things."[35] The boundary crossing, a flow of connection, is effected through violation and destruction, a sacrificial death, that restores a sense of the sacred to the profane world. "Sacrifice destroys an object's real ties of subordination; it draws the victim out of the world of utility and restores it to that of unintelligible caprice."[36] Sacrifice is a gift-giving ritual that connects the profane world to the sacred but, especially in Christianity, that sacramental sense requires death.[37] Dworkin implicitly recognizes this connection between the sacred and death, for he writes a book about life's sanctity through discussions about abortion and euthanasia, but again, from his limited theological purview, wasteful deaths cannot serve the sacred and instead stand in need of sanctification.

Dworkin wants to shift the abortion debate from a narrowly secular focus on the strictly legal question of whether and when the fetus should be regarded as a person deserving constitutional protection to a more wide-ranging discussion of what counts as a domain of "the sacred"—a discussion, in other words, that will necessarily engage religious and metaphysical sensibilities. That shift will presumably help illuminate our deep-seated differences and may in turn help break the impasse over constitutional issues about personhood and fetal protections. Yet I would like to see a similar wide-ranging interrogation on the *religious* side of that equation.[38] What, for instance, are the *religious* ramifications of denying personhood to fetuses? Does destroying the fetus prematurely result in condemning an innocent soul (not just the souls of the perpetrators) to eternal punishment? Are eschatological concerns driving hard-line political beliefs? In particular, pro-life forces need to clarify the theological status of the fetus's soul and its otherworldly destiny, especially if those background beliefs bear implicitly on the secular question of personhood. I suggest that Christian theologians and activists do some internal soul searching because, as far as I can tell, the doctrinal question of the fetus's *religious* status is anything but settled. Dante Alighieri had to create a special place in his underworld for innocent unborns, because Scripture provides no reliable guide on this issue. The Bible enjoins against killing, but no biblical decree that I can find states that fetuses are necessarily better off born into mortal existence than not. Job, in fact, curses the night he was conceived and the day he was born. Catholic theologians, from Jerome to Augustine to Aquinas to the Council of Trent, more or less followed Aristotle's distinction between "unformed" and "formed" or "animated" fetuses to argue that ensoulment, and therewith fully human life, begins not at conception but at some later point in embryonic development. The current Church position (since 1869) does *not* teach that ensoulment begins at conception but, rather, that since we humans cannot be sure when a soul is infused, we should act as though it commences at conception, lest we risk murder.[39] In short, the Church's doctrinaire policies on abortion seem to grow out of profound *theological* ambiguities, reservations, and compromises—and those questions need to be explored, not preempted.

Bataille does not address abortion explicitly, but he discusses at length the connection between death and procreative sexuality: "We must never forget that the multiplication of beings goes hand in hand with death. The parents survive the birth of their offspring but the reprieve is only temporary. A stay is granted, partly for the benefit of the newcomers who need assistance, but the appearance of the newcomers guarantees the disappearance of their predecessors. . . . Death is waiting in the long run, made necessary by multiplying and teeming life."[40] These macroscopic or "objective" elements do bear on subjective consciousness: "the objective fact of reproduction calls into question with the subjective consciousness the feeling of self, the feeling of being and of the limits of the isolated being. It questions the discontinuity with which the feeling of self is necessarily bound up because that furnishes its limits."[41] This perceived connection between eroticism and death gives rise to theology,[42] an attempt to address the crisis of discontinuity. Bataille offers a theory about how Christianity responds to this crisis by purging orgiastic sacrifice of violence and by proposing that "in Christian sacrifice the faithful are not made responsible for desiring the sacrifice. They only contribute to the Crucifixion by their sins and their failures."[43] Yet this supposedly benign restoration of the sacred is not wholly successful under Christianity: "Christianity could not get rid of impurity altogether"[44] and thus had to demarcate and attack certain unclean elements within the profane Christian world: witches, cults, prostitutes, pagans. "Desire for harmony and conciliation in love and submission"[45] was never far from transgressive violence typically manifest in forbidden erotic practices. The "mental agonism" of Christianity often escalates beyond hateful humiliation into the dirtiest cruelties.[46]

Christianity, for Bataille, is deeply ambivalent about the profane world, and thus over the course of its history Christianity has always developed innovations, both theological and practical, in order to adapt to changing earthly conditions. In view of that history of adaptation and of the theological uncertainty surrounding the status of the fetus's soul, we might suggest that it is not inconceivable that mainline Christianity could be reinterpreted in a way that accommodates and even condones, from a slightly reworked religious point of view, the legalization of abortion under certain circumstances. Such a paradigm shift would derive from similar Church logic, as stated above: if we humans must assume that, for all functional purposes, ensoulment takes place at conception, then it behooves us, if we are faithful Christians, to look after the fate of aborted souls subsequent to their destruction. From that vantage, then, it would not take much negotiation to inspire greater religious respect for abortion, prompting a theologically *affirmative* view (that would help justify, but not incite, actual abortions). One could point out, for instance, that abortion might hasten and virtually guarantee the fetus's blissful reunion with its holy Creator. Putting the case in even bolder terms: greater spiritual recourse to abortion could even be viewed as providing a solution to the problem that Bataille analyzes as Christianity's "ambivalence" toward the profane world, which manifests in violence in one form or another. In short: make Christianity more "efficient" in general economical terms via greater theological respect for abortion. In the Christian imagination, the soul informs life at or around conception but then is forced to descend further into the profane world at birth. The aborting of fetuses, however, need not wreak eternal damage upon the souls of fetuses and overall could effect a greater recycling of souls (in Bataille's terminology) back to the holy Creator. More abortions, viewed as sacramental rather than unholy, could represent a more efficient Christian theology than even the "Great Return" espoused by Aquinas. Instead of viewing abortion foremost as an impure act connected to illicit sexuality, the focus instead could be directed toward the belief that one more soul has been saved, and saved in the purest fashion.[47] Instead of viewing the act as simply sinful, an implicated woman might be able to find some mitigating solace in the theological speculation that no eternal damage will be inflicted upon the soul of her aborted fetus—she might even be doing it a great good. Indeed, Christianity could be reconstrued as *preferring* a teleology of abortion: a death sacrifice prior to living would be the happiest, or least violent, Christian reconciliation with the sacred possible.[48] Better that death teleology in Christianity than an apocalyptic one deferred until Armageddon.[49]

In the near future, abortions will likely increase in rate and number,[50] if only because new technologies will make them easier and more accessible; global population pressures will likely promote more drastic birth control methods; and the breakthrough medical benefits of fetal tissue will surely place an exchange premium on aborted matter as a highly sought, marketable commodity among the living. Although they are pro-choice, Dworkin's and Wolf's response to this impending onslaught is to deploy religious language apparently designed to accentuate women's guilt as the primary agents of destruction. Dworkin and Wolf want to underscore that such deaths are indeed tragically wasteful and morally wrong, even if sometimes necessary, and only through other sacramental gestures could any sense of religious atonement be forthcoming. But Bataille offers an ingenious way to see waste as a luxury, more in keeping with a fast-track, consumption-driven world. Moreover, fundamentalist Christianity simply will not be able to keep pace with new reproductive technologies and demographic developments, and thus orthodoxy will become more entrenched and is liable to meet the same fate as ascetic communism analyzed in the third volume of Bataille's trilogy.[51] My modest (if factitious) suggestion is that abortion could be viewed as the *perfect* fate for Christian souls, that it actually aids certain theological problems of circulation, and a theological reevaluation of abortion could underscore that all souls, aborted or otherwise, are tending toward the same goals anyway.

[*Note:* a pro-abortion or pro-death practical psychology or sociology does not necessarily follow from the above renegotiated metaphysics. It should not be assumed that a reevaluation of the theological benefits of abortion will actually lead to an increase in abortions. As Max Weber pointed out in his famous study of the effects of Protestantism, a worldly ethic of fatalism or hedonism did not follow historically from Calvinist predestinarianism, as might be predicted on the basis of theology alone.[52] Similarly, commentators about Islam often claim that Qur' ānic doctrines of perfection, such as the injunctions toward *jihād* (warfare) or *shahada* (martyrdom), do not necessarily nourish violent, radical, or terrorist movements but largely sustain reformist and compromising practices.[53]]

What extra benefit might accrue to the fate of women who abort, according to this reconfigured Christianity? As survivors, they would likely experience reduced psychic cost for having committed the violent act of destroying some form of life. They could begin seeing this squandering not simply as a necessary evil but as a potentially sacramental gesture, a saving of the fetus's soul and a perhaps slightly longer reprieve from death for themselves, the living, or as a direct way of helping others, for instance, bone marrow transplant patients, live. Bataille's reflections on economy can help in still another way: classical economics understands exchange only as barter, but Bataille draws on Marcel Mauss's study of potlatch and repositions potlatch as being central to the workings of creative/destructive consumption.[54] Bataille associates potlatch with the marriage bond and procreative sexuality (though, again, he does not apply his reflections to abortion). Women are traditionally the gifts given in potlatch: "Marriage is not so much the act of the betrothed couple as it is that of the woman's 'giver,' of the man (the father or the brother) who could have freely enjoyed this woman (his daughter, his sister) and who gives her away. The gift he makes of her is perhaps a substitute for the sexual act; the exuberance of giving, in any case, has the same meaning—that of an expenditure of resources—as this act itself."[55] The gift giving in marriage reveals marriage as a festivity of transgression that overcomes and absorbs erotic taboos into a now-purified world: "In this movement, humanity's *purity*, which the prohibition establishes—the *purity* of the mother, of the sister—slowly passes, in part, to the spouse who has become a mother. Thus, the *condition* of marriage reserves the possibility of a properly human life, pursued in respect of prohibitions opposed to the free satisfaction of animal needs."[56]

But abortion could redefine women as the primary gift givers.[57] Giving the gift of death could be viewed, for women, as a *better* gift than giving the gift of life. The gift of death could be viewed as a luxurious offering to the fetus, the guarantee of redemption without any bodily pains involved. If, as Derrida contends, a true gift can never be returned,[58] then the gift of premature death would be a better, more efficient gift than bestowing the gift of life, which contains an ambiguous legacy and merely defers death anyway. Moreover, the gift of death, as a nonreturnable purchase, eliminates the cycle of gift-giving escalation characteristic of potlatch: accelerating rates of abortion, should they increase for whatever reasons, could therefore be viewed as helping stave off Christian apocalypse, promoting human welfare and the quality of life for those currently living.[59] "Pro-life," viewed in these general economic terms, would turn out to be "pro-abortion."

A quandary for some pro-choice feminists is that with new prenatal screening technologies, compounded with global pressures for population control, proto-female fetuses are liable to receive the disproportionate brunt of abortion in the same way that female infanticide seems to account for huge gender imbalances in certain regions of the globe.[60] Yet a new moment of Christian utopianism could view this imbalance as a luxury: Heaven would be disproportionately gendered in favor of formerly female fetuses. Besides, those surviving bodies that must suffer the vale of terrestrial tears would be disproportionately represented as male: such male body/souls would need to experience a slower death, and according to most Christian schema, they still would need to earn their salvation in one way or another. Thus, females would hold both the power of sacramental death and would be the primary beneficiaries.

The point is, if we accept the Christian narrative that proclaims that human existence ends in a bodily death that does not extinguish an abiding soul that wishes finally to reunite with its Creator, then a more efficient economic outlook on that general plan would recognize that we humans are all oriented toward the same ultimate goal anyway, and such a perfectionist insight, in Christian terms, might narrow the "substantive" gap between pro-life and pro-choice forces. The comparative worth of living versus not living is not covered by Rawlsian originalism, largely because Rawls deems such speculations procedurally out-of-bounds. Quasi-religious or metaphysical or perfectionist language *must* be reintroduced into the Original Position, however, in order to eke out such invidious life-or-death judgments as called for by the abortion issue. But Bataille's innovative political economics also suggests that in attempting to fill in that gray zone of speculation, we do not need to accept received religious language at face value, without inside modification whatsoever.

Is it so far-fetched to imagine a practicable transvaluation of Christian values regarding abortion? In fact, religions innovate all the time; the major religions constantly devise new rituals, alter orthodoxy, and adapt traditions to changing times. It is not so unbelievable that Christian clergy today might start offering religious services and sacraments designed to cope with the practice of abortion (a few already do)—and changing attitudes could evolve accordingly. If religious activists started dwelling upon *religious* forms of so-lace regarding abortion, instead of concentrating their main efforts on politi-cal and legal remedies, then I could imagine more churches offering baptisms after the fact, or memorial and burial services for aborted fetuses (as fetuses), or the construction of religious spaces and rituals for grieving survivors—including women who abort. Reportedly, one of the most traumatic experi-ences for many women who undergo abortion in the United States (and elsewhere) is that they have few people with whom they can talk about it afterwards and few acceptable public institutions where they can freely go in order to grieve, cope, talk, and survive.[61] One could argue that the appropri-ate venue for such services should be religious in nature, or at least that churches should be offering those services to women (and men) who would prefer a religious response to abortion. If the Religious Right is serious that the fetus should be treated as a person in the secular realm, then such advocates should probably first prove those convictions by providing in their own houses of worship full sacramental and memorial services for aborted souls.

Japan presents a perfect comparative case where traditional religion has been altered significantly to accommodate the modern practice of legal abor-tion, and the innovative accommodation—metaphysical, not political—works nonetheless to the benefit of the political sphere. In stark contrast to the United States, Japan is not polarized politically over abortion, and it boasts strong family values, even in the face of relatively high abortion rates.[62] Traditional Buddhism takes a strong stance against the taking of any life—the "First Precept" of Buddhism is a vow of moral behavior that states, "I will not willingly take the life of a living thing"—and Buddhist scriptures also are very clear that babies in wombs are lives to be respected. Yet in recent decades, Japanese Buddhists have become largely accepting of the practice of *mizuko kuyō*, a religious service commemorating dead fetuses, complete with rituals, prayers, and burial services, and the right to legal abortion simply is not made into a pressing political issue by religious opponents.

William LaFleur has argued that Buddhism has reconciled itself and adapted to the exigencies of contemporary abortion through a kind of moral *bricolage*, an acceptable and a useful assemblage of fluid metaphors and folk practices whose bits and pieces borrow from various sources, traditional and contemporary, and altogether renegotiate a pragmatic course of action between orthodoxy and circumstance.[63] In charting this path, LaFleur contends that "religious metaphysics made the difference."[64] Drawing upon common water myths and related metaphors, as well as older Buddhist notions of the transmigration of souls and also an indigenous belief in a kind of "recycling" of dead children, the contemporary practice of *mabiki*, or "returning" the *mizuko* or unborn, starts to make sense. An adumbrated cosmology of "returning" an unborn child back to a limbo world, where in waterly repose it awaits again rebirth under better circumstances, or a return to the abode of the gods and the Buddhas, performs several functions. First, the mabiki puts a favorable spin on the abortion. It suggests that the return of the mizuko will ultimately be to a place far better than that of a family that does not want it: the abortion is good for the unborn. It also is good for a society, for it is beneficial to control the entry of children into the world: abortion is a kind of family planning, and in contrast an unchecked "fecundist" religionism can prove extremely detrimental to a country with population pressures. Families are thereby encouraged to see the "liquidation" of children as something other than an act of finality, they can conceptualize what happens to the fetus and maintain an ongoing, responsible relationship with those unborn souls, and living survivors are provided with public rituals designed to mitigate (though not eliminate) their sense of loss and guilt. LaFleur thus explains the apparent paradox that abortion, with the right metaphysical tweaking, can be seen as compatible with strong family life and practices that aim to maximize both societal and spiritual happiness.

Yet the notion of moral bricolage stands in jarring contrast to the idea of moral perfectionism—ritualistic and cognitive "muddling through" could hardly be equated to perfection. In light of LaFleur's analysis of mizuko kuyō, I submit that a reimagined Christianity could better accommodate, in a perfectionist mode, the practice of abortion than even a reworked Buddhism. LaFleur touches upon some of the crucial metaphysical differences between Christianity and Buddhism on this issue:

> . . . whereas the Christian cosmology assumed a *one-time only* creation by God of a soul for each fetus and a strictly forward movement from that point on, the Buddhist one entertained the possibility of a wider range of potential moves—including backward and lateral ones. Analogies are never exact here, but perhaps one from the world of games may help to show the difference here. Life as understood by Europe's Christians was invariably a forward movement—till death—and in that is not unlike the game of checkers. Japan's Buddhists, by comparison, saw life as a kind of ontological chess; its movements could be forward, lateral, or backward on the board. This opened up a wider range of possibilities.[65]

Key to the Buddhist reconciliation with abortion, claims LaFleur, is *adumbration*: what exactly happens to the dead child is left ambiguous and sketchy, and no one associated with mabiki wants to press for greater details. "There is just enough detail to keep the concept rich and open to variant interpretations. The point is to avoid so much specificity that the notion gets hardened into a rigid—or refutable—doctrine."[66] Instead of consigning the aborted unborn to a vague limbo that eventually, after several revisions, will more or less work to everyone's advantage, a Christian linear teleology of direct reunification with a Creator would provide a more "efficient" circulation between the living and the aborted dead. LaFleur even notes that a good deal of the public criticism of mizuko kuyō rites in Japan arises from a sense that such rites are a "waste," and defenders of the practice have a hard time explaining the benefits of wasteful expenditure in Bataillean terms.[67] He also notes that Japanese Christians, especially Western Catholics residing in Japan, seem to be fascinated with the mizuko ritual, and they are now moving beyond criticism toward an "understanding" of these rites. It is "not unreasonable," he proposes, to expect that the practice may eventually be accepted into the Christian context itself: "Mizuko kuyō may, in time, prove to be a context wherein the Catholic Church's adamant opposition to abortion comes—at least in Japan—face to face with what some perceive to be the emotional and ritual needs of persons who, rightly or wrongly, have had abortion."[68]

> However, it is not, I think, insignificant that Westerners who have lived in Japan—including persons who are Christian—have increasingly come to the view that there is an appreciable level of psychological and spiritual sanity in the practices of mizuko kuyō and that aspects of these practices should be introduced into Western society and the ambit of the West's religious modalities. Although, given the official positions of the Roman Catholic Church on abortion, there is a reluctance to articulate such things overtly, a growing number of Catholics in Japan, I am told, have an interest in exploring what of the mizuko kuyō could be transferred into Christianity. There are also, it appears, members of the clergy who share this interest, and this all seems to arise from a sense that the churches that condemn abortion wholesale have in many instances proven unreasonable and impractical.[69]

One of the reasons Western political theorists might want to study the Japanese case is that *religious* acceptance of abortion has enabled that society to avoid the kind of political divisions and disruptions over abortion that we have experienced in the United States, whereas we seem hopelessly deadlocked over abortion, even at the theoretical level.[70] In light of mizuko kuyō, Rawlsian liberalism might want to redesign the original position so that it takes into account family planning, providing an intergenerational purview that distributes entry into the world in an equitable and a reasonable manner.[71] But once we start tinkering with the benefits and timing of worldly entry, we have left the strict realm of political economy and entered the proper sphere of metaphysics.[72]

My own recent work has tried to extend Rawlsian contractarianism into a death construct by imagining a Final Position in a land of the shades, wherein democratic contestations occur between and among the awakened dead, postponed until after the fact of living, and thus judgments about justice may be imagined as bestowed (or anticipated) post hoc, after all information has been put on the table, as it were.[73] Such a death conceit gives greater voice to consent as an aspect of justice, I argue, whereas Rawls, in the original position, freezes consent (as one-shot bargaining) and places it under conditions of imperfect information about our lives to come. Thus I propose that we can better address issues of intergenerational justice from a Final Position than from the Original Position, or we can better address the public dimensions of forthrightly death issues such as suicide assistance or murder. As my colleague, Daniel Conway, brilliantly suggested to me, Rawlsian originalism can be modified by including zombies and ghosts at the bargaining table—those who do not know whether they have lived yet and died, or not. At one point I include the unborn in this death perspective of the Final Position, but I now must say that aborted fetuses pose a special case for Rawlsianism constructivism. The dead-who-have-lived can be more easily imagined as speaking and consenting for themselves, but those who have been aborted cannot be granted quite the same constitutional status as persons-to-be, even in a land of the shades (which traditionally features all sorts of former life-forms, including the unborn). Abortion, then, poses special problems of democratic consent, even in a constructivist mode. Dworkin dismisses the issue when he says that only the living can have rights, but the problem is rather one of *representation*: who speaks for the fetus? The pro-life movement presumptuously claims to speak somehow for the unprotected unborn, and the pro-choice movement reserves choice for women but not for dependent fetuses, however imagined.[74] My book ends with an imagined conversation between a mother and her aborted fetus in the land of the shades, wherein the fetus is allowed to speak for itself or can be imagined, in any case, as "mutely self-representative,"[75] but I do not elaborate on my cryptic suggestion.

Now in retrospect I think I was attempting to bring together, in one collapsed vision, the rival concerns of what are called the "justice" and the "care" perspectives. Carol Gilligan, famous for her contribution of a care ethic, spoke not just about the games that little girls and boys play but also about women and their concerns about pregnancy and abortion.[76] Women who abort, she contends, consider the circumstances of abortion around issues of care and responsibility, not simply or primarily around arrangements of formal morality—such women seek recognition "of the continuing connection between the life of the mother and the life of the child [sic]."[77] My own view is that my conception of an imaginary conversation between a woman and her fetus captures some of the intimacy proposed by the "care" perspective, but as construed from the semi-detached, semi-deferred death perspective as if located in a land of the shades or a "final" position, that conception retains a dimension of impersonal justice as proposed by the Rawlsian construct, a kingdom of ends.[78] This displaced Rawlsianism, which features afterworldly, democratic, face-to-face confrontations instead of judgmental deities, does not rank moral virtues from a universalist vantage, which is the main Gilliganesque complaint about Kohlberg–Rawlsian analyses, but it does prompt deliberation about closures and hard judgments, justice as relational but also blindly binding.[79] Although it gives some independent voice to fetuses,[80] it still views women as empowered and accountable, the primary choosers of life or death from the perspective of abortion.

This neopagan but democratic afterworldly account can be put into respectful competition with Christian afterworldly accounts, even those modified via Bataille, as above. Pluralizing afterworldly conceptions (in the hope of introducing morally deep, life-or-death language about political issues such as abortion) runs the risk of returning to a nonperfectionist Rawlsianism, but I suggest rather that the issue of justice conceived from a final rather than an originary gambit better accommodates rival perfectionist claims: "Pro-choice" could thus become the preferred political stance out of deep *religious* respect, a spiritual reconciliation,[81] instead of a contrived and contentious proceduralism. Displacing their dispute from courts or congresses to the metaphysical heavens, erstwhile opponents might find that they can first forge considerable agreement or mutual concessions about the ends of life (or rather, about the ends of an afterlife), after which viable political and legal accommodations are more likely, if ever, to obtain.[82]

6

Political Philosophy
in the Twilight
of an Idol

I t gives me great pleasure to attend this symposium, "Nietzsche and Modernity," on the happy occasion of the publication of Professor Daniel Conway's
book, *Nietzsche's Dangerous Game: Philosophy in the Twilight of the Idols*.[1] My
association with Professor Conway dates back to 1985, when we both found
ourselves, as new Ph.D.s, teaching in Stanford University's infamous and
now defunct Western Culture Program. Our three years' teaching in that
program happened to coincide with the last three years of the program—
although we weren't *directly* responsible for the demise of the program. But
yes, it can now be safely revealed, we were two of the thickheaded goons
who had been teaching Homer, Shakespeare, and Cervantes to politically
unsuspecting and culturally vulnerable Stanford undergraduates who consistently rated our classes as among the most valuable in their Stanford education, even while celebrity protesters marched outside our windows chanting,
Hey hey, ho, ho, Western Culture's Got to Go. Little did the critics realize
that inside those classrooms we were teaching Marx, Freud, and Nietzsche,
whose inside attacks on Western Culture were much more devastating than
those purporting to emanate from the outside. Yes, it was a time that gave
rise to irony. Our interim solution to the absurdities in our midst was to bite
our tongues and go underground. One of my first conversations ever with
Dan was when he came to my office to talk about the use of irony as a
teaching tool during dark cultural epochs. "What a strange but enterprising

---

Talk delivered at the Pennsylvania State University, October 29, 1997.

fellow," I thought to myself. Eventually we would publish a couple of articles together on irony, and then a book together,[2] and emboldened, we took our campaign on the road. We gave papers jointly at a couple of conferences at the end of which we would propose, modestly, or perhaps falsely modestly, that we sought funds to establish The Irony Institute, a think tank that, according to our wildest dreams, would relentlessly shadow the Rand Corporation with a series of rival recommendations on policy issues of the day. Well, it didn't go very far. Back at home, Professor Conway and I also co-founded the Stanford Orpheus Society, a subterranean faculty reading group comprised of a motley collection of misfits and malcontents who somehow found wayward inspiration together in tracking the exploits of infernal travelers in the Western tradition of descent literature, those epic figures emulating Orpheus—namely, Odysseus, Aeneas, Dante, Faust, Zarathustra—who descended figuratively into Hades to seek solace and insight via poetic communion with other underground sojourners. Ah, those were the days! And to think that we even succeeded in winning school sponsorship for our crepuscular activities. I mention all of this background to suggest to you that it should come as no great surprise, in light of his checkered past, that Professor Conway today should be publishing a book once again dedicated to the grand themes of cultural demise, pent-up resentment, and self-implicating decadence.

Let me rehearse the barebones argument of Professor Conway's book, *Nietzsche's Dangerous Game*, and then I will mention a few issues that the book raises for me, and perhaps we can use those issues as a starting point for discussion. The book is situated in the field of political philosophy, and it takes seriously the idea that Nietzsche's writings should be so considered, rather than belonging properly to the fields of, say, existentialism, philology, ethics, or even today's fashionably catchall cultural studies. Nietzsche had *political* aims and strategies, often grandiose ones, and his work must be assessed on those terms. Hence, Conway's book undertakes a critical appraisal of the political philosophy that informs Nietzsche's post–Zarathustra writings, namely, in that three-year period just before he goes mad, 1885 to 1888. To that end, Conway first reconstructs what he calls Nietzsche's revised critique of modernity—and already Conway's thesis is complicated, because his reconstruction requires that he explain how Nietzsche's critique of modernity changes and evolves from his earlier writings to these post–Zarathustra works such that the latter constitute a period on their own. The second aim of the book is to situate Nietzsche's post–Zarathustran political thinking within what Conway calls the "self-referential" context of Nietzsche's revised critique of modernity. The notion of self-referential critique is key to Conway's analysis at every turn, and it makes for an extremely provocative reading of Nietzsche. Basically, Conway's claim is that Nietzsche at times knowingly implicates himself in his own analysis of modernity's decadence—

and thus we are left with quite an interpretive challenge: How much of the analysis of decadence can you trust when it issues from a self-avowed decadent, whose own terms of analysis invite suspicion and mistrust? Conway also adduces evidence that at other times during this period Nietzsche seems to exempt himself from his own diagnosis of decadence, or rather, he fails to follow his own prescriptions, all of which again complicates our understanding of Nietzsche, because maybe his signal failures confirm as much as they betray the original analysis. Hence, the book operates at several levels of interpretation. It isn't simply a book, a formal exegesis, about Nietzsche's writings as such, but rather the analysis of self-reference requires that we readers make inquiries after the author and his intentions, an old-fashioned, non-Derridean move at this point. But more, a book about self-referential decadence necessarily implicates Nietzsche's interpreters, hence, Conway's book becomes a book about Nietzsche's scholarly commentators and about today's academic Nietzsche industry, the fact that there are so many books and articles published in various attempts to understand this nineteenth-century figure, so it is also about reader-response and the dubious relation of those responses to the supposed aims of the author. Finally, I want to propose, a book that analyzes Nietzsche's self-referential aims, his successes and shortcomings, as well as the successes and shortcomings of Nietzsche's readership necessarily implicates Conway in the snare of self-reference. I'm not going to say flatly that this book is finally about Conway, but the book does raise the question of self-reference with respect to Conway's authorship, and it behooves us, his readers, to seek an account of Conway's reading in relation to past Nietzsche scholars and in relation to Nietzsche's purported intentions. Anyone who writes a book about self-reference makes himself vulnerable to those lines of inquiry. We have, therefore, a challenging, intricate project on our hands and, indeed, Conway is a strange and enterprising fellow.

Nietzsche's later writings, contends Conway, constitute his mature political thinking, for they are marked by Nietzsche's growing awareness of his own complicity in the cultural malaise that earlier he presumed to diagnose and to treat. Other commentators who have been keen to Nietzsche's concern about his own complicity in decadence have construed these problems of self-reference as vicious, but Conway takes the problem of self-reference as the starting point for his investigation. Nietzsche understands not only that a philosophical confrontation with modernity must appeal to immanent standards of evaluation, but also that an immanent critique of modernity must apply to the critic who advances it—but here is the catch, another catch-22, for clever Nietzsche. Nietzsche has no idea, says Conway, where his self-referential critique of modernity may lead. He cannot know, because, as the avatar of his own theory of decadence, he is perhaps in the worst position (and perhaps the best position) to evaluate decadence objectively or to cure others of the cultural ills that beset him, if indeed cures are called for. Other commentators have depicted Nietzsche as a champion of the heroic will, someone who entrusted the redemption of modernity to super-human acts of almost aesthetic affirmation or a new post–theological ethics. But Conway thinks otherwise. Modernity is an age, for later Nietzsche, characterized by advance decay, and modern agents, including Nietzsche, lack the will and the wits to reverse or arrest such downward spiraling. Any attempt to implement a political solution to the problem of modernity would only compound the decadence of modernity and possibly hasten its advance. But Nietzsche, despite his own acute awareness of his own shortcomings, can't resist trying. Conway quotes a passage from *Beyond Good and Evil* in which Nietzsche describes certain philosophers who throw their philosophic caution to the wind, who yield to temptations, take risks, and play "a dangerous game."[3] That passage becomes, of course, the basis for Conway's title. Nietzsche plays a dangerous game with his readers. In order to extend his influence into the next millennium, when cultural conditions may become more sanguine for political rejuvenation, Nietzsche, in the interim, must cultivate a readership that inevitably, because instructed and goaded on by Nietzsche, will likely turn their own decadent analyses against him. In order to deliver his teachings to the mysterious "philosophers of the future," Nietzsche must recruit wily emissaries who display some cunning and late-modern initiative on their own but who also will probably distort his teachings; but that's the best Nietzsche can bargain for, hence, he must play a dangerous game of authorship, which will involve a tussle with his careful but impertinent and similarly decadent late-modern readers. Although Nietzsche prefers to depict the dangerous game as a heroic agon, a test of wills between brave author and daring readers, Conway intervenes to propose that Nietzsche's predilection for disciples and fawning sycophants is a manifestation and betrayal rather than a neutralization of Nietzsche's own decadence and ultimately prevents him from cultivating the perfect readers who might safeguard his teaching for a better day. Nietzsche hoped that his teachings would be remembered after his death, so that posthumously he might be reborn (as it were) and remembered as the original Antichrist during a later epoch that will be more receptive to post–Christian sensibilities. In the name of the Antichrist, grand political upheavals might ensue. Nietzsche's grandiose political ambitions haven't, however, come to fruition and most likely won't, yet he seems to have partly succeeded in training a significant collection of decadent Nietzscheans in the late-modern world— a lot of people read him and study him, and he indeed got himself remembered through nothing but provocative rhetoric—and thus we have to pause to evaluate what kind of double-edged success Nietzsche perhaps unwittingly has won for himself. Why, in short, are we academics so enthralled with Nietzsche?

Conway's book is the first book I have read that explains Nietzscheanism in the late twentieth century, and the answer is indeed compelling. In fact, I consider the book nothing less than a tour de force, which probably, given the analysis, reflects poorly on my own mental health. Nonetheless, Conway's book is an extraordinary, impressive accomplishment. He has read, digested, and synthesized an enormous body of difficult primary and secondary literatures—and his scholarship to my eye is impeccable—and yet, he goes beyond simple analysis to issue his own comprehensive and original thesis that puts all of the material at hand into a new perspective. That is a stunning feat, especially since the field of Nietzsche studies is crowded and complex. I particularly admire the fact that while Conway builds on the work of those before him and often takes issue with prior interpretations, he relegates most scholarly infighting to the footnotes and even therein resists much of the *Widersagen* and rancor that characterize most academic positioning. The main text of the book is devoted to his extended argument about Nietzsche, and what emerges is a rare, even-handed, balanced reading of Nietzsche—Conway presents himself neither as a cheerleader for Nietzsche nor as an enemy. But the balanced reading isn't a tepid reading: Conway doesn't domesticate or tame Nietzsche, and he alerts us, indeed, to Nietzsche's dangers and excesses. By the end he urges us to appreciate Nietzsche's perverse genius without, however, becoming ourselves disciplic. By the end Conway also emerges as a new kind of reader of Nietzsche: someone who isn't simply using Nietzsche for his own purposes, as a template on whom the reader can map his own hopes and resentments, someone, in other words, who hasn't been an easy mark for all of Nietzsche's underhanded ploys.

Conway makes a great deal out of Nietzsche's critique of modernity as performative: Nietzsche not only describes decadence, but he exemplifies, enacts, and reacts to it. We've heard others talk about philosophy as performance—from Austin, of course, and more lately from Derrida, Rorty, and Butler—it's all the rage—but no one has heretofore explored the self-referential implications of a performative decadent. To this end Conway invents his own term, *parastrategesis*: Nietzsche deploys various experimental rhetorical strategies aimed at a presumptive audience, which indicate directed authorial intent, and yet his intention is to cultivate the kind of reader who might resist his intentions and venture beyond the sphere of his influence. Nietzsche gambles, in other words, on recruiting apostates to himself. But then he can no longer depend on his own strategic mastery, his own intentionality, and thus the prefix *para* added to his risk-taking techniques.

I wonder about how many philosophers, or scholars in general, think about their formative influence on their audience, or think about the different kinds of audience they might attract. We all do so implicitly—some of us might want to write in a more popular vein, others want to exchange arcane jargon and shibboleths within a coterie of secret initiates; but what

Conway's analysis of parastrategesis makes me realize is that all sorts of moves are possible beyond simple admiration and acceptance. I think artists are usually more aware of the audience than we academic writers. So often, it seems, when I'm reading a scholarly work these days, the not-so-secret subtext is, "I've read a bunch of books; respect me as a scholar!" and I'm supposed to be bored or beaten into submission. So much academic writing has become predicable and perfunctory in form; we've abandoned style, we've emulated the natural sciences, we pretend that we are testing hypotheses and arriving upon demonstrable results. Our results validated, we want approval and applause. I'm reminded of a story about opera impresario enfant terrible Peter Sellars—after one production in Los Angeles of one of his operas, the cast members came out, and the audience gave them thunderous applause, the orchestra received a similar greeting, and the same for the entire production company; and then, at the very end, Peter Sellars walked on stage, and an extraordinary thing happened: the audience stopped clapping, and in unison, shouted, *boooo*. I know Peter fairly well, and I can guess what he would say about that reaction: it was a *great* day. He had succeeded. He had touched a nerve, affected many people deeply. Sometimes you want boos, or should be doing work that draws widespread ire, not acclamation.

I also think artists are more often apt to think about affecting an artistic accomplishment that achieves some kind of permanence, of an influence that lingers through several ages, of their own artistic efficaciousness. Scholars, writers, philosophers—especially those writing after Max Weber's famous "*Wissenschaft als Beruf*" speech—hardly ever anymore aspire to crafting some influence beyond their immediate scholarly circle. We pedants seek to score points, to be cited in other journal articles, to be invited to conferences, to get paltry merit pay raises but the idea of exerting historical influence via writing seems hopelessly remote and romantic. Nietzsche, according to Conway, thought otherwise, which was hubristic and decadent, but Nietzsche was also somewhat successful, so the hubris was perhaps justified. Maybe we should reclaim the performative dimensions of our own writing, while writing still has an audience before the multimedial epoch takes over entirely. To do so we must not fall prey to a complete cynicism about authors and their intentions; writing is not simply the dissemination of signifiers. It can also be, though need not reducible to, a test of wills, an exchange of sentiments between authors and readers.

Conway explicates superbly Nietzsche's critique of agency—Nietzsche rejects all moralities that trade on the metaphysics of agency, will, responsibility, blame, and guilt. *Pace* many interpreters, Nietzsche is not, according to Conway, a radical volunteerist, a German-style Emersonian individualist. Thus the political rejuvenation of Western culture cannot depend on the efforts of willful decadent moderns. The analysis of heroic will confuses cause and effect, puts the cart before the horse. Instead, the emergence of healthy

individuals already presupposes the flourishing of a healthy, vital epoch.
Nietzsche's critique of modernity's decadence is thus sweeping and wholesale: there is no intentional way to get from point A to point B, no way
to redeem modernity from within. Conway explains that Nietzsche believes in an organic, vitalist model of cultural formation: the health of an
epoch frames, informs, even determines the health of particular individuals
in that age. But that determinist theory raises questions about Nietzsche's
own privilege: How can one analyze broad cultural preconditions when
those preconditions are largely invisible to agents acting within those ages?
Conway explains that Nietzsche employs symptomology: Nietzsche takes
representatives exemplars of an age and works backward, via symptoms, to
assess cultural preconditions.

At this point my own social scientific background intervenes to raise all
sorts of methodological questions. Why isn't the background causal notion
of a people or an epoch or an age as much of a grammatical fiction as the
willful subject? How can Nietzsche, sitting in his cubicle, his isolated place
of garret, accurately assess the health of all modernity, all Western peoples,
for the next 200 years or so? Conway admits that the theory of symptomology
is dubious, and he sees Nietzsche's broadside critique as evidence of Nietzsche's
own decadence: Nietzsche anchors his theory of decadence in a sweeping
account of Western history, even though Nietzsche knows that all such
metanarratives are epistemically bankrupt. But I want Conway to say more
on this. My own view is that great thinkers often reduce complexity to an
elegant insight that doesn't seem at first reductionist, and it takes us a while
to step back from the sly metanarrative—with Christ, all becomes love, with
Marx, all is class struggle, with Freud, sex and eroticism, with Foucault, you
begin to see every relation as power, with feminism, everything is a function
of patriarchy or gender, and even with Weber, everything in modernity seems
to be a result of Western rationality that ends up in an iron cage. Heideggarians
these days are also in a foul, nasty mood about everything. Here's my backhanded compliment for Conway on this score: his account is perhaps too
successful, too sweeping, it makes too much sense of both Nietzsche's successes and shortcomings, and thus Conway delivers insufficient resources to
us to critically evaluate Nietzsche's project. The image of Nietzsche as a self-
betraying decadent covers too conveniently his own tracks; it explains or
resolves his witting and unwitting contradictions, makes sense of his excesses
and lapses—or else, if we can't make sense of some of Nietzsche's efforts, that
limitation then redounds to our detriment, for as readers we are thus unable
to discern his secret teachings, or else we are caught up in denial and bad
faith. Either way, any response that we might have to Nietzsche can too
easily fit the broad thesis of decadence that frames Nietzsche's claim. But the
problem is that there is no way to test, in order to confirm or to falsify, what
is essentially Nietzsche's speculation or his bad mood about modernity. Just

as modernity cannot be redeemed from within, neither can Nietzsche's thesis, as Conway presents it, be confirmed or confuted from within. Once stated, I fear that we just can't do much with it, because it is so all-encompassing, or else we just reach a stalemate. Conway merely shifts the burden of proof back upon Nietzsche's critiques of his doom and gloom. He writes: "Indeed, if [Nietzsche's] critique of modernity is to be exposed as a genuinely fraudulent mismeasure of the age—as opposed, say, to an unpopular, curmudgeonly assessment of our collective failures—then his critics are eventually obliged to produce actual (as opposed to theoretical) counterexamples to the descensional trajectory he purports to chart."[4] I don't know, I think $E = mc^2$ is pretty impressive and is leading to an interesting understanding of the universe. What would Nietzsche say about Einstein? Isn't our postmodern episteme more Einsteinian than Pauline?

Finally, I wonder about the performative dimensions of Conway's own project. Conway is clearly a recipient of the dangerous game; he is a distinguished graduate alumnus of Nietzsche's educational training ground—and I'm tempted to start calling him Dangerous Dan. It's not that Conway is claiming himself to be Nietzsche's chosen reader or his most worthy enemy, nor is his claiming to be a future lawgiver. He's learned from other Nietzscheans before him, but he is not just casting his lot in with theirs—he's positioning himself as a new kind of reader, one who steps out of the game and can identify the game as such. His book, I want to say, is a better read, it is an improvement. We are learning more about Nietzsche. We probably should give Nietzsche a good deal of credit for this ongoing legacy. We should also give Conway a good deal of independent credit. The quality of Conway's work militates against the dark conclusion that everything written in the twilight of the idols is for naught, or is simply a last-gasp expression of active nihilism, those who make a go of it despite their limited volitional and cultural resources, those who press on with Weber's "In spite of all!" as their refrain. We could, of course, defer to Nietzsche's decadent mood and find fault with professors who apparently have nothing better to do with their time than to peruse the writings of a perverse malcontent such as Nietzsche, and to comment on writers who are paper mache Übermenschen; we could say that there is something misbegotten about academic institutions that celebrate such books, and so on. Nietzsche may be right, we are decadent, and there's little more to say about this endgame of ours; but there's something about the quality of Conway's exposition, the integrity of the analysis, that belies the book's own conclusion. It's too clearheaded.

While reading the book, I kept coming back not to Paul and the New Testament, but rather I kept thinking about the Hebrew Bible or Old Testament. Much of post–Zarathustran Nietzsche seems like a jeremiad, but more, the dangerous game reminded me of Genesis. Both are about genius authors who suffer from an anxiety of influence, who want to create rebelling readers, who want to exert their influence millennia henceforth, who want to be worshipped but are ambivalent about their devotees, who present some coy promise of distant redemption. Max Weber ends "Science as a Vocation" by suggesting that if one can't accept the disenchantments of modernity, one can return to old-time religion, quietly, simply, and plainly. And he says:

> In my eyes, such religious return stands higher than academic prophecy, which does not clearly realize that in the lecture-rooms of the university no other virtue holds but plain intellectual integrity. Integrity, however, compels us to state that for the many who today tarry for new prophets and saviors, the situation is the same as resounds in the beautiful Edomite watchman's song of the period of exile that has been included among Isaiah's oracles: He calleth to me out of Seir, Watchman, what of the night? The watchman said, The morning cometh, and also the night: if ye will enquire, enquire ye, return, come.[5]

One way to view the great chain of Judaism is that these communities have tarried foolishly within the fairy-tale metanarrative of a creationist God; another way of viewing such activity is that communities of faith don't really need ultimate redemption in order to hold together and to hold significance from generation to generation. In that light, Conway's book won't redeem us, I'm sad to say, but neither should it need to redeem us in order to deserve our celebratory mood today.

7

Grant Wood's
Political Gothic

As a rule, American political life does not accommodate irony very
well—which is not to say that American politics is devoid of or
even lacking in what pundits generally deem "ironies," namely, those
consequences unintended by some hapless party, those reversals of fortune
that undermine initial expectations, those witticisms that wryly mock the
arrogance of power. Rather, the above-stated rule—to which there are very
few exceptions—should read more to the point: American political life has
welcomed few full-time ironists, and no self-respecting ironist I know would
make American politics the main subject of his or her attentions, let alone
affections. Americans simply don't elect arch-ironists to office, and if an
American Socrates were somehow to gain widespread public celebrity, he or
she would likely stay far away from our nation's capital. Even the judicial
branch shows little interest these days in putting ironists on trial for their
alleged transgressions to the democratic order. More generally, Jean Baudrillard
is probably right to observe about America that "the irony of community is
missing here."[1] To be sure, American intellectuals talk a lot about irony,
especially in the last few decades, but there are few public practitioners of
the trope, and even fewer who direct their missives toward national political
life.[2] Most academic analysts, such as Richard Rorty, wish to confine ironology
to appropriately *private*, as opposed to public, venues.[3] Irony, for Rorty, can
only be corrosive of public life, and even when he attempts to fashion a
pragmatic truce between public liberalism and private ironism, he names no
American as an exemplar of irony (he names Baudelaire, Darwin, Derrida,
Foucault, Hegel, Heidegger, Kierkegaard, Nabokov, Newton, Nietzsche, Proust,
and Swift as ranking ironists). For Rorty and most others, irony is a gesture

of detachment and subversion; it is largely European and elitist; and it is un-American and undemocratic. Irony's self-referential attractiveness in arcane academic circles thus confirms its elusive distance from American public life.

Given this power vacuum, pop culture frequently steps into the irony breach. Irony is all around us, in music, film, cyberzines. *Spy Magazine* and *The New Republic* both named irony as the cultural trope of the 1980s,[4] and despite some backlash, it continues. In *Reality Bites*, the 1994 film about Generation X-ers, Winona Rider is asked in a job interview to define irony, and although she was an English major in college, the question stumps her. Alanis Morrisette achieved musical stardom with her hit, *Ironic* (the real irony of which, some critics sneer, is that the lyrics contained little of the stuff indeed). Barry Sonnenfeld, director of *Men in Black*, confides, "I'm going to stick with irony, because that's where I started."[5] Multimedial pop irony achieves mainstream box office success by banking on a coy conceit of pretended self-marginalization: the hip jokester, the inside spoofer, the postmodern prankster, the straight cross-dresser, the passive-aggressive cynic. The gesture of knowing detachment, of a smirking distance often ambiguously struck, informs various pop strategies from Andy Warhol to David Letterman. To the extent that such aloof ironists make occasional forays into American political life, their cool commentaries remain marginalized and merely parasitic, a smug snicker or two from the peanut gallery. "Pop irony" thus signifies an American deformation of Thomas Mann's wistful notion of "political irony,"[6] namely, that rare irony which, unexpectedly and therefore in nearly perfect keeping with its hidden political character, contributes precariously yet productively to the public good.[7]

The hard truth of the matter is that we have an extremely difficult time identifying any outspoken American practitioner of political irony. Have we ever produced such a mutant beast, a political animal sporting a Sphinx-like smile in artful service of lowbrow republican ideals? One would never accuse Whitman or Emerson of committing irony: their paeans to our democracy are, after all, too pious; their soaring celebrations reveal few simultaneous moments of parodic self-subversion; their transcendentalisms would hardly qualify for Friedrich Schlegel's definition of irony as "transcendental buffoonery." Allen Ginsberg may have been an irreverent gadfly, but his anger in the end outstripped his humor. I want to suggest one possible candidate for the title of American political ironist laureate—and quite by definition, the designation will and should seem, on its face, inappropriate.[8] I nominate twentieth-century artist Grant Wood. In the best scenario, my claim probably would require an elaborate rehearsal of the definition of irony, and then an elaborate definition of politics, and then a conjoining definition, and so on. I want to sidestep those crucial steps for now, or rather leave them implicit,[9] in order to devote the remainder of this chapter to a reevaluation of Wood's artistry. I submit that Wood should be seen in the main as a national political commentator, not simply as a regionalist painter (as is the wont of art historians), and that something akin to what we would conventionally call "irony" informs his political paintings. In the spirit of full disclosure, I should add that I am attaching to the term *irony*, however, the capacity for political affirmation, *pace* Rorty's (and Hegel's) understanding of irony's thoroughly corrupting character as applied to politics.

For more than six decades, Grant Wood has been called an American "regionalist" artist. Take a standard art history survey course or pick up any introductory art history textbook and there you will find Wood listed under the heading "American regionalism," along with Thomas Hart Benton and John Stewart Curry. The term apparently designates, in part, the extracurricular fact that these artists all hailed from the Midwestern "region" of the country, although painters from other "regions" of the country usually are not similarly identified.[10] We seldom learn about the Southern agrarians, or New England specialists as such, or Northwestern provincialists. Some commentators even use the qualifying, almost redundant, term *Midwestern* regionalist. All of these artists, at one time or another in their painting careers, featured bucolic landscapes (albeit, never exclusively), and all of them attracted some wider attention in their day. But what painter has not painted landscapes? The sheer coincidence of having several painters, situated in the heartland from Kansas, Missouri, and Iowa, who achieved some kind of national prominence seems to have constituted, for some, a back-to-the-earth "movement"—and the rural designation "regionalism" apparently stuck.[11]

Moreover, the appropriateness of calling Grant Wood a "regionalist" has gone largely unchallenged, probably because Wood willingly grew into the term, to the point that he defiantly accepted and promoted himself as a regionalist.[12] But the record is mixed. Early in his career Wood dabbled in all sorts of styles and subject matter. He studied in Minnesota, Chicago, and Paris and traveled four times to Europe in the 1920s to study the masters; there he painted his fair share of buildings, fountains, and nudes. Eventually he painted a good number of farmers, barns, and cornfields—though he painted the great majority of these "regionalist" works *after* he had already become famous supposedly as a "regionalist."[13] Early on, he apparently viewed his own Midwestern activity as *unrepresentative* of Midwestern life: although situated in the Midwest, he sought to import influences from elsewhere and to emulate artistic circles in New York, Paris, and Athens. He tried to found outlying pockets of artistic creativity, little anomalous oases in the art desert that was middle America. In the late 1920s, he attempted to turn a group of old barns located around a Cedar Rapids mortuary into an artist colony that might become the "Greenwich Village of the Cornbelt," with "the only true bohemian atmosphere west of Hoboken."[14] He did much the same thing again in the summers of 1932 and 1933, attracting a group of Midwestern artists to a backwoods art colony in Stone City, Iowa. At various times he imagined Cedar Rapids as a "New Athens" or as a potential "Latin Quarter" in Iowa. But as soon as he became a national figure—some called him the Christopher Columbus of American art—he began to decry the borrowing of culture from elsewhere, and he repudiated his early emulation of outside artistries. He dropped one affectation for another: in Paris, he had donned a beret and sported a goatee; now he started wearing overalls—even though he had never worked as a farmer. At a New York exhibition, he told the story that while sitting in coffee shops in Paris, he had been reading H. L. Mencken, who had lampooned the Midwest, when it occurred to him "that all the really good ideas I'd ever had came to me while I was milking a cow. So I went back to Iowa."[15] The critics howled, and thereafter most viewed Wood as a sentimental hayseed. He reacted by digging in his heels, or so it seems, as an unapologetic "regionalist." In 1935, he painted a self-portrait, *Return from Bohemia*, which thematizes his having left Paris for Iowa, and he started to give lectures across the country on the importance of regionalism. As a professor at the University of Iowa, he published a manifesto in defense of regionalism—"Revolt Against the City"—in which he claimed that artists needed to liberate themselves from the "colonialism" of European influence, which still, he contended, unduly affected commercial art houses on both coasts.[16] In a talk that he gave at the Beverly Hills Hilton in Los Angeles, however, he explained that the term *regionalist* was not a particularly fortunate name, but that nothing better had been found to take its place: " 'Regional,' " he said, "sounds almost geographical, and there is nothing essentially geographical about the work."[17]

But critics and art historians apparently have never forgiven him for his retreat back to the Midwest. By the mid-1930s he was criticized as betraying a Paris-based modernism in favor of a decorative, even reactionary regionalism, an art of country folks and pastoral landscapes—and by the late 1930s he was seen as an isolationist. More recent critics typically have read his work as a precursor of sorts to Norman Rockwell's squeaky-clean, Boy Scout boosterism, and it is fair to say that he is far more patronized than celebrated in the established art world. He has never shaken the title "Regionalist," with all of its provincialized, country-bumpkin connotations, yet what is odd about this trajectory is that Wood became famous *not* for his later regionalist paintings and polemics but rather for paintings the consistent subject of which were *national* themes, allegories, and fables.[18] To read too much regionalism back or forward into this body of work may be to localize those paintings too much, and thus to distance ourselves from them so that they cannot make claims upon us. In particular, critics tend to read Grant Wood's most famous painting, *American Gothic*, as a regionalist commentary. Robert Hughes, for instance, in his recent *Time* magazine synopsis of his PBS series and book by the same name, *American Visions*, describes that painting as a "satire on the denizens of Iowa."[19] The reach of Wood's satire evidently does not extend as far as New York, Hughes's main observation post. Yet I want to note that Wood did *not* call his painting *Iowa Gothic* or *Midwestern Gothic*,[20] nor by a similar token did Hughes call his television and book series *New York Visions* or *City Visions*. (He seems to presume that his *commentary* about *American Gothic* says something about America, whereas the painting does not.) In fact, soon after the showing of *American Gothic*, Wood responded to queries about the painting, and in particular he insisted: "The people in American Gothic . . . are American . . . and it is unfair to localize them to Iowa."[21] So why do Hughes and others apparently fail to see themselves, or refuse to admit to seeing themselves, implicated in that painting? Reading Wood's *American Gothic* thus raises all sorts of geographical, cross-projectional questions of authorial intention versus audience reception, and I turn to some of those issues presently.

Grant Wood's 1930 painting, *American Gothic*, is one of the world's most widely recognized portraiture paintings. It has been called the American *Mona Lisa*. Ever since winning an award at its unveiling, the painting has enjoyed unusual popularity—or at least notoriety. In the 1940s it was used as a war recruitment poster, requiring only the added caption, "Government of the people, by the people and for the people shall not perish from the earth." From the 1960s on, cartoonists and ad pitchmen have reworked and parodied the painting so that it has become installed in popular imagination as a national icon that allegedly depicts enduring American values.[22] Critics and admirers have generally agreed on a converging interpretation of the painting, namely, that *American Gothic* supposedly depicts a Trinitarian iconography of depression-era, Midwestern ideals: work, family, and religion.

Only a few art historians, most notably Wanda Corn and James Dennis, have broken with the conventional view of Grant Wood. According to Corn, although Grant Wood was indeed attempting to found a new regionalist style, he was always a *mischievous* painter—yet commentators, including Corn herself sometimes, seem to have a hard time reconciling Wood's regionalism with his satire if they detect it. Corn gives an evolutionary account of Wood's transformation into a regionalist, and she views his moments of spot humor as good-natured and not malicious. She insists that Wood did *not* intend *American Gothic* in particular to be satirical, and that geography may best explain its uneven reception: "By and large, the farther a critic lived from the Midwest, the more predisposed he or she was to read the painting as satire or social criticism. Local commentators usually saw the painting in a more benign light."[23] Her account responds to Matthew Baigell's, another art historian, who in 1974 contended that *American Gothic* is a "vicious satire" that depicts the couple as savage, exuding "a generalized, barely repressed animosity that borders on venom."[24] James Dennis sees *American Gothic* as an eclectic hybrid that somehow combines "personal iconography drawing upon a visual pun, portrait caricature, comic satire, and rural regionalism."[25]

He eventually settles upon calling Wood a "cosmopolitan satirist," who in his own day dared explain to a New York audience the wider appeal of the rural Midwest as an urban yearning if not envy for an uncomplicated American existence.[26] More recently, Robert Hughes has carried forth this two-pronged line of criticism: He calls American Gothic a "mild satire" of Iowans' "fetishized values of sobriety, moral vigilance, patriarchy and the rest." Yet Hughes also acknowledges, without any explanation, a completely contradictory view of the painting: "But," he adds, "millions of Americans have thought Wood was praising those qualities."[27]

So was Wood a satirist and/or a regionalist? What was/is American Gothic? How are we to understand that work? Why is the interpretation of American Gothic, and of its artist's intentions, so elusive upon analysis? Gertrude Stein reportedly warned about Wood: "We should fear Grant Wood. Every artist and every school of artists should be afraid of him for his devastating satire."[28] At the same time, while warning against Wood's satire, she also was said to have loved it: "He is not only a satirical artist, but one who has a wonderful detachment from life in general—a necessity for creating the best of art."[29] Wood himself gave an elliptical response to the question whether American Gothic was satire: "There is satire in American Gothic, but only as there is satire in any realistic statement."[30] He admitted that there was at least a double aspect to the painting: "I admit the fanaticism and false taste of the characters in American Gothic, but to me, they are basically good and solid people."[31] He often emphasized that he had "no intention of holding them up to ridicule," but also claimed that "these people had bad points, and I did not paint them under."[32] Wood expected the painting to generate controversy: Instead of showing it first at the 1930 Iowa State Fair, he submitted it to the Art Institute in Chicago.[33] He also worried about hurting the feelings of the subjects who modeled for the painting. Once the painting was exhibited, it was praised but also viciously attacked, and Wood defended himself and the painting against many of the attacks—but he also seemed to relish the storm of controversy as a potential source of "good fun"[34]: "I'd rather have people rant and rave against my painting than pass it up with 'Isn't that a pretty picture?' "[35]

A many decades' long, popular interpretation of American Gothic has understood the term gothic in the title as referring to the "carpenter Gothic" architecture that is recognizable in the window of the white house in the background of the painting.[36] Grant Wood had studied Gothic cathedrals in Munich, Paris, and Naples; in 1927, he was commissioned to design a stained glass memorial window in Cedar Rapids, which he completed in 1929, and earlier in his career he had designed residential homes and thus was keen to carpentry styles.[37] Observing the Gothic allusions on simple farmhouses in Iowa, Wood was therefore making some kind of commentary about the transplanting of thirteenth-century European religiosity into the cornfields of middle

America. But the confluence of religiosity and architecture extended beyond the steepled window in the painting. The formal features of the elongated Gothic window are echoed in the two subjects' long oval faces; the sloping shoulders, the oval broach worn by the woman, and the curves of the pitchfork's tines all repeat this Gothic theme, suggestive of visual punning. One commentator has even mentioned that the pitchfork is reminiscent of a medieval candlestick holder.[38] Other religious cues seem to reinforce the *religiosity* of the Gothic theme: there seems to be a church spire in the distance; the Gothic window seems to hang like a Christian cross between the two faces; and the man's overcoat is black, about which many have said (including Grant Wood) that the man may be a preacher or at least may be a churchgoer who is wearing his Sunday best. Hence, we tend to look at the *people* in some way as Gothic. Some commentators have viewed the painting as little more than a formal exercise in elongated verticality,[39] but Wood himself seems to have imagined a Gothic sensibility as animating the *subjects* of the painting: "Any northern town old enough to have some buildings dating back to the civil war is liable to have a house or church in the American Gothic style. I simply invented some American Gothic people to stand in front of a house of this type."[40]

Yet the term *gothic* admits another connotation, far less reverential, namely, that sense of ominousness characteristic of the Gothic romance novel—and Baigell, Corn, and Dennis have all drawn attention to these dark forces looming in the background of the painting. Dennis suggests that Wood might have been familiar at this time with the mansion description in Edgar Allan Poe's *The Fall of the House of Usher*,[41] and later paintings in Wood's career certainly would play upon literary works (Horatio Alger, Sinclair Lewis, and Henry Longfellow were among his prominent targets).[42] Comparing an earlier study for the painting, we know that Wood replaced a rake with the now-famous pitchfork. The three tines of the pitchfork, one starts to notice, are repeated eerily in the man's overalls. Baigell emphasizes the unmistakable *devilishness* of that instrument: "Might we look upon the man with his pitchfork not as a religious farmer—the mythic New Jesus of the mid-west—but as the Devil himself, or as a symbol of the Devil's presence in Iowa?"[43] Some have read the pitchfork as a simple, perhaps unassuming, commentary on the preindustrial, premechanized era of agriculture that had already passed by the 1930s—yet the threatening violence of a pitchfork, ostensibly thrust at us as the centerpiece of a very stylized work, echoed repeatedly throughout the work, is hard to ignore. The black coat, on second thought, could be either preacherly *or* devilish, and that the man seems to be blocking our visual entrance to the house gives the painting an unwelcoming feel at the least.[44]

If the term *gothic* admits of countervailing senses, the reverential *and* the horrifying, then much depends on whether and how the couple is a couple.

As Hughes remarks, millions of Americans have assumed that the couple represents a husband and wife—and the iconography of hard-won, enduring family values would seem to depend on such a read. The controversy has taken on a new life today, but it began decades ago. Shortly after the opening of *American Gothic*, one newspaper mistakenly called the painting *A Farmer and His Wife*, and almost all newspaper reports in the aftermath described the painting as depicting a farmer and his wife. A storm of protest ensued. People wrote letters to editors as well as to the curators of the Art Institute of Chicago. Grant Wood received more than 100 letters of protest and numerous angry phone calls. Reportedly, more wives than farmers complained about the depiction. The woman's face is so sour, one woman objected, that the painting should be hung in an Iowa cheese factory. In response to this outpouring, Grant Wood issued a few clarifications. He explained that the man was not necessarily a farmer—but could be a small-town businessman, a druggist, a postmaster, or perhaps a preacher. Wood's sister jumped into the fray and insisted that the woman was not a wife but his daughter—and she continued that line of interpretation in her 1993 book, *My Brother, Grant Wood*. Corn and Hughes have repeated that sisterly testimonial. When the subject was raised at the 1996 Davenport Museum exhibition,[45] Corn responded, "I thought I put that to rest in my own book. I believe firmly it was intended to be the daughter, on all kinds of grounds."[46] Hughes similarly concludes that the painting was meant to be a daughter.

If authorial intention holds some remote interest even in this post–Derrida era,[47] then I would like to make a few observations of my own on this controversy. In my own research, I have found no direct quotes out of the mouth of Wood claiming that the woman in the painting was necessarily a daughter. In fact, it is perhaps telling that he often insisted that the man was not necessarily a farmer but on the same occasions did not make a parallel disclaimer about the woman.[48] Brady M. Roberts recently uncovered a direct quote by Wood that mentions that the woman is supposed to represent a wife:

> I saw a trim white cottage, with a trim white porch—a cottage built on severe Gothic lines. This gave me an idea. That idea was to find two people who, by their severely straight-laced characters, would fit into such a home. I looked about among the folks I knew around my home town, Cedar Rapids, Iowa, but could find none among the farmers—for the cottage was to be a farmer's home. I finally induced my own maiden sister to pose and had her comb her hair straight down her ears, with a severely plain part in the middle. The next job was to find a man to represent the husband. My quest finally narrowed down to the local dentist, who reluctantly consented to pose. I sent to a Chicago mail order house for the prim, colonial print apron my sister wears and for the prim, spotless overalls the dentist has on. I posed them side by side, with the

dentist holding stiffly upright in his right hand, a three-tined pitchfork. The trim, white cottage appears over their shoulders in the background.

When the picture was printed in the newspapers, I received a storm of protest from Iowa farm wives because they thought I was caricaturing them. One of them actually threatened, over the telephone, "to come over and smash my head."[49]

Nan Wood Graham claimed that all articles referring to "the farmer and his wife" upset her brother, and in her book she quotes him as saying, "My sister posed as the woman. She is supposed to be the man's daughter, not his wife."[50] She cites those lines as part of the Wood quote I mentioned above about localizing *American Gothic* to Iowa—but in the original interview, *no such lines appear.*[51] It would seem that sister Nan had a particular investment in reinforcing her role as the model of an unmarried daughter, not a wife, in the painting. Wood might have told her that, but he apparently told interviewers another story as well.[52]

What difference would it make? Hughes interprets the painting as a father protecting the virtue of his not-so-alluring daughter. Corn mentions a more scandalous background possibility but then retreats a bit from its implications in favor of a more kindly reading of Wood's intentions. The couple was supposed to be an "odd couple," says Corn, for Wood was drawing upon the literary works of friends in his Midwestern circle, namely, Ruth Suckow and Paul Sigmund, both of whom were playing with the "spinster" daughter theme in their works.[53] Such daughters stay unmarried out of excessive duty to family, in order to care for widowed or aging parents, and often they wither as social creatures, become unbending in their judgments, and also become the subject as well as purveyors of town gossip. Corn points out that Sigmund and Suckow depicted the spinster as sexually stunted, old-fashioned in dress, and overly fastidious in behavior. Originally Wood wanted to ask a Cedar Rapids "spinster" to pose for the painting,[54] but he could not work up the courage to ask— and thus he asked his sister to step in. She was thirty at the time, and the dentist who posed as the man was sixty-two at the time; hence, the disparity in ages, which may be ambiguous yet discernible in the painting upon close inspection, seems to confirm, on Corn's read, the father-daughter motif.

Corn concedes that the characterization of the woman in the painting is at best ambiguous, but she contends that the ambiguity betrays Wood's "affection" for the country couple:

He could not bring himself, as Sigmund did in his poem "The Serpent," to characterize his spinster as a "sexless" monster. For Sigmund, the spinster was a "smug and well-kept" woman with a "saintly smile" that betrayed her hypocrisy, an "arch-assassin of reputation" whose fangs were no "less cruel and deadly for being hidden."[55]

That literary stereotype *does* lay behind Wood's portrayal, adds Corn, but somehow she also wants to claim that Wood was not intending after all to be mean or mocking. Spinsters just happen to look older than their years, hence, the daughter might be mistaken for a wife—and that was the popular perception of spinsterdom at the time. The beautiful goddess on the cameo reminds us of the way she ought to look.[56] Her flattened bosoms and flattened apron suggest her repressed sexuality. The serpentine strand of hair falling out of her tight hair bun and the "snake plant" on the porch in the background do indeed recall Sigmund's metaphor of the spinster as serpent, but Corn thinks this reference is "far-fetched." The averted gaze, a feminine gesture, looks both passive and active, both saintly and meddlesome. Corn does see gender conflict in the relations between the man and woman. He is protective of her, and he stares at us "menacingly." The pitchfork is phallic, a symbol of male sexuality—but Corn sees him as protective of *her* virtue, not his reputation. And then she reads Wood's echoing of the pitchfork in the man's overalls as a parody of his aggressive virility—and Hughes repeats in copycat fashion this theme of parodic limpness.

Both Corn and Hughes seem to want to resolve the ambiguity of the woman figure in favor of a father-daughter theme, the effect of which is to desexualize the relations between the two as potential husband and wife, and that tends to soften the theme of small-town ridicule.[57] But the apron pattern seems to rhyme with the pattern of the closed curtains behind the Gothic window upstairs—and so we naturally wonder, what goes on behind those closed curtains? The storytelling features of Wood's painting draw us in and raise more questions than they resolve: What kind of family is this? Even if the woman is a daughter, what happened to the mother? How did the threes become twos? Are not we not to wonder whether the spinster daughter acts as a wifely substitute, out there on the isolated plains, in more than merely housekeeping ways? That averted gaze could be saintly or could be meddlesome; it also could tell the story of abuse.[58] Gothic tales of fathers and daughters surely would recall the story of Lot and his daughters (and Ruth Suckow played upon this Lot theme in her writings about the Midwestern spinster[59]) and thus raise the theme of incest—and the devilish details in the painting would compound that scandal.[60] We know that one of Wood's favorite stories was Shaw's "Androcles and the Lion"—so he was not averse to scandalously blasphemous material.[61] The woman-as-serpent theme, with all of its larger biblical temptations, cannot be so simply revoked or resolved into a local issue about town gossip or bad hair days.[62] Hughes and Corn both domesticate and soften the pitchfork so that it parodies overall(s) male violence, but to my eye, the prongs of that grasped pitchfork are still very sharp.

Hughes suggests another sexualized dimension of *American Gothic* and its artist, which I find outrageous but intriguing. He claims that "far from being a sturdy son of the soil, Wood was a timid and deeply closeted homosexual."[63] *American Gothic*, moreover, is allegedly the expression of "a gay sensibility." The critical passage at length:

> Today one is inclined to see it *[American Gothic]*, like so much of Wood's other work, as an exercise in sly camp, the expression of a gay sensibility so cautious that it can hardly bring itself to mock its objects openly. Was Wood poking a quarter of an inch of fun at the denizens of Iowa and their fetishized values of sobriety, moral vigilance, patriarchy, and the rest? Or was he, as millions of Americans have thought since the painting won a prize in Chicago in 1930 and was catapulted into national fame, actually praising those virtues? The answer, in a sense, is both: a mass audience was intrigued by the image because it couldn't quite decide, just as Grant Wood couldn't quite decide either.[64]

The claim is outrageous, because Hughes does not explain himself, nor does he adduce any evidence or cite any supporting documents to back his claim. In an interview, Brian Lamb asked him whether others view Wood as a "closet homosexual," and Hughes responded that he believes it is widely known in the literature—but I have not found a peep to that effect.[65] Hughes's explanation of Wood's homosexuality—though Hughes adds that he has "no actual knowledge" of whether Wood was a "practicing gay"—is that Wood was not "a sturdy son of the soil" (whatever that means) but had "refined and Victorian tastes." He mentions only Wood's interest in Flemish painting as being symptomatic of such tastes. In the book he contends that Wood retained a memory of a Chinese willow-pattern plate in his mother's house, and that he wanted to reinstitute a dollhouse, child's world of make-believe when he established his art colony in Stone City. The "timidity" of his "deeply closeted" homosexuality apparently is revealed by the indirect, ambiguous nature of his social criticism (a more courageous or an out homosexual, or a straight painting man, presumably would not pull his punches?). Hughes ends his ramble on Wood by making a few last distancing digs: "Generally, the assumption that American Gothic was a satire tends to increase in direct proportion to one's distance eastward from Cedar Rapids. But *ogni dipintore dipinge se*, as Leonardo once remarked: every painter paints himself. Of none is this truer than Grant Wood."

Let us pause to reflect on Hughes's analysis. His improvised theory of gay camp certainly needs work.[66] It cannot be that any social criticism that is couched or cleverly concealed represents a "gay sensibility." The details he draws from Wood's life are refracted through Tinkerbell, interior decorating stereotypes. Certainly we could dwell, if we wished, on better performative evidence: almost all of the members of the collaborative art colonies that sprung up around Wood consisted of other male artists; neighboring farmers complained about the live nude models used at such colonies; Wood painted a good number of nude male paintings and featured a "coming of age" painting about his protégé, Arnold. In short, Wood's dreams of relocating the bohemian activities of Greenwich, the Latin Quarter, or Athens into the middle West may have been about more than merely aesthetic collaboration. Adding to Hughes's account is that *American Gothic* is surely about gender conflict, conflict that manifests in odd couples, odd families, and subaltern sexualities. Certainly it is a valid, though perhaps a limited and an unguaranteed, line of inquiry to venture into Wood's personal life and to ask whether and how those sexualized narratives that we are reading into *American Gothic* relate to his own story. In his final sneer, Hughes says that Wood painted himself into that painting, and thus he now must wear it as some kind of albatross around his neck, just as Leonardo will forever be remembered for his Mona Lisa.

But Wood had already admitted the self-referentiality of the painting. He once said that the characters were "tintypes from my own family album."[67] If it is true that Wood's own family is somehow represented in the piece, we should note a few interesting cross-dressing substitutions or superimpositions.[68] Wood himself was the spinster figure in his own family at the time of the painting. His father had died when he was eight, and he looked after his mother from that time on. He built a small cabin for her in Cedar Rapids when the family was shelterless, and later she moved into 5 Turner Alley with him, his studio in Cedar Rapids, where he painted *American Gothic*. His "bachelorhood" was a source of continued speculation in town.[69] Nan Wood Graham repeatedly disparages Darrell Garwood's biography of Wood, but some of the anecdotes in that early volume are particularly telling—and in contrast Nan's version seems to omit crucial details.[70] According to Garwood, after army service, Wood needed a job, and one of his cousins pressed a junior high school principal, Miss Frances Prescott, to hire Wood.

> "What have I ever done to you that you want me to take Grant Wood as a teacher?" she demanded.
>
> "Well, he was in the army, and he needs a job."
>
> "Why, he might go off with the children and get lost somewhere. He may be a Pied Piper for all I know."[71]

Later, when he was in his thirties, Miss Prescott asked him about his marriage prospects. Writes Garwood:

> There were times when people thought he might marry, but there were no sound reasons for these expectations. He took girls to parties and on picnics, but seemed uneasy at the prospect of being left alone with them

and too deliberate for the pace of events. Besides he was still planning to study abroad.

"Do you think you'll ever marry?" Miss Prescott once asked him.

"I don't think so; not while my mother is living," he told her.[72]

The subject comes up again in Garwood's account. Now in his mid-thirties, Wood discusses the matter of marriage "seriously" with Vida, the wife of a friend of his, and Wood "seemed puzzled about himself": "I guess I'm just not interested in women."[73] Later, at 44, he finally married, over the objections of his close friends, a woman five years his senior, a woman who was already a grandmother at the time, an artist herself who cared for Wood's ill mother in his celebrity absence; the marriage, virtually doomed from the start, ended three years later, at which time Wood confided to fellow artist Marvin Cone, "I'm a free man again."[74]

American Gothic contains other substitutions seemingly drawn from Wood's life: the cameo worn by the daughter/wife, which was worn in real life by model Nan, was a gift Grant Wood gave to his mother upon his return from Italy.[75] The apron, which Wood had picked out of a mail-order catalogue, had the same jagged braid as Wood's mother's apron. A painting finished shortly before *American Gothic, Woman with Plants,* is of Wood's mother, and the plants depicted in that painting—a snake plant and a begonia—reappear on the porch of *American Gothic.* In short, Oedipal, generational, incestual themes haunt the picture in many directions.[76] The question of Wood's own spinsterdom is not necessarily a *personal* one of concealed homosexuality, as it probably ought to be seen as representing larger issues of competing masculinities, and alternative erotics under terms of patriarchy: How was a man in the 1930's, or in the 1990's for that matter, supposed to portray his caring if sexually stultifying relationship to his widowed mother?[77] (A friend once described the strong bond between Wood and his mother as "excessive."[78]) Hughes insists on a final resolution of the daughter-wife issue, and he demands that Wood make a "decision" about his ambiguous sexuality. Yet if Hughes is right that a painter always paints himself, then perhaps a critic's criticisms also apply auto-referentially: Hughes evidently feels it necessary to distance himself from "timid," Midwestern, sexually ambiguous men, and we as his readers naturally wonder why.[79]

I find it vastly more interesting to leave the ambiguities of *American Gothic* intact and unresolved, to the extent that I wish to ascribe or imagine an authorial intentionality that deliciously invites and deviously reinforces such ambiguity, though such logocentric imputations are not really necessary to retain the pleasures and confusions of interpretive indeterminacy. Generations of Americans have reportedly read stability into the piece, arresting its irresolution into a construct about national iconography, even while they appreciated caricatured elements thereabouts; but they evidently assumed that Wood was the unwitting victim of his (or the painting's) own parodic tendencies. Yet with a little background prompting, a little analysis, for instance, of the serpentine strand of hair falling out of the woman's hair bun, the spell breaks. Six decades later, the painting virtually deconstructs itself before our very eyes! What was once a cartoonlike painting about work, family, and religion now becomes a scandal possibly involving hypocrisy, repression, and denial, and even abuse, incest, violence, devilishness, gender terror, and, at the least, threatening body language. The woman's averted eyes now tell an untold story, and the man's defiant stance no longer looks like straightforward American self-reliance in the face of dashed dreams. On second view, the pitchfork becomes menacing, not just an emblem of rural living and a work ethos clinging to a premechanized era. The black Sunday jacket starts to disturb. Play the painting backward, scratch the surface, and the "Gothic" elements start to look quite devilish, now suggesting yet another pun: these are "Goth" people—coarse, uncivilized, and maybe even barbarous. Exceeding its representational limits, the painting reproduces the experience of, and the difficulties in talking about one's family secrets in public. I would prefer, however, to see and talk about those shortcomings, those unspoken and virtually unspeakable sexual and gender conflicts, as a *national* issue, an American Gothic story, and not simply as a local Iowa concern.

I want to say that the painting, from its inception, was always "about" masking, masquerades, and cover-up. The figures are posing for public purview, the technology of imagined camera surveillance is already upon them,[80] and the rivalry between photographic realism and representational art is surely one of the painterly conceits that modernist Wood is deploying: families facing family album photos. These figures, we know, lead double lives: public and private, indoors and outdoors, past and present, town and country, high culture and low culture, secular and sacred, Old World and New World. They have work clothes and dress-up clothes; the painting features both. The aprons and overcoats, the blocked entrances, the closed windows, the tight lips, and the differing stares all bring into public light that which has been, and continues to be, kept under wraps. The painting has always generated discussion if not controversy, but the history of its reception is one in which the viewing public typically replicated, or deferred to, the masking and cover-up that stood as spectacle in front of them. Learned commentators, keen to its self-subversive and underground elements, have seemed unusually nervous about the topics it apparently broaches, a canvas with cues and clues that seems to invite unlicensed projection, a Stephen King mystery novel that unfolds within a single frame, and they tend to retreat from a double or an ambiguous reading in favor of an overly affectionate or an overly aggressive authorial purpose. Somehow, such commentators seem to presume, Grant Wood cannot be both affectionate and scandalous; such extremes must be mutually exclusive; likewise, his simple painting cannot be truly Janus-faced, a projection of projections, of reciprocating gazes that withhold and mask as much as they insinuate and reveal.

What do such matters have to do with American politics? On the most obvious level, the painting is important in its ongoing second life as an icon of pop culture, and thus it continues to figure into our nationally mediated cultural politics. Since the 1960s the painting has been reproduced endlessly in popular media, reworked and parodied in magazine cartoons, films, and ads, to the point that, contends Wanda Corn, the couple has become "a barometer of our times."[81] Very often, she observes, these reworkings involve explicitly political themes: the heads of First Families and politicians are routinely grafted onto the American Gothic bodies; Wood's couple is frequently redeployed "to address major social and political causes."[82] Moreover, she notes that odd recouplings are mobilized to make "statements on contemporary relations between the sexes,"[83] and one branch of the American Gothic industry consists of lewd and off-color versions.[84] The painting in popular fashion is used, in other words, to ventilate some of our national suppressions and repressions—political, gendered, sexual, racial—although Corn contends that it is seldom used in service of radically divisive social causes. More recently The New Yorker contends that an American Gothic style—where "the worthy clashes with the sinful, the high-minded with the debased"—is the prevailing form of news reporting in our sensationalist, tabloid society—and that much of the reason "the Gothic mode is ascendant" is that our undramatic, post–Cold War politics neither excites nor engages any longer.[85] In our liberal boredom, we are now always on the lookout for hidden scandal or underlying conspiracy.

Hughes provides another point of political departure, an offhand comment on Wood's own political tendencies, though Hughes points us in the wrong direction. He avers that Wood himself was politically "on the right" along with other regionalists, whereas the social realists of the time were on the left.[86] But the stereotyped assumption about Wood simply is not true. According to all accounts, Wood was a lifelong liberal.[87] He was a "New Dealer before there was a New Deal,"[88] someone who supported Roosevelt when and where it was not fashionable. At numerous times in his artistic career, he pressed for and received federal support for promoting public art programs. He was named director of the Public Works Art Project in Iowa, and he supervised the painting of a number of post office murals. His political manifesto in defense of "regionalism" turns out to be an appeal for federal funding for supporting the diversity of American art, a competition among different districts, a competition in much the same way, he explains, that the Gothic style of architecture first started in Europe. At every turn his regionalism was voiced in support of a heterogeneous Americanism, yet with the rise of the Nazis his nationalism fell into disfavor in some camps. It should be noted, however, that early in the growing international concern about fascism, in 1938, Wood's sketchbooks already include a caricature of Adolph Hitler as a devouring wolf.[89]

But Hughes may be right in another regard, for Wood kept his political leanings closeted. He felt he could not talk politics as a liberal Democrat in a Republican stronghold, so he kept mostly quiet about such matters.[90] Yet a great number of his works, as we shall see, take up explicitly national political themes and motifs; such works though are conveyed via the kind of indirection or doublespeak we see obliquely exhibited in *American Gothic*. I want to call this technique "political irony" in an American liberal mode, an attempt to bring into public light that has been relegated to the private sphere under the split terms of liberalism, terms that tend to preempt or deflect open discussions. I am not the first to ascribe representational irony to Wood and to attach it to his political tendencies. Dennis writes: "As Wood gained command of irony and comedy as instruments of social commentary, his career following American Gothic seemed to take on a new cosmopolitan air."[91] Whereas Richard Rorty views irony as destructive of political life, best therefore kept out of public view altogether, Wood found gentler ways to introduce ironic critique into our public ponderings: "Because reality often begets irony, Grant Wood preferred light comedy to caustic criticism in commenting on fixed patterns of traditionally tailored behavior or belief."[92] Another painting of his, *Daughters of Revolution*, came under great attack for its seemingly devastating depiction of the Daughters of the American Revolution (DAR), yet Wood insisted that the painting was, according to Dennis, "a sympathetic but determined exposé of their 'great inconsistency' as Americans."[93] Said Wood: "They [the DAR] were forever searching through great volumes of history and dusty records, tracing down their Revolutionary ancestry. On the one hand, they were trying to establish themselves as an aristocracy of birth; on the other, they were trying to support a democracy."[94] Likewise, Wood insisted that his portrayal of the figures in *American Gothic* was a loving one, yet it also was a rendering that did not shy away from exposing their faults. How can this be?

The Gothic window situated between the heads of the two figures in *American Gothic* invites a comparison to the mirror that Foucault analyzed in Velàquez's *Las Meninas*.[95] Wood's window is of course a window on liberalism, that observance of a distinction between public matters and private spheres. It is a window that formally holds the couple together, a window that is presented to our public eye; but in the painting, it is covered from inside, so that we cannot peer any farther inward. An apron-pattern curtain shields our eye; we are no longer looking through stained glass as in other Gothic windows, toward some colorful, ecclesiastical, other world. For Fou-

cault, the mirror in *Las Meninas* engenders a fascinating movement of rico-
cheting gazes between invisible painter and invisible spectator. The sovereign, albeit invisible, gaze of the absent painter imposes order on its diverse
publics; it cleverly constructs and organizes a universalized subjectivity by
purportedly mirroring a common absence. *American Gothic*, too, plays with
similar framing devices of exchanged stares, windows within windows, the
staging of stagings, and posed poses, thus the offstage spectator tends to
inquire after the absent painter, who presumably once occupied the same
frontally scrutinizing position. Yet I want to suggest that Wood is not trying
to discipline us into a new spectatorial regime, and this demurral or forbearance is the key to his irony. Irony, in this context, could be defined as a
disruption of the sovereign gaze, a choral *parabasis*,[96] a knowing pause in the
transfer of imaginary feints and glances. The ironic artist cedes some ocular
control by calling attention, through winks and puns, to his mock inscruta-
bility; so goaded, we no longer can stand there spellbound.[97] True, we, the
American viewing public(s), have characteristically looked to *American Gothic*
hoping to find a mirror, hoping to learn something, to see something reflected
about ourselves, a common and stable American subjectivity or narrative, a
solvent identity or destiny. We have, in other words, internalized the family
photo album experience. But Wood does not play it straight. We cannot take
the painting completely seriously, which may be the reason it continues to
recur parodically in pop fashion. It lives on. Indeed, the central irony of this
gag-piece painting may be that it somehow lives on and retains interest,
accommodating over many decades a running succession of stabilizations,
subversions, and cover-ups, and back again.

   That ironic movement turns, I propose, on the covert suspicion that if
this painting is about concealed family dysfunction or spinsterdom in some
whispered way, then this couple is one contemplating a childless future—
wifeless Lot's gaze is now grim—yet we latter-day Americans are somehow
still implicated, are somehow nonetheless the children of Lot, the legatees of
this sometimes sinful, sometimes virtuous biblical story. The painting is surely
about American ancestors and their possible failings, their bleak futures, and
yet we spectators also stand in living contradiction, partial mockery, to that
narrative. History, generationalism, or survival—what Stanley Cavell might
call Emersonian perfectionism[98]—in America is never simply continuous but
occurs in fits and starts; pioneering breaks from the past hardly ever deliver
redemption, renegotiated beginnings in their stead open futures that are far
from certain.[99] Grant Wood's distant affection is to remind us that we are still
here, as sympathetic and inquiring observers, that we have not yet suc-
cumbed to dark forces in our collective past.[100] (Irony, I have argued elsewhere, often is invoked by Orphic artists as a creative response to death—and,
after all, *American Gothic* was painted over a mortuary garage.[101]) As one
commentator, perceptively and presciently, wrote in 1931:

Let us present Grant Wood of Cedar Rapids, Iowa. You will notice he is a rotund, compact stoutish chap with a disarming puckish grin and a soft deprecatory voice. But keep your eye on that grin—it's going somewhere. . . . In the meantime, Grant Wood smiles mystically like a benign Buddha and plans other canvasses.[102]

So what to call Wood? He disliked reductive labels and unqualified terms attached to his work. He gave lectures across the country about regionalism, at which times he would disclaim that regionalism had anything to do with geographical regions. Those who believed he was poking fun at his own Midwestern region typecast him as a "satirist," but he disliked that term too; yet he also kept people guessing by disclaiming his disclaimers:

Because I have painted a few "satirical" things, the classifying school of critics has labeled me as a satirist. And they go on finding satirical meanings in things that do not have any satire in them. Of course, I have been satirical; but I have to keep on insisting that I am not a satirist so that people won't get an easy and incorrect notion of what I am about. It is always easier to judge an artist by a label than by what he does, and often such judgment is worn-out and irritating to an artist.[103]

Politically, Wood was called a flag-waving patriot, a nationalist, an isolationist, especially by those who viewed "regionalism" as a rightward movement compared to the left-leaning social realists. As with his art, however, the political reception of Wood's work divided into antithetical lines of interpretation. Several of his "satirical" works were attacked as anti-American, and not infrequently he was condemned as being "disrespectful" if not "destructive" of American traditions.[104] *American Gothic* raised many hackles, but other paintings—*Daughters of Revolution, Midnight Ride of Paul Revere, Parson Weems' Fable*— also provoked violent reactions in many pro-American circles. Matthew Baigell continues this line of criticism of Wood-as-vicious-attack-dog:

Grant Wood has been so closely associated with corn of one sort or another for so many years that we are prevented from seeing the artist who in a handful of paintings dating from the early 1930's attacked American institutions at least as bitterly as any other American artist.[105]

What I will say about Wood is that he seemed preoccupied with *American* themes over virtually the entire course of his painting career. Baigell is right to note Wood's fascination with American institutions, but Baigell confines that interest to a two-year period, and he may be overstating Wood's hostility, or at least assuming that severe criticism presupposes embitterment and precludes affirmation. To my eye, which is schooled in political theory

and not art history, the term *regionalist* is particularly unfortunate with respect to Wood's apparent political purview. Wood invokes explicitly and
expansively political material on numerous occasions, from revolutionary to
presidential subject matters, but even more startling is the great *range* of
American institutions that he examines—the practical basis for American
citizenship according to theorists from Tocqueville to Ben Barber—to wit:
presidents, professors, poets, pioneers, patriots, workers, teachers, youth,
Masons, Shriners, women, villagers, Main Streeters, gentry, Victorians, home
owners, real estate developers, even golfers (one might even see his *The
American Golfer* as a companion piece to *American Gothic*). Space limitations
prevent me from analyzing the following works in any depth—and Corn and
Dennis have already done those analyses superbly—but I present here a
selective list of what could be called Wood's "nonregionalist" and largely
political corpus in order to indicate his abiding concern with *Americanism*
extending over the span of his career:

1903–1904	Return of Columbus from Amer(ica), March 15, 1493
1917	Democracy Leading the World to Victory
1921	First Three Degrees of Free Masonry
1921–1922	Adoration of the Home
1923	East Coast View of the West: Buffalo Stampede Cowboy Chases Indian Indians Steal Long Johns
1925	The Shop Inspector, Coppersmith, etc.
1928	Portrait of John B. Turner, Pioneer
1929	Veterans' War Memorial Window[106]
1930	Arnold Comes of Age American Gothic Overmantel Decoration[107]
1931	Midnight Ride of Paul Revere The Birthplace of Herbert Hoover Victorian Survival
1932	Daughters of Revolution Arbor Day[108]
1933	Portrait of Nan[109]
1935	Death on the Ridge Road[110]

1936–1937	Main Street: e.g., Booster,[111] The Radical, Practical Idealist, The Good Influence, Village Slums
1937	Honorary Degree
1938	Charles Manson as Silenus[112] sketchbook caricatures of Hitler and Chamberlain
1939	Parson Weems' Fable Shriners' Quartet (planned: Captain John Smith and Pocahontas)
1940	Adolescence The American Golfer, Portrait of Charles Campbell Henry Wallace Bundles for Britain[113]

Many of these paintings display apparently whimsical techniques which, on second thought, reveal or require more critical attention. Wood's sly hand is apparent even in *The Adoration of the Home*, one of his earlier and lesser-known works. Receiving a commission in 1921 from a Cedar Rapids realty company, Wood painted *Adoration* as an outdoor mural that served as a sign advertising the realty company, and it was hung in the doorway above one of its new model homes. The painting allegorizes the building of the new suburban home, a miniature version of which is in the painting held aloft in the hands of a female figure symbolizing the city of Cedar Rapids. The painting looks like an altarpiece of a Madonna and child surrounded by saints, but the plan is decidedly secular: the inscription announces that the painting depicts the local realtor's vision of Cedar Rapids as a "city of homes." Wood thus pokes a bit of mythological fun at his self-aggrandizing patron, but his wit seems gentle and harmless, not severe. Mixing hype with sympathy, he also incorporated local persons into the painting—as farmers, workers, and builders—evidently to offset the mythic proportions of the Madonna, Mercury, and Silenus figures in the painting. All in all, the work looks like a throwaway commercial piece featuring amateurish and pretentious techniques (and Wood once said that he wished it had been burned), but we also have to pause to consider the implications of the seemingly humorous idea that the American suburban home has now displaced the traditional worship of Jesus: does home ownership, the American Dream, provide a functional equivalent for old-time redemption?[114]

Was Wood celebrating or mocking the American Dream? Whither his "Americanism" if that indeed was his lifelong preoccupation? What was he saying about American institutions? In "Revolt against the City," Wood (with Mott's help) explains that, "Your true regionalist is not a mere eulogist; he may even be a severe critic."[115] Wood often seemed to be playing it both ways, straddling some political or artistic middle ground: he disliked Ameri-can chauvinists and superpatriots, even while he promoted a "post–colonialist" American aesthetic; and he disliked American "debunkers" as well as Ameri-can "romancers."[116] But what would be the point or points of such double-edged commentary? Dennis explains Wood's elusive position as such:

> The strict supervision of social standards, attitudes, and customs by aging matriarchs in the community, and a fundamentalist belief in patriotic leg-ends on the part of the American public at large, prompted Grant Wood's most controversial paintings. His ability to transform his amused disaffec-tion for both areas of orthodoxy into gentle yet effective satire gave him a means of expanding his painting into an art of national expression. Behind an easygoing amiability, he displayed a healthy skepticism to-ward individuals or institutions who concocted or perpetuated deceptive elaborations of historical truth, sentimental imagery, affectations of taste, or social pretenses in the name of tradition. Not committed to an ardent program of cultural conservatism, he freely exercised his imaginative prowess in his parodies on favorite fables in American folklore.[117]

Dennis nicely settles upon calling Wood a "cheerful iconoclast" and a "cos-mopolitan satirist" who employed satire and comedy to draw renewed atten-tion to American fables, political allegories, and national mythologies. But again, as Wood himself insisted, *satire* is not quite the right word. As one commentator remarked in 1932 about *Daughters of Revolution*, a painting that most critics view as Wood's most clearly "satirical" work: Just when you think Wood's main purpose is to mock the revolutionary-elitist pretensions of these old women, he pulls that rug out from under you:

> The trick in the admiration of "Daughters of Revolution" is not to appre-ciate it too comfortably—that is, if you are in a position to snicker instead of snort—for you can't tell when your pet project might bask in the same light. And we all have them, you know.[118]

That prompting toward self-referentiality, a forced juggling of hetero-geneous if not contradictory perspectives,[119] usually is a telltale sign of an ironic hand at work. Dennis sprinkles numerous references to irony into his analysis of Wood, but a possible clincher, a rare smoking gun, is a 1931 article he cites in which Wood describes his own ways of employing ironic methods:

> The story of American life of this period can be told in a very realistic manner, employing sympathy, humor, irony or caustic criticism at the will of the painter, and yet have decorative qualities that will make it classify,

not as an illustration, but as a work of fine art with the possibilities of living through the ages.[120]

We have, then, a self-betraying ironist preoccupied with American institutions and often political motifs, thus let us ask the Richard Rorty question: Was Wood up to any public good? I'll just end with a few possible suggestions. In "Revolt against the City" Wood calls for a Jeffersonian revival of America through federally supported regional art schools. Such art schools would provide artists not just with technical training but more importantly with a broader education in the liberal arts. Gradually that liberal arts education, along with art exhibitions, would "greatly enlarge our American art public," making us eventually "a great art-loving nation." That hope for an "art-conscious America" would not be wed to any particular style of art but instead would showcase the great diversity of America's "drama." Wood ends the piece claiming that what he has "at heart [is] a deep desire for a widely diffused love for art among our whole people."[121]

Irony, claimed the late Gregory Vlastos, puts a heavy burden of participation upon the interpreter.[122] Wood wanted the democratization of art, call it the Americanization of art, and irony probably would be the most auspicious prompting toward that unlikely end.[123] His circle of friends included many poets and friends of democracy—John Dewey, Robert Frost, Carl Sandburg, Sinclair Lewis, Langston Hughes, Henry Wallace, Paul Engle, and of course the Whitmanesque insurance-selling poet, Jay Sigmund[124]—so it should come as no great surprise that Wood was so disposed.[125] But it is easy to mistake irony, especially of a democratic and homespun variety.[126] Teaching at Coe College, Marvin Cone remembered his friend thus:

> We never discussed politics, but he was a great believer in democracy. He liked people, common people—loved to talk to them anywhere, everywhere. He detested insincerity. But he and I had too many technical problems about painting to have time to discuss politics. His unfailing cheerfulness and good humor always impressed me. He always enjoyed a joke on himself. I guess you know that once, just for fun, we painted portraits of each other. Grant was Iowa's greatest artist, but he never took himself too seriously.[127]

8

Do Media Studies Belong in a Liberal Arts Curriculum?

D o media studies belong in a liberal arts curriculum? I am not the most qualified person to be addressing this question. I was a Johnny-come-lately to the Media Studies program at Pomona College; I jumped on the bandwagon only recently. I wasn't one of the original signatories to the Media Studies proposal, and I didn't have strong feelings one way or another at the time of the debate. I can't claim that Brian Stonehill and I were close drinking buddies, but we were close *colleagues*—thanks to his generous overtures, I must admit, and not to my efforts, I'm sorry to say. I'd like to begin my talk by indulging in just a few personal remembrances of Brian; such memories continue to bring pleasures and consolations.

To my mind, Brian and I were often uncannily on the same wavelength on certain matters, except that Brian always seemed to have the volume turned up louder on that frequency; he was always ahead of me. When I first came to Pomona, I had my freshman seminar screen Truffaut's *400 Blows*, and the word got back to Brian, and he approached me and said, "Are you into Truffaut?" I blathered on as if I were some expert, and he humored me at the time. Only later did I learn that he was a Truffaut *ringer*, that he had produced an entire laser disc devoted to the guy.[1] And then, I had been teaching Thomas Pynchon's *Crying of Lot 49* for several years before coming to Pomona, and thus we found another idiosyncratic interest in common— though I was again a little shaken to learn that he had an entire course

Talk delivered at Pomona College, March 28, 1998.

139

dedicated to Pynchon, not to mention a Website up and running. And then I had another class view D. W. Griffith's *Birth of a Nation*, only to learn—well you get the idea.[2] But then I asked Brian, "Have you read Michael Rogin's chapter on *Birth of a Nation?*"[3] Brian was never competitive or patronizing with me, he just relished that comraderie, but he did admit softly, "Yes, we've already obtained the rights to Rogin's piece for a forthcoming CD-ROM that we're putting out."

I found that I'd bump into Brian in the nooks and crannies of college life. There he'd be sitting in Lyman Hall attending an evening organ concert by Bill Peterson, so we would sit together, just listening, enjoying each other's quiet company. There he was at my tenure party in La Cañada, hosted by Leo Flynn. There he was at the Scripps Humanities Center, explaining to the Berkeley historian, Martin Jay, that I had just published a book, acting impromptu as my unpaid promo man and taking obvious pleasure in the chance to showcase his junior colleague. The reason so many of us became passionate and proprietary about Brian is that he *embodied* the liberal arts ethic—Media Studies was but an institutional vehicle that might formally reap the cross-fertilizing, cross-disciplinary fruit, the seeds of which he had already planted. Brian was a person of letters, but his spirit came first. Spirit must always precede the letter, and spirit indeed lives on.

Do media studies belong in a liberal arts curriculum? The question seems rhetorical today. Of course it does. But it wasn't always the case here at Pomona. Only five years or so ago Brian had to fight with college committees, college administrators, the faculty at large—and he suffered some personal and professional recriminations as a result. In thinking back about our common interests—Truffaut, Pynchon, Griffith, Rogin—I realized that those were wayward, odd preferences. I dare say that if you put forward for approval those quirky pedagogical selections in front of a faculty curriculum committee, they'd be turned down or toned down. Committees can kill the spirit of liberal arts. Committees aren't creative. Committees compromise, they play it safe, they regress to the mean, they routinize, they homogenize, they regulate, they enact procedures, they castigate, they obstruct initiative, they aren't entrepreneurial, they aren't visionary. The real question we should be asking today is, do committees belong in a liberal arts curriculum? Ah, but maybe another day for that purely rhetorical inquiry.

Back to the matter at hand. What has changed so that Brian's vision is now taken for granted? Surely technology has changed the equation and changed our collective outlooks. But not all technological changes are equal; some, more than others, change the order of things fundamentally. When I took my first typing lessons in eighth grade, I had the choice of whether to learn on a manual typewriter or a newfangled electric one. The received wisdom at the time was that one should learn on a manual, because then your fingers will press down harder, and so you can be bi-keyboardal—you can type on either a manual or an electric; whereas if you learn first on an electric, your fingers won't press down hard enough to revert back to a manual. When I finally got an electric typewriter, as a sophomore in college, I was so proud to enter a new era—the old manual seemed so hopelessly antiquated. Imagine, an unmotorized mechanical contraption with an array of arms that slap ink onto a page. It was digital only in the sense that each of your digits got quite a workout pressing down those keys. I was very proud to be the first person to hand in a laser-printed dissertation in graduate school. I've kept up a bit with the times—though only earlier this year, after many years of gathering dust, did my old college electric typewriter get thrown into the Goodwill pile. And I still have an old Apple computer, a clunker, gathering more dust on the shelf. Now I read in the newspaper that keyboard entry will be obsolete in five years. They won't even be teaching typing in schools anymore. Keyboards will go the way of abacuses and slide rules. All words, all information, will be entered into our computer screens by voice commands alone. I understand that Brian was already ahead of the rest of us at the time of his death by starting to experiment with voice recognition software.

The point I want to make is that the technological shifts I have experienced in my lifetime, from a manual to an electric to a computer keyboard, are pretty much continuous innovations, but the loss of keyboards altogether will represent a new order of things; we will be crossing a new threshold. Scholarly pundits tell us that Homer, or whoever Homer was in the ancient world, consolidated a shift from an oral culture to a written one; the Gutenberg Press, along with the development of rag paper and other technical innovations at the time of the Reformation, democratized that access to written matter. And now, to make another jump, we are leaving a preciously written cultural world, or at least a world in which most cultural producers still type their own words onto their screens, and will be entering into a truly multimedial world of production and appropriation, where we combine oral, aural, visual, and written modalities into one whiz-bang enterprise—or at least that's the hype. The main argument, then, for studying this new multimedial world is that it is unavoidable, it is ubiquitous, it is intractable. We have crossed a threshold, and there's no going back. Even if you want to remain a Luddite in theory, you can't do so in practice—the computer is here to stay—and a protest against the computer-processed world of ours would be something like saying that you don't like to read Gutenberg Bibles and want to read only hand-inscribed Bibles. Good luck with that lost cause.

In the 1980s, when most or many English professors in the United States were enthralled with Jacques Derrida's often brilliant attempts to elide the distinction between oral and written materials, or rather, to recuperate the importance of the written word against the presumed primacy of the spoken, Brian instead was watching and thinking about television. I suspect this is why many of his colleagues were initially skeptical about media studies as a discipline warranting serious study. Most professors were lamenting the coming dummied-down TV generation of Pac-man playing students; and after the decanonization of the canon, and the new exultation of popular and postmodern cultural materials, many of us were worried that our classes would be populated by Beavis and Buttheads, the MTV generation. Media studies, read, TV studies, would thus be *tawdry*, a pandering to the Bart Simpson mob. But Brian turned to Aristotle's poetics and rhetoric to start to make some sense of the new narratives that he viewed on the screen in front of him. He started talking about visual literacy, the need to become studied, savvy, and critical regarding the rhetorical strategies of moving visual images in TV and film. In their own day, classical tragedy and comedy were seen as low forms of entertainment; only in hindsight, thanks to Aristotle, do we start to appreciate the educational, civic, and artistic dimensions of these once tawdry, bacchanalian spectacles. But Aristotle, Brian insisted, needed an update. The forms of spectatorship in theater are different from the forms of spectatorship in film and television. D. W. Griffith, as Rogin has argued, replaced the dramatic scene with the camera shot, as the modal unit of storytelling in moving pictures; and jump cutting, editing, altered camera angles, and other technical innovations meant that this new mode of storytelling could defy almost all space and time limitations.[4] Films, unlike theater performances, could be replicated and widely and uniformly distributed, which meant that film could attract larger audiences, national audiences, hence, we were on our way to mass media, the new global village. Marshall McLuhan argued in the 1960s, of course, that the medium was the massage.[5] Stanley Cavell at Harvard was one of the first professional philosophers to argue that American film should be seen as high art, even high philosophy, maybe even high religion.[6] Alexander Nehamas at Princeton was one of the first to argue that the aesthetics of television should be taken seriously.[7] Brian was one of the first, I believe, to argue that media studies was appropriate in a liberal arts environment, and particularly appropriate for Pomona College, given our proximity to, and remove from, Hollywood.[8]

He and his colleagues here recognized early on that we are becoming bombarded with images, both moving and still. Texts and images are intermingled, but our words are no longer *printed* words; they are electronic bleeps, encoded in invisible binary systems. These words move, too. Ours is a discourse-rich world; words flow at an accelerated pace from one screen to another. Pictures speak a thousand words, true, but now they can be accompanied by literally thousands of instant-access words. Increasingly our public life has become mediated; our constitutional representative democracy is representational in new digital and cybernetic forms. Brian understood that if we are going to reclaim our national public life, we will have to confront and try to understand our increasingly mediated politics, these brave new virtual communities. In fact, we members of the politics department considered Brian to be a charter member, you could say a virtual member, of our department; it is no coincidence that he was scheduled to teach one of our senior seminars this year.

Lately grand academic theorists, big bookish thinkers, have jumped into the fray and joined the discussion about what our mediated public life means and should mean; note that recently Jürgen Habermas has started to view the Internet as a real-world public realm.[9] Derrida has been talking recently about the hauntology of electronic interactions.[10] Our Brian had already been writing about Rodney King videotapes and their legal repercussions,[11] about O. J. Simpson and our mediated racial and gendered relations,[12] about military euphemisms deployed during the Gulf War,[13] about presidential politics in our tabloid society,[14] about corporate takeovers of our major print and broadcast journalism networks,[15] and about the poetic incantations of our astronomical explorers.[16] Media studies, in other words, is no longer merely the study of a fourth estate, of an unofficial branch of government comprised of a vigilant and voyeuristic group of muckrakers out there; it is, rather, the study of our own public circuitry, our wired relations as a people, and our increasingly globally interconnected interactions with the rest of the planet. The word *media* has become a protean, expansive, catchall, corrosive, cancerous, even imperialist term, to the point that we really should be asking, media studies as opposed to what? Media Studies—newspapers, the Internet, e-mail, film, video, photographs, television, computers, graphics, holograms, radio, cyberzines, laser discs, digital disks, midi sound systems—has infiltrated every part of the curriculum. The late John Cage, a Pomona product (or dropout), wrote in a 1991 poem: "I think now of Marshall mcluhan/the world has become a single mind/we have extended the central nervous system/electronics our technology/makes the revolution for us/we can change our minds/we share only one the planet/the planet has become a single person."[17]

The central question for us today is really not about what constitutes media studies and whether it is important, but rather, how does media studies fit into a liberal arts environment? I think that what we are really doing is begging the question of what a liberal arts education should be, given our media-saturated world. Will we, should we become a bunch of technocratic, computer geekish, cyberjockies? In the context of Pomona, there is an easy answer that suggests itself. Our liberal arts curriculum is officially defined by our general education courses—our PAC system of skills[18]—and media studies fits well, it might be argued, with that notion of a skilled studentry. The answer is simple then. Add visual literacy to the list of skills that we require of our well-rounded students and, presto, we are off and running.

Tempting though that quick fix might be, I want to submit that the language of skills, of which many have become enamored here recently, represents nothing less than a betrayal of the liberal arts ethic, a failure of nerve, a crisis of confidence. What is a liberal arts education? It is not just the taking of a bunch of courses from different disciplines; it is not the acquisition of an array of skills. We do not, I repeat, we do not teach skills. Our approach to education—and there are other approaches to education, perhaps equally valid, perhaps even more important for other purposes, for other people, trade schools, vocational schools, technical schools, extension schools—our approach is that we have relaxed utilitarian and instrumentalist considerations in our teaching. College for our kids is a pure luxury, an absolute privilege; someone (usually their parents) has decided that these kids will be fortunate enough to suspend, for four years, pressing concerns about the mundane aspects of life, about getting a job, about putting food on the table, about cleaning the washroom. It is a time of almost unadulterated freedom, of free inquiry, free speech, free contemplation. Reading a book in almost any other context is an absolute waste of time; here we encourage that waste of time. Read your Shakespeare, read your Toni Morrison; go to professional school later. We tell our kids to think, to ponder, to question, to venture. The skills we teach—to use that awful language, a language for those boorish souls who believe that education can be measured, plotted, and tracked—our skills are intangibles. We teach brooding, living with ambiguity, passionate ratiocination, discovery, adventure, risk, curiosity, listening, negotiating paradox, mystery, joy. Those are our skills. We teachers trust, we have faith, that these seemingly wasteful pursuits will serve our students well in the long run, for they will instill in our students the capacity, and the desire, to give meaning, not skills, to their lives and to those lives around them. We try to equip them with good judgment, good sense, independent and rigorous thinking. I find that there's a lot of confusion these days about liberal arts—college administrators seem reluctant to sing our praises; they try to sell us to the accountants of the world, to pretend that foundation and corporate sponsors will see some tangible return on their investments, some bang for their bucks. Oh ye of little faith.

What do we do, what is the heart and soul of our enterprise? We read. We are readers. There are different ways of reading, there are different technologies and strategies of reading, there are different contexts and purposes for reading. But it all comes back to reading. I tell my students, if they want to become successful at anything, they should read. In music, they must read scores; in drama, scripts; in dance, other bodies; in athletics, the ball or one's teammates. In science, they must read the natural world, and they must read many, many scientific texts. Science is not, strictly speaking, a matter of method—there is no scientific method, no formula for good scientific results. Science requires risk taking, a receptivity for serendipity, for novelty, for revelation, for contingency, for failure; it requires a faith in the integrity of one's collaborators, for no single individual can empirically replicate every experiment or proof. Scientists—those who believe in an ongoing process of skeptical observation, testing, and falsification—are perhaps the most faithful of all of us, faithful that all of these patient yet persistent steps will amount to something down the road, of a belief in verities and eventualities that will probably always elude them. We are readers, of the world, of scripts and scriptures, of ourselves. All our other activities—all that talk about collaborative learning and speaking intensive and service learning—all of that is derivative, all of it is prefatory, all of it second order, and the only question is whether that busybodiness enhances or detracts from our reading moments in repose.

Small wonder, then, that Brian, an English professor, a reader par excellence, should turn his reading purview to visual matters, to television, to film, to computer screens. There was never such a thing as the self-conscious novel[19]; there are self-conscious readers, and Brian exuded that readerly self-awareness of one who continues to read and reread himself and others. His vision of Media Studies at Pomona wasn't about sharpening communication, journalistic and public relations writing and computer and video skills; rather, he talked and wrote about how media studies might promote, in his words, knowledge, wisdom, and beauty. Like all good readers, he was critically engaged with his subject matter; he wasn't just a cheerleader for the cyberworld. He worried that, without critical scrutiny, our media world will overwhelm us, will manipulate us, will dominate us. Other voices have warned us about the mediating dangers of technology in the twentieth century—Heidegger, Arendt, Horkheimer, Foucault, Haraway—and we should indeed worry that our liberal arts environs are vulnerable to becoming mere digital diploma mills, a cyberplace of automated and processed, rather than reflective and deliberative, learning. Liberal arts colleges may be the only places where old-fashioned study and face-to-face learning and wasteful thinking, reading, and talking can survive and thrive in the teleconferencing on-line virtual university environment that masquerades these days as higher education. In some ways these are the dark ages for readers, and liberal arts colleges are modern-day monasteries, places of refuge and sanctuary and devotion. We are scribes, we are monks, and our students are our exegetical initiates who still come to us to learn how to pore over passages. But now we are monks watching monitors, Benedictines wearing beepers. We must keep up with the latest innovations while preserving our heritage. Likewise, Brian, who called Aristotle the first media expert, updated and modernized Aristotle's definition of the arts of persuasion, translating Aristotle's pathos, logos, and ethos into hearts, smarts, and sparkle.[20] I would suggest that that update—hearts, smarts, and sparkle—would make a rather nice motto for our liberal arts college, or a helpful mantra for those who waver in their faith in the liberal arts. I might end by saying that when I listened to one of our new Media Studies professors, Kathleen Fitzpatrick, give a talk here a few weeks ago, I was struck by how *perfect* her topic was for the occasion, for an audience of largely English professors—a talk about the anxiety of readers at this historical juncture of ours, a readership worried about fighting a rearguard battle against the Rupert Murdoch media moguls of modernity—and, sitting in the back of the room that day, I thought to myself, tuning in to his wavelength, Brian Stonehill would have been thrilled by this talk.[21] Welcome, Kathleen! Are you into Truffaut?

9

Unremembered Acts Remembered

C lass of 1999. I am honored and humbled that you have asked me to speak to you on this glorious day. But I am also a little perplexed about why you selected *me* as your speaker. I am *not* funny. I am *not* profound. John Cleese is funny.[1] President Stanley is profound. Well, maybe I *am* a *little* funny, but not everyone appreciates my wisecracking ways. Still, I'm flattered to be here, especially since I learned that I beat out Keanu Reeves in the balloting.

Truth be told, I really don't feel funny at this time of year, I usually get depressed the day after graduation. My students are leaving me, and my entire constitution doesn't quite understand why. We professors fall a bit in love with our students—that love isn't parental love, nor is it romantic love, but it is a species of love nonetheless. That's the secret reason we professors wear robes on graduation day—it is to hide our emotionally fragile selves, because underneath those gowns our knees are knocking. So tomorrow, I ask you, after graduation, first, hug your parents and relatives, then hug your friends and classmates; but then, find a professor and hug that poor, pathetic creature. You are abandoning us, and we are starved for affection and affirmation. Besides, it is the one day when we can enjoy a holiday from sexual harassment laws, so please, hug a professor or two.

Instead of dispensing advice today, I am going to engage—uncharacteristically—in unabashed boosterism. My solemn contention is that your class, the Pomona College Class of 1999, is the greatest class ever, the greatest class in the history of the college, the greatest class perhaps anywhere in

---

Talk delivered at Pomona College, March 15, 1999.

history, the greatest class ever on the planet. (Actually, I think next year's class might be a tad better, but never mind that.) First, by all politically correct criteria, you have progressed well beyond your forebears—collectively you are the most environmentally conscious, the least racist, least sexist, and least homophobic class ever to leave these grounds; you are the most globally connected, the most technologically adept, the most appreciative of diverse peoples and ideas. And more of you are vegetarians than ever. But I don't want to lecture to you, I just want to sing your praises. Today I want to indulge in telling you of some of the displays of greatness I have witnessed from your class, and I'm going to name names. Please wave to the crowd if and when I call your name.

Sarah Kerbescian played alto saxophone for four years in the concert band at Pomona, and I can tell you that she didn't do it for the fame or glory. Few of you, frankly, ever attended those concerts, but you missed one of the most beautiful saxophone voices I have ever heard. Sarah's tone was always clear and vibrant, her facility graceful and quick. I had the pleasure of playing with Sarah a few years ago in a quartet that we unofficially called, The Pomona College Coed Naked Sax Quartet, and our little group somehow inspired the great composer and Professor Emeritus Karl Kohn to write a piece dedicated to us.[2] My huge regret, Sarah, is that I have been unable to play that piece with you—fatherhood intervened—but I will remember your tone and good cheer in future years. For the rest of you, find a way to keep music in your lives, as Sarah has, who plays for the sheer love of playing.

Ben Johnson—this guy is a national chess champion, a national master, and yet he never told his classmates—maybe he wanted to hustle them, I don't know. But as his professor, I saw his prodigious abilities of concentration at work. In our senior seminar this year, Ben would listen intently to his classmates, quietly plotting moves three steps ahead of their ideas, and finally he would break in and speak. What he did not say, and what his peers never realized, is that he had just checkmated them. Somehow he forgot to bring me back a souvenir bust of Lenin as promised from his semester abroad last year in St. Petersberg—so much for those abilities at concentration—but I guess he was busy learning Russian and playing international grand masters. Ben's going back to Russia, to play more chess, and then he'll go to law school. I pity his future courtroom adversaries who try to outmaneuver his legal gambits.

Mahvish Jafri told me earlier this year, incidentally and without fanfare, that reading Emerson's essay on friendship had literally changed her life.[3] The essay made her realize the importance of cultivating friendships during her college years—such memories are the most important treasures that you will take away from here—and so she and her housemates started a practice whereby they would invite fellow students they did not know particularly well over to the house for dinner and conversation. Emersonianism is talked about with great pretension on the East Coast, but methinks it is better practiced here.

Aaron-Andrew Bruhl is a champion athlete, Phi Beta Kappa in his junior year, he's our Downing Fellow next year, he's been admitted to Stanford and Yale law schools—and on top of all of that, he's modest! I asked him why he didn't apply for a Rhodes Scholarship, and he said, "Ah, I really didn't want to spend *two* years in England." People have been wondering around here about why Pomona students haven't won any Rhodes Scholarships in a while, and has anybody thought about the weather factor? Or that Pomona students just have their sights set on other goals, less glitzy but no less grand? One of my mathematics colleagues who sat on the Downing Committee said that he wouldn't be surprised if Andrew is the fifth deciding vote out of nine someday. I can say that, because I know that it won't go to Andrew's head.

Lea Scheppke is one of those Penny Dean swimmers[4] who swims about forty miles every day, and she performs arcane lab experiments on limpids or something like that in biology, and *she's* funny. Known as the female Dave Barry, Lea is an aspiring humor columnist. After reading one of her columns about how dirty her dorm rug had become, I gave her an old Hoover vacuum cleaner of ours. I'm not sure she really appreciated receiving an old dusty vacuum cleaner from a professor—who would?—so once I realized that I had embarrassed both of us, I tried to say that it was a metaphor for her continuing education. But she humored me, and forgave me, flashing one of her famous endorphine-induced smiles.

I've had the privilege of seeing *Jordan Snedcof* representing his peers on the Academic Procedures Committee, speaking his mind, questioning convention at every turn—in fact, I can say, without violating confidentiality, that a few of you are graduating tomorrow thanks to the intervention of your Academic Affairs Commissioner, Jordan. But I most remember a special faculty meeting called last year to discuss the candidates for dean. The faculty was squabbling about whether to look to outside candidates for the position, or to insist on our own internal candidate. A moment I'll never forget, a student observer, Jordan Snedcof, dared to raise his hand and spoke to the group, sorting out the issues with a clarity that had eluded the professoriate at large. What courage! To my mind, it was a turning point in our deliberations; and so, Dean Palmer, you should know that to some significant degree you owe your job to the extraordinary leadership and eloquence of one Jordan Snedcof, and many of us will be thanking him for years to come.

Shellie Sewell was in a class of mine that went on a field trip to the Roy Rogers Museum, and I expected somewhat that these savvy undergraduates would deconstruct and sneer at Hollywood's notion of yesteryear's cowboy. But Shellie wrote a piece afterwards that moved me to tears. She had shared a cigarette with an older white couple near their RV in the parking lot of the museum, and they all talked. And she speculated later that probably no where else in the Los Angeles area would this couple initiate such a conversation with an African-American woman, and she thanked Roy Rogers for that experience. Later I sent Shellie a photo of Dale Evans that I noticed she had secretly been admiring in the museum gift shop. I can also say that this past semester the best class in my Political Freedom course was conducted by Shellie. An Oxford historian was visiting that day, and afterwards, he didn't want to speak with me, he made a beeline for Shellie Sewell; and the rest of the day, I am told, that's all he talked about during his visit to Pomona—Shellie Sewell, Shellie Sewell—and I'm sure he's still talking about her back at Oxford. Although she's now an international academic star, Shellie is eschewing that limelight next year and will become a labor organizer instead. Integrity doesn't need an audience.

Dean Campbell—this guy's smile can charm the pants off anyone, and indeed he somehow coaxed me out of mine. It's not what you think; he convinced me to play inner tube water polo, where I became a man more dunked against than dunking. But I got the chance to see Dean's goal-tending tenacity that lurks behind that winning smile—this guy is the Mark McGwire of intramural sports around here[5]—and yet he also brought that cheerful ferocity to his academics. Dean managed to write a senior thesis this year that my economics colleague, Eleanor Brown, called one of the best uses of empirical research she's ever seen. The thesis was on the legalization of drugs. But hey, I know Dean's clean. Clean Dean, the transfer student dream.

When *Francisco Duenas* wasn't making agitprop posters this past semester, he was writing brilliant scholarly papers for my Idea of America class. Frankie often presented himself as a sharp but thoughtful critic of American society, favoring for instance Robert Pinsky's critical poetry over Walt Whitman's unchecked exuberance,[6] but he never told the class that he was most proud of having helped his mother pass her naturalization exam a while back (and I learned this again only within the safe confines of the Roy Rogers Museum). I noticed in the school paper that he wanted some speaker at this year's graduation to say something in Spanish, so for you and your mother Frankie: ¡Felicidades a todos los estudiantes! Y a los papás de Francisco, gracias por mandarlo a nuestra universidad. Francisco era un estudiante muy excelente. Eso es todo lo que puedo decir. ¿Bien dicho, no?

Ponytailed *Paul Kahn* has the gift of gab—not just any gab—he can quote lines from Shakespeare at the drop of a hat, or he can launch into an extended political analysis. Talk to Paul about the PAC skills curriculum—forget about it, don't get him started!—Paul hates the PAC system, which suggests that our curriculum hasn't completely suppressed intelligence and good sense. Earlier this year Paul offered to organize a student petition drive—he said that he could come up with a thousand signatures—calling for an ice rink here at Pomona College—but I suggested that we had to put that visionary idea in cold storage for the time being. Paul's going off to drama graduate school at NYU next year, and you better get his autograph today, because next time you'll probably be begging for tickets on Broadway. I say, we should all support Paul so that he can become rich and famous so that he can donate lots of money for the Pomona College Ice Rink in the next capital campaign, after the current one peters out.

Amy Teng was the first student who ever received an A+ from me, and I've now taught for something like eighteen years, at Berkeley, Stanford, Santa Cruz, Tufts, and Pomona. I've taught future Rhodes scholars, Marshall scholars, Watson scholars, many amazing students along the way. But Amy was the first to crack the Seery code. She'll be going to Harvard Law School next year, and I'm supremely confident that that A+ wasn't a fluke—and I can say that, because Amy confessed to me a few days ago that she did not vote for me for Class Day speaker.

Finally, *Fernanda Baretto* creatively combined media studies and politics into an interesting double major, but more than that, Fernanda competed for four years in ballroom dancing. She invited me to one of her dances, and whoa, was I treated to a visual feast. Here's a woman who can tango, can rumba, can cha cha, and she holds her own in the waltz—she didn't win the competition that night, but I blamed her partner, who just couldn't match her style, romance, discipline, and dignity. Fernanda just upstaged him, the poor freshman shmuck. Fernanda will be studying entertainment law next year or she might become a film director; either way, she's going to be continuing her dancing at the competitive level, next year for the USC dance team.

Ladies and gentleman, I am proud to say, the spirit of liberal arts is alive and well at Pomona College! It lives on. Believe it or not, there are skeptics even among us, doubting Thomases, who question the merits of liberal arts, who want proof, and so I want to tell you, the Class of 1999, you must remember what went on here. I know that you will continue to be exemplary in your personal conduct, but I want you to stand as clear examples for others. I want Pomona College students to seek out and to occupy positions of leadership. I want Pomona College people to rule the world. I want the world to be run by persons whose greatness consists in many understated virtues, persons who listen, persons who need not be ostentatious or self-aggrandizing, who need not wear their talents on their sleeves, persons who know the inner wisdom of those lines from Wordsworth about a good person's "little, nameless, unremembered, acts of kindness and love that have no slight or trivial influence on that best portion of one's life."[7] Accomplishment, hard work, and ambition can indeed go hand in hand with friendship, kindness, and humor—that is who you are, Class of 1999. And so, I want you to evangelize, I want you to spread the word. If you can't find passion and conviction about what went on here, you will never awaken to the rest of life. So hereby, starting today with you, I pronounce the next century to be *the Pomona Century*. You've got to make it happen. If you must, make Pomona

College and liberal arts education into a religion. Let only the eager, thought-ful, and reverent leave here. This is a community of faith. From here on out, wherever you are, whenever you hear anyone say the name of your great college, Posoba College, no CalPoly Pomona, no, Panama College, Palomino College, no Pomona College, I want you to raise your hands into the air, and imagine that you can see Mt. Baldy off in the distance, just like now, imagine that you can see Mt. Baldy off in the distance, and when those sweet words ring out, you must shout, *Hail Pomona Hail,* Not Oh hell Pomona, but Hail Pomona Hail. Let's try it, altogether. Pomona College. Pomona College. Pomona College. Amen. Congratulations! Go well, be good, see you tomorrow!

10

Castles in the Air

An Essay on Political Foundations

> If you have built castles in the air, your work need not be lost; that is where they should be. Now put the foundations under them.
>
> —Thoreau, *Walden*

Rereading Judith Butler's 1990 essay, "Contingent Foundations,"[1] has prompted me to ask a few foundational questions about foundations. Her essay, which has been reprinted subsequently in several high-profile feminist anthologies,[2] provides a spirited reply to certain unnamed critics of so-called "postmodernism" who evidently portray that movement as naive and nihilistic. Responding to the reputed relativism and political listlessness of postmodernism, such critics wish to reassert the need for certain basic starting points—foundations—that will lend coherence and rigor to political theory and activity. Poststructuralism and its illegitimate cousin, post-modernism, have destabilized the subject, have undermined the notion of agency, have deessentialized every meaningful identity, have detotalized every narrative and diffused every norm and, well, burst every bubble and deflated all phallogocratic balloons so that it may be time to return to primary premises—"For politics is unthinkable without a foundation, without these premises."[3]

Butler's response is engagingly curious, for she does not mobilize a defense of "anti-foundationalism," but instead she maintains that foundational thinking is indispensable to politics and yet, somehow at the same time,

I am deeply grateful to George Shulman for pointing out the above Thoreau passage to me after the article originally appeared.

should be viewed as "contingent" and "contestable." What then for Butler is a "contingent" foundation? Whereas most foundational thinking implicitly presents its foundational premises as unassailable (which is why, supposedly by definition, they are foundational), Butler invites us to challenge these purportedly unchallengeable presuppositions, even though we continue to posit foundations and often remain committed to many of their consequences: "the point is not to do away with foundations, or even to champion a position that goes under the name of anti-foundationalism. . . . Rather, the task is to interrogate what the theoretical move that establishes foundations *authorizes*, and what precisely it excludes or forecloses."[4]

Butler, as I read her essay, is in a roundabout way responding to a question that has nagged feminist theory for the last decade or so: If the subject is dead, if agency is multiple, if identity is performative, if the signifier "woman" is itself an essentializing and thus self-discrediting symbolic, if feminism on the whole is a totalizing metanarrative, have we not deconstructed ourselves out of a job? Third-wave feminists no longer call themselves feminists (especially after feminism was revealed to be a white, heterosexed, middle-class, academicized subject position); for a short while, some writers started calling themselves "womanists," but that *nom de guerre* never took hold. Feminism as it evolved started incorporating queer studies and also made occasional overtures toward masculinities studies, hence, "gender studies" emerged for a spell as the prevailing rubric—and lately all of these sites of interest have been subsumed under the catchall "cultural studies." But then, back to basics—as a former feminist, can you still maintain unreconstructed loyalties to universal sisterhood, or must you succumb to sophisticated situatedness? Butler's answer: "One might ask: but doesn't there have to be a set of norms that discriminate between those descriptions that ought to adhere to the category of women and those that do not? . . . To establish a normative foundation for settling the question of what ought properly to be included in the description of women would be only and always to produce a new site of political contest. That foundation would settle nothing, but would of its own necessity founder on its own authoritarian use. This is not to say that there is no foundation, but rather, that wherever there is one, there will also be a foundering, a contestation."[5] In sum, in offering the language of foundering foundations, Butler is giving fellow feminists a "have-your-cake-and-eat-it-too" formulation—but that paradoxical approach, turning on clever locutions, seems to my ear oddly reminiscent of Ronald Reagan's similarly disarming 1980s doublespeak slogan: "Trust, but verify."

While I greatly admire Butler's overall insistence that we should question even the unquestionable, and I readily confess to becoming spellbound by her impressive language and intricate turns of phrases, I nonetheless find myself, after finishing another reading of her essay, scratching my head in wonder: is there something more, after all, to this deconstructive critique than simply a thoroughgoing skepticism, now applied to politics? Let us examine what she means by "foundations" before we accept her uncanny contention that foundations can founder. What is a foundation?

Clearly Butler borrows on a scholarly tradition that deploys the word *foundation* as a trope for philosophical certitude, though usually she directs her particular critique toward the knowing *subject*, thus toward the notion of a stable and an unquestioned subjectivity, which leads her to direct our attention toward the power dynamics that reportedly constitute the self; hence, Butlers focuses more on identity politics than on epistemology proper.[6] But the metaphor of foundational stability, whether epistemological or identitarian, is used in the same way. The Oxford English Dictionary (OED) defines *foundation* as "the act of founding or building upon a firm substructure"; it is an action of "establishing, instituting, or constituting on a permanent basis." Building metaphors and construction analogies pervade the OED definitions of *foundation*. Building an edifice is apparently a two-part process: there is the above-ground, constructed edifice but underneath is the "solid ground or base" on which "an edifice or other structure is erected." In successive definitions, the OED seems to build its own case for how bedrock foundations become the bases for more abstract edifices: "6. *fig.* A basis or groundwork on which something (immaterial) is raised or by which it is supported or confirmed; an underlying ground or principle; the basis on which a story, fiction, or the like is founded."

In writing about the foundations of subjects, Butler too deploys these building analogies, but she mixes her metaphors. On the one hand, she grounds her use of *foundation* in references to earthy groundedness and figures connoting physical stability: She defines "foundations" as "those premises that function as authorizing grounds."[7] A grounded foundation has "weight;" it is located in a "site" or "field"; it is a stabilizing "position" that one "lays down" or "shores up"; it is placed, anchored, grounded, even "buried."[8] But then Butler often switches language, from the physical to the metaphysical. Now a foundation involves "metaphysical commitments" and "metaphysical lodgings."[9] The topography, or architecture, becomes top-down, not bottom-up: the foundation, we learn, is a "transcendental ground" or "transcendental anchor."[10] Eventually she offers a new formulation: the "foundering foundation" is also an "ungrounded ground"[11]—an unmooring that I guess will help us scale the heights of a new, free-floating politics.[12] But now I am lost in verbiage. To be sure, I do not want to lose sight of Butler's main point, which I take to be a broadside challenging of the presumption that feminism needs a unitary self-definition in order to enact a transformative politics; but her playfully loose language to that end may not be, upon close inspection, the most effective strategy for building her own constructive case.

I want to return to my own roots for a moment, not in order to draw undue attention to my person, nor to recommend an ontology of the everyday, nor to invoke Robert B. Reich's working observations that some people get paid for analyzing symbols, whereas other people get paid for pouring concrete.[13] Rather, I happen to have thought a good deal about foundations in my past, for reasons that will become apparent later, and I want to draw upon that experience. It so happens that my first job as a teenager was to work on a small carpenter crew in the Midwest. On my first day, the foreman drove me out to a job site, gave me a shovel, and told me to dig the footings for a foundation for a building. With neither the help of a backhoe nor any coworkers, I started digging—in 90° humid heat, in the middle of an old farm pasture. Suffice it to say, to this day I take the idea of foundations quite personally, and therefore I want to hold commentators rather strictly to their language about foundations. In this first concrete example, I dug the footings far too wide and none too straight. Who, after all, would really want a crooked or an unlevel building? But my mistakes were soon rectified. My boss, with the help of a few tools—a plumb, a chalk line, a level, a tape measure—straightened out my work and nailed into place the 2 × 4 and 2 × 6 footings. The next day a cement truck and driver came by and poured the concrete mix into the footings, and I helped place some anchor bolts into the hardening mix. Once the concrete sets, you knock away the wood molds (the footings), and there you have a basic foundation.

It gets more complicated, I learned. On my second assignment, I was dropped off at another job site, where the foundation had already been poured for a house-to-be that would be built over a subterranean basement. The basement area had already been excavated, and the concrete floor and the concrete walls—a fake brick pattern—had already been poured. Worried that forecast rains would cause the foundational walls to collapse inward, the carpenters had earlier erected a temporary network of supporting wood beams and braces that would help shore up the walls until the floor joist could be installed above. My job, with just a claw hammer in hand, was to dismantle this crisscrossing network of supporting beams and braces—but to do so in a way that the walls would not come tumbling down. Foundations, I discovered, even concrete ones, do not necessarily stand on their own—but rather need the support of backfill on the outside in addition to the floor beams on the topside—and often we would call in a crane operator to drop in a steel I-beam (fashioned at a local foundry) for extra support. Moreover, the composition of the surrounding soil also matters—if the soil is sandy or rocky, then the foundation and the basement probably will remain pretty dry; but if there is a fair bit of clay or ground water, the foundation may eventually crack and leak, and the basement will become dank.

I left the Midwest many years ago, but I have continued to keep my eye on foundations in various parts of the country, and on various building techniques from region to region. I now live in California, where few residential homes are built over basements, since houses with basement foundations cannot well withstand earthquakes nor can they, over time, ride the lesser undulations of the shifting earth. California contractors make do in a variety of ways. In graduate school I lived in several houses built on stilts, which featured crawl spaces between the dirt ground and the wood floor of the house. In the Berkeley hills, some houses are built on steel beam platforms that sit atop encased posts that sit upon large internal ball bearings, which allow the entire platform to move. Near the ocean, houses are built on top of piers driven deep into the ground. One hopes, of course, that the ball bearings or the piers can withstand earthquakes and pounding sea tides, but often these structures fail. During the year of El Niño, several California hilltop houses, along with their foundations, came crashing down, as rain-saturated grounds gave way underneath.

My current house, a commonplace 1970s' era tract model, is built on a concrete slab foundation. The idea is that a slab of concrete can ride pretty well on top of the waves of the earth, and that it would take a rather strong jolt to shake the house off its foundation. But often these foundations need reinforcement, and California home owners pay lots of money to have extra bolts and braces installed. Moreover, one has an ongoing relationship with one's slab foundation. Some slabs are only three or four inches thick and thus are prone to cracking through normal wear and tear. In my neighborhood, some people have had problems with water spouts leaking upward through cracks in the foundation. In my own case, I have had a problem with sub-terranean termites coming up through the foundation cracks and eating away at my edifice. The solution, a temporary one at best, is to treat the underside of the foundation with a chemical barrier—otherwise my concrete foundation is virtually porous to these pests.

Older houses in my town of Claremont have foundations built out of large stones. Often these older foundations need some tuck pointing repair. In one section of the town, a village built by Russian immigrants, the foundations are made from mud bricks, which are noticeably more crude than the smooth, sun-baked adobe bricks featured in some of the California missions. On one summer trip to Hawaii I noticed the many foundational uses to which lava rock has been put—which is amusing, because one big eruption from Kilauea could wipe out those air-filled foundations, much as those entire islands once bubbled up volcanically in the middle of the ocean. On another summer trip, this time to Alaska, I learned about Native American Eskimo igloo foundations cut out of glaciated ice—a cooling effect that invites spectral comparison to lava rock. Yes, foundations are fashioned from many materials—bricks, stones, mud, mortar, adobe, clay, wood, concrete, steel, ice—and some foundations work better or last longer than others. Even the composition and quality of concrete vary from place to place. My office sits on the ground floor in a former Carnegie library, a building that was the first steel-reinforced concrete structure in California. But when that building was recently renovated, we learned that the consistency and quality of the concrete were uneven throughout and contained many big chunks of stone, and that the steel was all reclaimed from various projects available at the time and thus had been jury-rigged into place—hence, the concrete structure looks monumental and uniform from the outside, but looks are deceiving (the entire building could come crashing down in the next earthquake). Back in the Midwest, many of those concrete basements are now erected from prefab panels instead of being poured on-site. Time will tell whether this cost-effective, assembly-line technique is a better building method than the custom-made foundations of yesterday.

Perhaps my experience with foundations runs somewhat deeper than others, but I have never understood them to stand, whether literally or metaphorically, for the purposes to which Butler makes of them. True, foundations provide a source of stability for edifices built upon them. More, one hopes that one's foundations are strong and durable. But problems with foundations arise constantly in the construction business, and builders frequently adapt their methods to changing circumstances. Butler, however, uses the term *foundation* as a marker for far more than anything suggested by the OED definitions, or that my own experience bears out. She uses the term as a virtual synonym for "metaphysical commitments," "unshakable premises," and "normative universality." What carpenter has ever actually believed that a one-size foundation fits all buildings? What contractor has ever laid a foundation without thinking about it and its relationship to the rest of the building? What mason ever believed that his wall was truly indestructible? And how did metaphysics enter the discussion (carpenters use sketches and blueprints, but few buildings are actually designed as monuments to God or Pharaoh)?

To my way of thinking, Butler, in asking us to question our foundations, has deconstructed a moving target, a floating signifier; she has projected undue stability onto that trope in order to claim for herself the broad gesture of destabilization. What kind of foundation is she actually thinking about she when recommends global subversion of foundationalism? My cousin, Richie, lived for a long time in a houseboat. Other people live in caves or tree houses or geodesic domes or space stations. Frank Lloyd Wright dared to build Fallingwater over a waterfall, on top of a hanging boulder. What would it mean to "contest" the above foundations, to see them as "contingent," or to try to erect new structures on "ungrounded grounds"? Following Butler in the same volume, Kirstie McClure, in an essay called "The Issue of Foundations," calls for political theorists to operate "without the security of foundations," which will open up more "breathing room."[14] What kinds of foundationless buildings would she actually construct? Are we talking about movable teepees or log cabins with dirt floors? My cousin, Richie, was a daredevil, but even he had enough sense to drop an anchor for his boat. Or by recommending foundering foundations, does Butler mean that we should intentionally build rickety buildings? Or are Butler and McClure indirectly advocating some vague dream about political institutions that require no borders, no walls, no floors, no stabilizing features? In talking about "open sites" and "breathing room" and "groundless grounds" are they talking about universal homelessness or nomadism as an existential possibility? My bottom-line question is: How did the foundation metaphor get so misconstrued?

Butler's essay is, of course, a late-coming intervention in a running academic debate between "foundationalism" and "anti-foundationalism," and many of her terms apparently are imported from that dispute, especially from the "anti-foundationalist" camp. Self-proclaimed anti-foundationalists seem eager to define foundationalism so that they can oppose it, thus this body of literature may be a good starting point for investigating the genealogy of the term *foundation*.[15] In the late 1980s Stanley Fish published a good summary of the anti-foundationalist argument, and his language on the topic of foundations is particularly telling. He begins his definition of *foundation* in terms and metaphors that accord more or less with my down-to-earth experience: "By foundationalism I mean any attempt to ground inquiry and communication in something more firm and stable than mere belief or unexamined practice. The foundationalist strategy is first to identify that ground and then so to order our activities that they become anchored to it and are thereby rendered objective and principled."[16] But immediately Fish starts attaching riders to his understanding of foundations that would make no sense to any carpenter I know: "The ground so identified must have certain (related) characteristics: it must be invariant across contexts and even cultures; it must stand apart from political, partisan, and 'subjective' concerns in relation to which it must act as a constraint; and it must provide a reference point or checkpoint against which claims to knowledge and success can be measured and adjudicated."[17] And then Fish, like Butler, takes flight into the transcendental heavens, and he leaves behind earthbound foundation metaphors altogether: "In the long history of what Derrida has called the logocentric tradition of Western metaphysics, candidates for the status or position of 'ground' have included God, the material or 'brute act' world, rationality in general and logic in particular, a neutral-observation language, the set of eternal values, and the free and independent self."[18] Foundationalism, explains Fish (and he calls himself a "card-carrying anti-foundationalist"), claims to transcend all historical and social circumstances and thus the job of anti-foundationalism is to return to "the local, the historical, the contingent, the variable, and the rhetorical."[19] "Anti-foundationalism teaches that questions of fact, truth, correctness, validity, and clarity can neither be posed nor answered in reference to some extracontextual, ahistorical, nonsituational reality, or rule, or law, or value; rather, anti-foundationalism asserts, all of these matters are intelligible and debatable only within the precincts of the contexts or situations or paradigms or communities that give them their local and changeable shape."[20]

But again I am confused. How exactly did "God" or "logic" or "the self" get mixed up metaphorically with the stone bases that anchor most buildings? How could a "ground" metaphor become the code for all "decontextualization"? Fish does not give us a clear answer; he sweepingly asserts that foundationalism now lies in ruins, because almost every important intellectual of the last half century has become an anti-foundationalist: ". . . in philosophy by Richard Rorty, Hilary Putnam, W. V. Quine; in anthropology by Clifford Geertz and Victor Turner; in history by Hayden White; in sociology by the entire tradition of the sociology of knowledge and more recently by the ethnomethodologists; in hermeneutics by Heidegger, Gadamer, and Derrida; in the general sciences of man by Foucault; in the history of science by Thomas Kuhn; in the history of art by Michael Fried; in legal theory by Philip Bobbit and Sanford Levinson; in literary theory by Barbara Herrnstein Smith, Walter Michaels, Steven Knapp, John Fekete, Jonathan Culler, Terry Eagleton, Frank Lentricchia, Jane Tompkins, Stanley Fish, and on and on."[21] For a proponent of localized categories, Fish uncharacteristically seems to be reading across many horizons: do all of these people really have a common enemy drawing them together, or is this another paranoid exposé of some widespread Freemason conspiracy?

The person who is most often credited with inciting a contemporary attack on foundations is Richard Rorty. Rorty, according to one commentator, established "anti-foundationalism as a slogan for a complex cluster of ideas previously lacking resonant expression."[22] He brilliantly gathered together a unifying story about Western philosophy, drawing upon and drawing together diverse thinkers such as Plato, Descartes, Locke, Kant, Nietzsche, Dewey, Wittgenstein, and Heidegger; yet that synthesis or overview might have been accomplished only with the help of some smoke and mirrors. Giving foundationalism its operational ambit, Rorty also is probably the main source for all of the mixed and muddled metaphors that attend the "foundationalist-antifoundationalist" debate. Indeed, Rorty explicitly approaches foundationalism via a metaphorical analysis. In *Philosophy and the Mirror of Nature*, Rorty explains that the "foundations of knowledge" tradition in philosophy, from Plato to the present, is "a product of the choice of a certain set of perceptual metaphors."[23] If we think of knowledge as a series of propositions, and if we reject the view that arguments are conversationally cumulative, we will likely look backwards to try to discover an originary reason or cause behind our series of claims, a privileged proposition from which all others subsequently derive. Drawing on Heidegger's use of ocular metaphors, Rorty contends that notions of objective truth or necessary knowledge spring from a long-extended Western obsession with "the notion of our primary relations to objects [i]s analogous to visual perception."[24] The "original dominating metaphor" behind all truth claims is the idea of being brought "face-to-face" with the object of our belief. We stand in the presence of a vision so compelling that its accuracy cannot be doubted, hence, truth is a spectatorial confrontation. The next stage is to try to improve upon this quasivisual faculty, a faculty that will accurately mirror the vision, and thus we start to look for a privileged class of representations—those supposedly immutable structures within knowledge, life, and culture—and these privileged representations will constitute our "foundations" of knowledge.[25]

Yet Rorty explains one metaphor by recourse to another metaphor, and the two metaphors do not work well together. A "foundation" metaphor draws its logic through a building analogy, and Rorty brings together his "complex cluster of ideas previously lacking resonant expression" with perceptual, visual, or ocular metaphors. How did a "ground" metaphor become an "eye" metaphor? I think a few steps are missing in Rorty's analysis. His great accomplishment in *Philosophy and the Mirror of Nature* is to bring Continental and Anglo-American philosophical traditions into play with one another, a grand merging of a Plato-Descartes-Kant-Nietzsche-Heidegger story with a Dewey-Kuhn-Sellars-Davidson story. He is quite explicit that the connection between the two traditions is a common recourse to ocular metaphors,[26] but herein may lie the confusion, the source of a conflation. Heidegger tries to show how the epistemological notion of "objectivity" derives from the Platonic visual imagery of *idéa*, a notion of face-to-face presencing. In Rorty's grand overview, *idéa* becomes a code for all subsequent metaphysics—the Platonic eye of the soul, religion's "God's eye" point of view, the Cartesian Eye of the Mind. Descartes, explains Rorty, turned his thoughts toward inner pictures that evidently were more clear and distinct than outward representations, whereas Locke reversed Descartes' directions and saw "singular presentations to sense" as what should grip us.[27] Locke was the first, says Rorty, to look for the foundations of knowledge in the realm of the senses. Kant, Rorty further narrates, tried to develop a propositional rather than a perceptual view of knowledge, but Kant failed to free us from Locke's confusion between justification and causal explanation—hence, the notion still lingers that a "foundation" is a "cause."[28]

Much like Butler and Fish, Rorty uses the term *foundation* as a shorthand for "first cause," "objectivity," "necessity," "permanence," "universality," "systematizing," and "transcendence." A foundation, in other words, is the main characteristic of the long-standing Western tradition that tries to shore up knowledge by a constant. Dewey emerges as a hero in the book, as a philosopher who gives up the hope for transcendence and causes and instead looks for edifying questions and pragmatic social solutions. Dewey accepted the world of appearances for what it was and did not attempt to look for a hidden reality beneath the play of appearances, hence, Rorty names Dewey, along with Wittgenstein and later Heidegger, as a leader in the anti-foundationalist movement. Rorty, I suspect, lifts the "foundationalist" vocabulary largely from the American pragmatists, along with the confluence of building versus ocular metaphors. As Charlene Haddock Seigfried has pointed out, foundationalist metaphors seduced even the pragmatists.[29] Charles Sanders Peirce, for instance, wrote: "To erect a philosophical edifice that shall outlast the vicissitudes of time, my care must be, not so much to set each brick with nicest accuracy, as to lay the foundations deep and massive."[30] William James spoke of grounding knowledge by plunging explanatory systems "into sensation as bridges plunge their piers into the rock."[31] Seigfried, however, insists that the pragmatists were using the foundation metaphor advisedly and ambivalently; they "continue[d] to use terms bequeathed to them by the philosophical tradition after having radically reinterpreted and revalued their meanings."[32] James, for instance, criticizes the foundationalist building-block metaphor as a way of understanding sensations—for he refused to believe in pure, simple, bedrock sensations as the ground of our experience—but he does make reference to quasifoundational language in writing about constructing our experiences piecemeal, experiences that can, at times, give us a sense of solace, closure, or security. But such "foundations" for the pragmatists are constructed and projected, not located and found in some originary realm.

Rorty, however, does not distinguish between the different kinds of foundations, pregiven versus erected. Rather, all foundations become part of the comprehensive critique of spectatorial knowledge, the notion of Truth as the accuracy of representation, as the correct mirroring of Nature. A foundation for a building provides, to be sure, some strong degree of stability, but in the philosophical tradition whose epistemology Rorty is challenging, a foundation apparently is an irrevocable guarantee that something will remain absolutely fixed and eternally unchanging. But note, stability is not the same as infallibility. Rorty has done us a great service in insisting that the vocabulary of "picturing" in philosophy has failed us, but that sense of arresting reality via a philosophical gaze, the "ocular" tradition, should not be conflated with all notions of foundational stability, namely, the building tradition (perhaps Rorty and other Western anti-foundationalists have been unduly influenced by the continued existence of Greek and Roman ruins, whose archaeological remains leave the mistaken impression that foundations are forever). Rorty, like Butler and Fish, has misappropriated a building metaphor and applied it, by false analogy, to selves, sensations, sentences, and knowledge. In turn, Rorty and others have taken the "death of God" or the "death of the subject" or the "death of logos" critique and applied it too indiscriminately, subverting all structures. Thus their political conclusions may not necessarily follow from their epistemological and linguistic deconstructions—and I hasten to add at this juncture that my ulterior purpose in questioning their political building techniques is not to bring down their respective houses of cards nor to propose that we must return to and shore up the old "foundations of knowledge" approach. Rather, I want to pursue a few alternative ideas about what I see as being more effective political uses of the foundationalist trope.

Purely for the sake of the argument at hand, thus falling far short of any exhaustive treatment of the matter, I want to propose a provisional but possibly helpful dichotomy. I submit that much of Western political theorizing can be categorized into one of two separate traditions: the "Edenic" tradition versus the "constructivist" tradition.[33] First a quick sketch of the Edenic tradition. The Edenic tradition, which is surely the most prominent tradition in the West, owing to its obvious biblical beginnings, posits separate spatial realms in which human activity takes place, spatial conceptions whose separated territories can be traversed only by some extraordinary, eventful temporal movement or transformative act, a complete relocation from one spot to another. The temporally prior realm, of course, is depicted as a pristine, harmonious, united, sacred realm, which also is described as a gardenlike state of nature owing to its creationist origins. Standing spatially opposed to the Edenic or natural realm is, as foil, the realm of civil or political society. Civil society is marked by its distance from grace; it is commonly depicted as sinful, secular, denatured, compromised, the realm of conflict, strife, diversity, and incompletion.

Edenic theorists (many of whom become secularized in their language) usually observe and respect strictly the distinction between the natural and civil realms and, depending on the particular theorist, they may prefer one realm over the over, or they may propose and favor different trajectories suggesting movement from one realm to the other, and/or back again. Temporalized motifs—metaphors of mobility—are highlighted in Edenic theorizing within their spatial frames: fall, exile, transformation, emancipation, preservation, recovery, and return.

So much for my crude setup. I rehearse the above in order to suggest further, somewhat contrarily I think, that Butler, Fish, and Rorty, as betrayed by their discussions about foundations, are all operating largely within the Edenic tradition. All three want to deconstruct the Edenic tradition, but try as they might, all three never quit that framework. For each of these writers, although in different ways, a "foundation" is always located in a naturalized, sacred realm—to be distinguished from a denatured, enacted, performed, and self-negotiated venue. To be sure, Butler, Fish, and Rorty are all constructivists at heart. They all claim, in short, that we must attend to humanly constructed edifices, but they always presume that grounding claims are "prior" claims about unquestionable or sacred or natural premises. Edenic grounding thus becomes the wellspring for their mixed metaphors about foundations, at once grounded yet transcendental.

Butler is most explicit on the need to challenge the particular *siting* of foundational grounding, and symptomatically her language continues to grapple with issues of Edenic versus post-Edenic temporality. She asks us to question the "pregiven" and the "preconditions" of our claims; she instructs us that by placing key political terms within quotation marks, we will help "denaturalize" those terms, which will help relocate these signs as "sites of political debate."[34] She wants to "emancipate" and "mobilize" certain signifiers.[35] The problem of foundationalism, she adds, is that it attempts to secure the norms of political life "in advance," and thus it attempts to ward off its strategies and exclusions from subsequent interrogation.[36] She asks feminists to ponder how a political field gets defined in opposition to a supposedly naturalized prepolitical or nonpolitical field, a "constitutive out-side," and she wants these grounding "parameters" themselves rendered contingent and thereby subjected to reabsorption into a politicized arena.[37] In short, how one frames a debate from the outset is all-important. But again, Butler's words start to creak beneath their own metaphoric weight, and I find myself wishing that she would philosophize more with a hammer—because as every carpenter knows, framing a house comes *after* laying the foundation, and framing is *not* the same as founding.

Fish and Rorty share Butler's suspicions about any theoretical foregrounding that subsequently structures political and scholarly activity, a worry that identifies them as Edenic theorists (or post–Edenic, same coinage). Fish explicitly associates foundationalism with Western religiosity, and he wants to replace providential guidance with a kind of rhetorical muddling through, a finding-your-way-as-you-go strategy to be applied to almost any discipline or activity, whether English composition or politics. Rorty, following Dewey, also is clear in his belief that Western philosophy has derived all of its crucial terms, insights, and gambits from Western religion.[38] Again, following Dewey, he recommends instead a can-do, edifying philosophic discourse rather than a know-it-all, systematizing approach. But throughout *Philosophy and the Mirror of Nature*, Rorty never explains how or why the philosopher's mirror is a mirror of *nature* rather than a mirror of God's eye. I believe the tacit linking of God to Nature reveals Rorty's underlying Edenic scheme of things; *foundation* is his corrosive term connecting, and thus obscuring, the two. The problem, finally, for these particular Edenic theorists is that while all three want to be constructivists, they never get very far in articulating (in advance or in hindsight) a politics much beyond their deconstructive projects and purviews. Even as they astutely diagnose the problems endemic to a nature-culture distinction serving as a political base, they repeat and reinscribe those categories and thus ever defer any understanding of political involvement that could offer direction in some poignant sense beyond critique, object lessons, or default possibilities. It is not simply a problem of endless Hegelianism, of being trapped in generations of negative terminology, but rather Butler, Fish, and Rorty offer no alternative sense of political foundations that *are not* metaphysical. Without such foundations, it is not that their politics are unthinkable, as Butler facetiously submits, but rather that their sketchy designs surely will result in shaky institutions. Back to the drawing boards!

THE POLITICAL FOUNDATIONS OF CHRISTINE DE PIZAN AND HANNAH ARENDT: A COMMON CORNERSTONE

The construction tradition, in contrast to the Edenic tradition, is mainly forward looking (albeit after surveying the entire landscape) instead of backward scrutinizing. It approaches political issues more in terms of architecture and city planning than in terms of metaphysics and selfhood. These are not unrelated issues, but characteristically one will find constructivist theorists building cities in words or imagining elaborate poetic underworlds, whereas Edenic theorists tend first to write didactic treatises about human nature, natural rights, and human identity before they get around to talking about politics per se. Constructivist theorists gravitate toward the poetically creative accounts of Homer, Plato, Virgil, Dante and More, whereas Edenic theorists seem to favor the philosophically ponderous treatises of Aristotle, Aquinas, Hume, and Locke. Typically, constructivist theorists will strike their own foundations or will build upon prior constructions; either way, they will view foundations as the result of human enterprise, even if manufactured out of natural materials. To constructivists, a foundation's primary purpose is to lend stability to building projects.

I want to dwell for a while on a constructivist theorist who might best lay out my case for foundations—political not metaphysical—namely the fifteenth-century writer, Christine de Pizan. Throughout *The Book of the City of Ladies*, de Pizan builds an elaborate architectural case in defense and in praise of women. To read her essentially as an essentialist woman-writer—as some later feminist commentators have—or to see her basically as a Christian apologist—as others have—is, I think, to miss her radicalism. In fact, I want to propose that de Pizan and Judith Butler have much in common: they both challenge prevailing (sacred) notions of gender identity, they both view gender identity as largely constituted through books and language, and they both wish to promote multiple definitions of women while retaining some general commitment toward improving women's overall lot. Both take matters into their own hands; they both know that they must take it upon themselves to rewrite gender identity, even though they believe that such designs must be practiced and performed, not just preached. The difference, I believe, is that de Pizan goes beyond mere excavation and, indeed, lays the foundations for a constructive case.

The Book of the City of Ladies, as avid readers of the book well know, is arranged according to a tripartite city-building motif. Three allegorical ladies—Reason, Rectitude, and Justice—descend upon de Pizan as she reflects in her study on the demeaning portrayals of women in literature. The three sibyls call upon Christine to build a city that will provide a fortress in defense of women and that will showcase the lives of exemplary women who, as it were, will reside there. The first division of the book, an extended exchange with Lady Reason, is explicitly occupied with the task of laying strong foundations for the city. The foundation must be deep and strong, says Lady Reason, so that the walls of the edifice can be built high. Lady Reason takes de Pizan to the "Field of Letters,"[39] where they begin a process of clearing and excavating before laying the foundation. The prefatory task of excavation will involve responding to the attacks on women as presented in the misogynist tradition of writing. Lady Reason provides arguments and answers that help diffuse the attacks on women as put forth by prominent male writers, but these arguments only clear the field. The process of excavating involves responding specifically to the attacks that women are not fit for politics, governance, and leadership, and Lady Reason adduces several examples of empresses and queens who actually did rule, as portrayed in literature and history. The "sturdy stones" of the foundation will be examples of strong, brave, and powerful women rulers whose stories Lady Reason will "throw" to de Pizan so that she can take the "trowel" of her pen and lay them down as bricks for the city's foundation. Once they lay the foundation with these bedrock examples of women rulers, they turn to constructing the "edifice" of the city, a question of women's mental capacities and accomplishments.

Commentators frequently note that de Pizan, in *The Book of the City of Ladies*, is playing upon, by imitating and rewriting, many male writers, both classical and Christian—notably Mathéolus, John of Salisbury, Petrarch, Ovid, Boccaccio, Augustine, and Dante. But I have not read any commentator state the obvious regarding this opening "foundation" section with Lady Reason, namely, that the major motif is Virgilian, à la Dante. As Dante follows his guide Virgil, the exemplar of poetic reason, through the infernal politics of Hell, so does de Pizan structure the first part of her architectural project by following Virgil's lead in appealing to reason in the basic task of disabusing readers of their misconceptions about feminist politics. But why is Virgil the foundational political poet for both Dante and de Pizan?

Dante's *Inferno*, of course, extends Virgil's basic lesson about love and its relationship to politics. Aeneas left Dido back in Carthage so that he could fulfill his mission of founding Rome; on the way thereto, in the underworld, he discovers her fate, namely, that she killed herself after he had left; and, to make an epic story short, he eventually learns about a greater love than romantic love, namely, his duty to God, family, and country. Dante the poet follows this structure by having Dante the pilgrim sympathetically confront lovers Paolo and Francesca at the outset of his infernal descent, at which time Dante the pilgrim cannot understand why such lovers would be condemned to Hell; by the end of his underworldly journey, however, he has learned from his guide Virgil how to be appropriately judgmental, now kicking the head of the politically treasonous Bocca Degli Abbati. These male epic poets have suggested (though their portrayals are arguably ironic) that political foundings require the repression of domestic, feminized attachments, and they both seem to suggest that Queen Dido's demise was due to her failure to put politics over love (Dante places Dido among the condemned lovers in his hell, whereas Aeneas escapes torment as one of the virtuous pagans). Responding to Virgil's and Dante's as well as Augustine's and Boccaccio's depreciating accounts that focus on Dido's person, de Pizan's version of this mythic tale reinterprets Dido's *political* legacy. In the *Book of the City of Ladies*, she writes that Dido was a strong and prudent ruler, the political equal of Aeneas, since both were founders and builders of cities, and she dwells upon Dido's political accomplishments, though she also accepts the view that Dido probably loved Aeneas too much, to her own detriment. The Virgilian Dido can thus serve as a basic role model for women rulers, even though Dido's own regime was not long-lived.[40]

De Pizan as writer must therefore build upon Virgil's example. In the next exchange with Lady Reason, right after they have completed laying the foundation for the city, de Pizan reviews several examples of female accomplishment in learning, which, as many commentators point out, are examples drawn mostly from Boccaccio's book in praise of women.[41] One of the first women de Pizan discusses is the Roman woman, Proba, who was a Christian poet who delved into all books of poetry, but, de Pizan tells us, especially those of Virgil. Proba's great accomplishment was that she Christianized Virgil's writings, adapting Virgil's poetry, in form and content, to fit the teachings of both the Old Testament and New Testament. As Patricia Phillippy points out, Boccaccio praises Proba's ability to rewrite the old books while adding her own stylistic flares; but Boccaccio's praise of Proba's own abilities is measured—she overcomes, to her credit in Boccaccio's patronizing view, her natural female shortcomings.[42] De Pizan, in a doubly self-reflexive move, trades on Boccaccio's authority and draws much of her own authority by appealing to his work, but she also alters his account significantly. Now she suggests that Proba's abilities as poet actually surpassed those of Virgil ("She would put small pieces together, coupling and joining them, all the while respecting the metrical rules, art and measure in the individual feet, as well as in the conjoining of verses, and without making any mistakes she arranged her verses so masterfully that no man could do better"[43]). She even beat Virgil at his own game of rewriting Homer! Phillippy contends that Proba's relationship to Virgil serves as a model for de Pizan's relationship to Boccaccio, for Proba's act of Christianization becomes the basis of de Pizan's "feminization" of Boccaccio.[44] I hasten to add, however, that de Pizan's revision is much more than a feminizing account, and her final target is Virgil, not just Boccaccio. De Pizan is establishing her authority in relation to the male poets, the entire epic tradition as well as the biblical tradition, but she also is obliquely announcing her own succession to the poetic throne of political founders. What Homer did for the Greeks, what Virgil thus did for Rome, what Dante thus did for Christian Rome, now de Pizan will do for an even more expansive empire, that of women, and a fortiori all gender relations, everywhere.

It is a grand conceit, a breathtaking hubris, though a poetic gesture much in keeping with the Homeric tradition onward. Dante certainly knew what he was doing when he wrote himself into the plot as the central character in the latest installment in a long-running spiritual odyssey. So too does de Pizan write herself as the heroic character in her own narrative, but now she writes her developmental tale as a builder, not as a pilgrim. That shift, from a spiritual odyssey to political endeavor, represents, I submit, the crucial distinction between the Edenic versus constructivist traditions. De Pizan has the audacity to radically rewrite Scripture, to rewrite pagan myth, to rewrite history and literature, and to use those revisions to her new end, the literary founding of a political city that celebrates women. She is not calling for emancipation, transformation, or redemption. Instead, she works with the flawed materials left to her from the misogynist tradition, and she fashions something creatively ennobling out of them. She is not telling her women readers, in effect, to seek compensatory justice for their sufferings in an otherworldly heaven; rather, the language, all the imagery, is decidedly political. Serving as the foundation of the city is the fact that women have actually served, the record shows, as successful rulers in the past; the walls of the city are erected to house examples of women's artistic, scientific, and other intellectual feats, and the roof of the city is capped by stories of exalted and sacred women. Apparently, certain heroic women should be viewed on par with comparably legendary male figures, for example, stories of Holy Mary should be placed along side stories of Jesus. Those critics who say that de Pizan's city is mere fiction, a clever utopia or allegory, are missing the point. As a self-appointed legatee of the poetic tradition of Homer, Virgil, and Dante, de Pizan knows that political foundings are related to one's skills of fabrication. Virgil's *Aenead* sets the stage not simply because he inured his readers to cruel lessons of imperial obligation but, rather, because he artfully drew a connection, in his underworldly time-space laboratory, between Troy and Ilium: to see Rome as an extension of an earlier human project with its origins in ancient Greece gives that later founding its historical depth and its particularly *political* meaning. Poets, not gods, are the real architects of these empires. Dante's tremendous talent was to conjoin the classical and Christian worlds, now substituting the poet for Christ, thus replacing theology with art.[45] De Pizan, in turn, announces herself not as a Christlike savior but as a prosaic builder of a newly configured, regendered world.

Back to an earlier point. Much of de Pizan's project resonates well with what I take to be Judith Butler's signature scholarship (and the politics of her scholarship): a joint concern with inherited language games, ongoing locutionary repetitions, bookish intertextualities, and, at the same time, novel performativities that break with or parody, even subvert, the disciplining effects of dominant linguistic regimes. Butler takes the work largely of earlier male writers—particularly Foucault, Lacan, and Derrida—and applies that vocabulary in new ways for us to understand gender politics. Short of announcing a modernist break with the past, she gestures nonetheless toward new possibilities—but her work remains parodic, parasitic, and mainly subversive, not quite creatively constructive because, I repeat, her notions of foundings and foundations, even contingent ones, remain metaphysical, not yet political. If poststructuralist feminism (or queer studies) has a hard time grounding its basic commitments to feminism, so too has Rorty run into trouble defending his pragmatic commitments to democratic liberalism—basically he shrugs his shoulders and says that it is not worth arguing about. Again, a quick contrast between de Pizan and Rorty may shed light on this dilemma: whereas Rorty spends many of his considerable energies uprooting the foundations of the "Mirror of Nature" tradition, de Pizan chooses to rework the "Mirror of Princes" tradition to her own advantage.[46] By building on exempla from the past, thus turning the Prince's mirror toward women, and by turning that mirror toward the reader as well (which is part of the tradition's writerly conceit, of course), de Pizan effectively parlays scholarly reinscription into political art. Rorty, in contrast, explicitly calls for cultural poets to replace professional political philosophers, but he fails to turn the mirror on himself, to enact his own summons, failing therefore to convert prose into *poiesis*.

My second example from the "constructivist" tradition is more complicated, because the theorist in question does not neatly conform to these oppositional categories. That theorist is Hannah Arendt. Metaphors of both mobility and construction recur throughout Arendt's writings, and both horizontal and vertical vectors intersect her spatial constructs on several fronts. It is hard to pin Arendt down to any one time-space model, or even to fit her theory into a modeling typology. The best commentators on Arendt today debate whether she is a modernist or an antimodernist, whether she resides reluctantly at home in modernity or rejects modernity wholesale in favor of a Greek conception of public glory.[47] I want to suggest that those temporal schemes, with their attendant spatial frames, miss an essential point that Arendt makes repeatedly about politics: political action steps into the liminal period of the present, but that moving occupancy assumes meaning, a thread of continuity, only by drawing upon the past and by anticipating the future. That lesson is stated, again and again, in Arendt's writings about foundings and foundations. The central figure Arendt always mentions in discussing political foundings is Virgil—although I have yet to find a single Arendtian commentator who discusses Arendt's fascination with Virgil.[48] In Virgil, according to Arendt, we may find "the purest form" of the political.[49]

The American "founders" were well schooled in Roman antiquity, Arendt tells us in *On Revolution*. From the Romans they learned that the act of foundation establishes its own authority and develops its own stability and permanence, and it does so by "augmentation," that is, by referring all innovations and changes back to the original act of founding.[50] The revolutionary act of beginning something new can thus be preserved in perpetuity by ongoing self-referentiality. The coincidence of foundation and preservation is best illustrated, she points out, in the Latin word for *founding, condere,* derived from an early Latin field god, Conditor, who presided over growth and harvest and thus was a founder and preserver at the same time.[51] Madison and other American "founders" were imitating and acknowledging their Roman forbears when they wrote in anticipation of their own successors, indicating a recognition that a kind of ancestor worship, or the passing of time itself, bestows veneration on the initial act of founding. The word *constitution*, Arendt adds, carries a twofold meaning—both the constituting act and the written document that attempts to capture, augment, and preserve the spirit of the original act.[52] Americans, Arendt muses, are deeply ambivalent about their Constitution worship; they are divided about whether respect for the Constitution should refer back to the original act, an ancestor worship of original intent, or should instead focus on the current readings of the written document as it has evolved over time.

That the American revolutionaries referred to themselves as "founders" indicates, Arendt continues, that they knew that the act of foundation itself would eventually become the fountain of authority in the new body politic—not an "Immortal Legislator" or "self-evident truth" or "any other transcendent, transmundane source."[53] Arendt insists that political foundations, for the Americans as well as for the Romans, were not located in the metaphysical heavens: "it is futile to search for an absolute to break the vicious circle in which all beginning is inevitably caught, because this 'absolute' lies in the very act of beginning itself."[54] The self-founding nature of foundations is hard to articulate fully in conceptual thought, she explains, because such beginnings usually are shrouded in mystery, and that is because they rely on the faculty of imagination, not on historical memory. Foundations attempt to solve the problem of human beginnings, the question of how an unconnected, new event—how a new "We the people"—can break into the continuous sequence of historical time.[55] This purported connection between the past and the present, between dead ancestors and live bodies, must always be speculative, even if it becomes authoritative. Thus foundations give rise to foundation legends.

In both *On Revolution* and *The Life of the Mind, Part II*, Arendt elaborates on what she says are the two main foundation legends of the West, and the only two foundation legends with which the American founders were acquainted, one Hebraic and the other Roman.[56] The first concerns the biblical story about the creation of the world, culminating in the covenant of God with the people of Israel. The second is Virgil's story of Aeneas, which results in the founding of Rome. Arendt's two foundation tales correspond well with what I have been calling the Edenic tradition and the constructivist tradition, respectively. For Arendt, both foundation stories recall a beginning at which a "We" is supposedly first experienced and articulated, both stories profess a love of freedom for exiles, and both gesture toward promised lands that will put an end to wanderings. While Arendt recognizes that it is tempting for some theorists, such as those who rely on Locke,[57] to see the founding of America as following mainly in the Edenic tradition, Arendt insists that the American founding had more to do with Virgilian notions of foundation.[58] Both the Pentateuch and *The Aenead* helped the early Americans think about taking action, starting something new, founding a new order—and that is because they both indicate the problem of a transitional hiatus between liberation and the constitution of freedom, a liminal zone between the "no more" of an old regime and the "not yet" of a new order. The legends indicate that freedom will not automatically follow upon liberation, and the temporal hiatus between the old order and new era reveals that the notion of an "all-powerful time continuum" is an illusion.[59] A "causal chain" is thus broken, and there is nothing for a "beginner" to hold on to,[60] but a beginner cannot begin completely from scratch, so the trick of a particular foundation legend is how it can present the arbitrariness of a new beginning against the background of ongoing historical time.

The Edenic tradition—Arendt calls it the "Hebrew solution"—resolves the apparent problem of political foundings by referring back to the creationist founding of the entire universe by a Supreme legislator who stands outside of time.[61] To be sure, the Americans often participated in such language: Lockeans appeal to "God in Heaven"; Jefferson to "laws of nature and nature's god"; John Adams to the "great Legislator of the universe"; and so on.[62] The Edenic explanation for a political founding works, explains Arendt, by analogy: just as God stood outside of his creation, so does the human founder imitate God when he lays the foundations of a human community.[63] Such foundations therefore lie "outside" or "prior to" or as a "condition" for "all future political life and historical development."[64]

But Arendt clearly believes that the American founders, on the matter of political foundings, were more influenced by Virgil than by the Bible.[65] The Romans at some point started tracing their descent not from Romulus but from Aeneas, who became "the fount of the Roman race."[66] What Virgil was teaching, what Machiavelli subsequently learned from Virgil, and what the Americans likewise learned from Virgil, according to Arendt, was "how to conduct human affairs without the help of a transcendent God."[67] Arendt, in both *On Revolution* and *The Life of the Mind*, dwells on Virgil's story of Aeneas at some length. Confronted with the riddle of foundation—"how to re-start time within an inexorable time continuum"[68]—the Americans turned to Virgil to learn that the starting point of Rome had already been a revival, the resurgence of Troy. "What matters," writes Arendt, "is that the notion of foundation, of counting time *ab urbe condita*, is at the very center of Roman historiography along with the no less profoundly Roman notion that all such foundations—taking place exclusively in the realm of human affairs, where men enact a tale to tell, to remember, and preserve—are re-establishments and reconstitutions, not absolute beginnings."[69] Virgil built on Homer's fabrications, and over time, the fabrications begin to build on each other. The "genius"[70] of Virgilian politics lay in the foundational idea that the alleged beginning was never absolutely new but rather was a reestablishment, which preserved a thread of continuity between a new human community and an older one. The Americans well knew that the hope of founding a "new Rome" was an illusion; they could at best hope to repeat the primeval foundation and found "Rome anew," which in turn was a refounding of Greece, as the tale goes. Arendt forcefully rebuts the Edenic scheme of things as an originary explanation for the speculative regress: "Whatever lay prior to this first foundation, itself the resurgence of some definite past, was situated outside history. . . . but whose own origin was of no interest because it was beyond the scope of action."[71] Even the "first" act, for the Roman foundation, was "already a re-establishment, as it were, a regeneration and restoration."[72]

Arendt draws superbly, in my view, the distinction between the Edenic and constructivist traditions, but toward the end of her sections on the American founding, she retreats from her own lesson about the importance of Virgilian reconstructions—which may explain why Arendtian commentators have ignored the centrality of Virgil in Arendt's thinking about political action in its "purist form." As the section evolves, she starts to express a worry about construction and architectural metaphors applied to politics (returning to an Arendtian motif prominent in *The Origins of Totalitarianism* and elsewhere). Fabrication involves violence, and latter-day political actors, such as Robespierre, may believe themselves to be in the position of an "architect" who "build[s] out of human material a new house, the new republic, for human beings."[73] Such architects will introduce the means of violence necessary for the purposes of fabrication, "precisely because something is created, not out of nothing, but out of given material which must be violated in order to yield itself to the formative processes out of which a thing, a fabricated object, will arise."[74] Little does it matter that Virgil's inversion of the Homeric progression from wrath to peace was meant to undo the wartime violence against Troy, or that the Aenead foundation legend attempted to displace the fratricidal legend of Romulus and Remus[75]; rather, Virgilian fabrication can be used all too easily to justify humanly self-inflicted violence.[76] The character, Virgil, as in Dante's *Purgatorio*, starts to fade out in Arendt's narrative, now giving way to discussions about Augustine. At this point, Arendt reverts, I believe, back to the Edenic tradition.

At crucial points in both *On Revolution* and *The Life of the Mind*, Arendt stops talking about foundational acts and instead starts talking about foundational actors. The importance of Virgil to her thinking about politics gives way to the importance of Augustine. Toward the end of the section on foundations, Arendt writes, apparently changing her mind about the value of political restorations: "What matters in our context is less the profoundly Roman notion that all foundations are re-establishments and reconstructions than the somehow connected but different idea that men are equipped for the logically paradoxical task of making a new beginning because they themselves are new beginnings and hence beginners, that the very capacity for beginning is rooted in natality, in the fact that human beings appear in the world by virtue of birth."[77] To be sure, Virgilian concerns with foundations, she contends, paved the way in Rome for "Asiatic religions which centred around the birth of a child-savior."[78] Birthing can thus convey the same idea of renewal. Moreover, foundings and birthings reveal a common concern with beginnings—but quickly Arendt starts to talk about the American founding as a birthing episode, in which the American founders, in rewriting Virgil, obscured his fundamental political contribution. The Americans at some point, contends Arendt, decided to vary Virgil's line from *magnus ordo saeclorum* to *novus ordo saeclorum*, at which point they were admitting that their founding was no longer a matter of founding "Rome anew"—a re-birth—but a founding of a "new Rome"—a birth.[79] The founders were concerned, she says, not only with the founding of a new body politic but with the "beginning of a specific national history"[80]—so much so that their concern with absolute novelty amounted to an "obsession." Absolute beginnings are impossible, according to Arendt, and now she introduces the Augustinian idea of natality as a foundational principle behind the American Revolution, thus the possibility that the American beginning could save itself from inherent arbitrariness by making self-validating reference to the sheer fact of having made "its appearance in the world."[81]

What explains Arendt's shift from foundings to birthings? At one point in *The Life of the Mind*, Arendt tries to explain her turn to Augustine in Virgilian terms, but I do not believe that she succeeds. She writes: "In [Augustine's] great work on the *City of God*, he mentions, but does not explicate, what could have become the ontological underpinning for a truly Roman or Virgilian philosophy of politics."[82] God created man, according to Augustine, as a temporal creature, and thus sheer entry into the world, via birth, can interrupt the time continuum: "That there be a beginning, man was created."[83] Augustine's notion of natality allows for an Edenic notion of foundation, based on a birthing motif of common creation—and once Christianized, and then secularized, birthing holds the potential for democratic applications via the Augustinian reading of worldly concern for one's neighbor. Birthing therefore becomes a more attractive grounding principle to Arendt, I believe, because it supposedly reduces the risk of tyrannical violence allegedly inherent in Virgilian foundings. Whereas the Virgilian tradition seems to emphasize the intertextual talents of ancestor-worshipping poets, that appeal to singular genius also can inspire the architectural violence of dictatorial political actors, while the Augustinian tradition of natality more likely inspires a mutually respectful concern for fellow creatures. The American revolution teaches a unique lesson, Arendt says, for it was beget not in violence but rather was initiated by men in common deliberation and on the strength of mutual pledges: "The principle which came to light during those fateful years when the foundations were laid—not by the strength of one architect but by the combined power of the many—was the interconnected principle of mutual promise and common deliberation."[84] Thenceforth humans could establish good government from reflection and choice, Arendt quotes Hamilton, instead of being "forever destined to depend for their political constitutions on accident and force."[85]

Natality as a temporal "in-between" fills the same void as that which all foundation legends address, the transitional hiatus between a "no more" and a "not yet." But in favoring in the end Augustine over Virgil, the biblical foundation tradition over the Roman foundation tradition, Arendt shifts the focus toward the self and away from politics, that is, toward the existential hiatus between not living and death instead of the political hiatus between liberation and freedom. The Edenic tradition wins out over a constructivist tradition ("The very capacity for beginning is rooted in *natality*, and by no means in *creativity*"[86]), but that emphasis imposes severe limits on Arendt's own capacities to inspire and to influence her readership. Commentators feverishly scrutinize her works from front to back hoping to find some glimpse of practicable politics that might withstand the dark technicism of modern society, but, as Dana Villa basically tells us, they search in vain.[87] The age of politics may be over, or at best our Arendtian political moments are but episodic and fugitive, and Arendt herself offers us scant political instruction about how we might jump-start our dead batteries and get moving into a new epoch. Instead we wait for the birth of some newly inspired actors, latter-day democratic redeemers, or else we ponder indefinitely our still-borne but supposedly ever-present possibilities. Lost and virtually forgotten in today's Arendtian commentary is, however, the specifically Virgilian notion that politics takes root by creatively reestablishing a meaningful connection to the humanly authored past while eagerly building for the worldly future to come. In insisting upon birthing, not building, as her main metaphor for political action, Arendt, at least in theory, is probably in good part to blame for the moribund state of Arendtian politics today. Or else, perhaps her scholarly interpreters, distracted by the taxonomic debate about whether to locate Arendt as an anti-modernist, a modernist, or a postmodernist, have simply overlooked her clearest, most proprietary language on the problems of modernity and on how to strike political foundations anew:

> For if I am right in suspecting that the crisis of the present world is primarily political, and that the famous "decline of the West" consists primarily in the decline of the Roman trinity of religion, tradition, and authority, with the concomitant undermining of the specifically Roman foundations of the political realm, then the revolutions of the modern age appear like gigantic attempts to repair these foundations, to renew the broken thread of tradition, and to restore, through founding new political bodies, what for so many centuries had endowed the affairs of men with some measure of dignity and greatness.[88]

Of course, Arendt is aware that her discussion may be misleading, her language provisional, for she notes that talking and thinking about foundations catch us in a "maze of abstractions, metaphors, and figures of speech."[89] She wishes to qualify her remarks about the loss of (Roman) authority in the modern world. Such authority, she writes, "resting on a foundation in the past as its unshaken cornerstone, gave the world the permanence and durability which human beings need precisely because they are mortals—the most unstable and futile beings we know of."[90] Which is to suggest that we mortals, as mortals, indeed need some stabilizing constructs, from time to time, even though today it is "as though we were living and struggling with a Protean universe where everything at any moment can become almost anything else."[91] The loss of authority is "tantamount to the loss of the groundwork of the world" that has "begun to shift, to change and transform itself with ever-increasing rapidity from one shape into another."[92] But Arendt ends her remarks by insisting that the loss of worldly reliability, the shifting groundwork, does not entail the loss of the human capacity for "building, preserving, and caring for a world that can survive us and remain a place fit to live in for those who come after us."[93] In short, a recognition of the loss of our "groundwork" does not destroy our capacity, or eliminate the need, for rebuilding the world. Arendt ends on a constructivist note.[94]

Asked directly whether she was advocating "groundless" thinking, Arendt chose instead to supply another "metaphor," which would be "less cruel" than the notion of groundlessness. She described her approach as "thinking without a bannister": "That is, as you go up and down the stairs you can always hold onto the bannister so that you don't fall down. But we have lost this bannister. That is the way I tell it to myself. And this is indeed what I try to do."[95] With this metaphor, Arendt has taken us indoors. Her staircase metaphor is an interior metaphor, and staircases, usually located within buildings or next to buildings, are quite grounded. She implicitly confirms her interiorized thinking by explaining that taking away their "bannisters" from people, their "safe guidelines," is something quite different from the complete breakdown of tradition, which would mean, she says, that "you really are out in the cold!"[96] But one wonders finally: Where was Arendt going, walking up and down that bannisterless staircase? What space, what building structure, was she imagining in which the freestanding stairs would be located?[97] Where did they lead?[98] It should be noted that Arendt's is a metaphor about balancing the self, and it combines in one image both Edenic and constructivist motifs, notions of the self's (still heroic) mobility, albeit situated within a constructed context while subject to the forces of gravity. Yet it is an imbalanced metaphor, confusing and cryptic at last, employing up-and-down movements that take us really nowhere.

The above contemporary scholars—Butler, Fish, Rorty, Arendt—have all been trying to limn the possibilities for a post–metaphysical politics but, worried about becoming stick-in-the-muds, they refuse to lay good alternative foundations and instead appear shifty in their political proposals. In my mind, they are still trying to settle large a priori questions, to settle old academic scores, before they get down to business,[99] and at some point even textbook theorists need to remind themselves of Weber's (constructivist) adage that "politics is the strong and slow boring of hard boards."[100] Instead of dwelling so much on the metaphysical subject and its discontents, today's theorists, I respectfully submit, should direct more (not all, but more) of their energies toward issues of architecture, interior design, and city planning— which might help prompt the political transition from critique to creation. I am not suggesting that we perform a wholesale recuperation of fabrication against Arendt's devastating dismissal of its politically contaminating effects, but I would like a better sense of the buildings that Butler, Fish, Rorty, and Arendt actually would build in which to house their wildest dreams. What would their cities look like? What institutions would they leave to their successors? What constitutions would they themselves sign? In what ways are their books laying the bedrock for these worlds to come? Theory, in its abstraction, often operates according to images, spectacles, and metaphors, and my sense is that Western political theorists have held themselves all too captive to open-air models of political interaction—the agora, the outdoor amphitheater, the stage, the garden, the village square, the town meeting, the marketplace, the bargaining table, the wandering motif, the sailing analogy—without giving sufficient attention to building metaphors and techniques.[101] If Foucault, following Bentham, is right about our panoptical regimes, then building designs have a great deal to do with constructing the self; yet poststructuralist Foucauldians cannot seem to resist taking one stab after another at merely deconstructing the world in various ways, even though their point, presumably, is to rediscipline it.

My point, finally, is not necessarily to recommend a mindless, mundane pragmatism, a theory of the concrete. Arendt, for one, believes that fabrication always produces ends-means rationality, an instrumentalism that can only reinforce our throwaway, consumerist, modern world.[102] My preferred architectural model is, rather, Virgil's netherworld, a fictive necropolis (which is just a mirror image of de Pizan's living model of dead exempla); here again I take leave from Arendt, who always insists that all constructions and inversions of Hell can serve only a utilitarian mentality.[103] In my political underworld, however, we the living continue to pay attentive homage to our ancestors, beyond their mere usefulness to us, and poised as well toward the future, we attempt to do right by those not yet born, most of whom we will never know face-to-face. Virgilian politics is founded on the insistence that commitments to justice ought to span across generations, a protracted dialogue between the living and the dead, even if such far-fetched notions of justice find a toehold only in poetry.

11

Political Theory in the Twentieth Century

My task in this chapter is to write about the enterprise of political theory in the twentieth century. I shall present the broadest and barest of overviews, a cartoonlike sketch, albeit bereft of any animated Hollywoodish special effects. Even summoning forth all of my faculties for theoretical abstraction, I simply know not how to serve as an adequate tour guide to an entire century, or even the latter half to which I personally stood witness. A few family anecdotes through the years are perhaps telling for starters, in order to get some kind of preliminary grasp on the century as a century.

My grandparents were farmers who farmed in the manner of their day in middle America, namely, with horse-drawn plows and pitchforks (while also making do without electricity, running water, telephone service, or regular mail delivery), although after the depression they bought both a tractor and their first automobile, a secondhand Model T, with crankshaft still intact. Counting backwards from 1920, I realize that my grandmothers could not vote in the United States when they came of age. My father as a very young man was a machine gunner on a navy destroyer during the Second World War, but he professed not to know whether he actually shot down any of those enemy dive-bombers amidst all of the ratta-tat-tat rumble. My older cousin, Donny, marched in the civil rights movement in Alabama, where we watched him back home on our fuzzy black-and-white television screens, and thereafter he scandalized the neighbors by marrying an African-American woman and, after she died of sickle cell complications, scandalized everyone a second time by becoming a gay activist in the 1970s in Chicago, where he eventually died of AIDS. For my own part, I was too young to become a hippie or to be drafted into the Vietnam War, but when I was twelve I did compose the following sign-o'-the-times poem (in longhand, because I did not learn how to type until the ninth grade, at which time I pecked away on a clanky manual typewriter):

Do Something!

Do something,
Before it's too late.
This world needs more love,
Not more hate.
There's a war going on.
Mud in our shoes,
Poverty in the mouth,
Crime makes the news.
Pollution is a word
Constantly used.
Come on, people,
Let's get united, joined, fused!
President Nix
Is in one hell of a fix.
Economy's down
And some whites won't mix.
Long haired kids
Run away from their homes.
People sit on their asses
Reading God damn poems.

My proud if perplexed parents tried to channel those early wayward tendencies of mine into an upwardly mobile law career, and so during my freshman year in college, I sought a resume-padding internship in the nation's capital with the upstart senator from my state, Dick Clark, whose report on U. S. corporate involvement in South Africa I helped distribute to the national press at its first release. Later in that fateful internship, all of us Iowans on staff in D. C. were invited to the White House for dinner and dancing to celebrate President Jimmy Carter's first year in office. Wearing my tan corduroy bell-bottomed three-piece suit and gum-soled shoes (the Reagan black-tie years were yet to come), I was the first on the dance floor when the U. S. Marine big band started playing In the Mood. Upon my return to campus, after watching my fellow students march in a protest calling for college divestment in those companies doing business in South Africa, companies named in Senator Clark's report, I switched my major from pre-law to a specially designed course of studies called political theory, which seemed to emulate a Nelson Mandela-like outlook on political possibility, wistful and realistic yet compelled onward seeking greater justice.

Having graduated into an oil-shocked, arms-escalating, downwardly mobilizing economy, I jumped coasts to California for postgraduate study in political theory. On my first day in Berkeley, Wavy Gravy (the clownish emcee of Woodstock and former merry prankster roadster) gave me a personal tour of his house after I knocked unassumingly on the door, having recognized his "Nobody For President" campaign bus parked outside. Thus increasingly keen to the theatrical politics around me, I started attending select street demonstrations, for instance, against U. S. involvement in Nicaragua or against nuclear weapons buildup. Soon after President Reagan announced his Project Democracy initiative, a graduate professor networked me into a modestly gainful position in San Francisco, where I eventually discovered that I was now working for a CIA front organization, funded by that same Reagan–Thatcher initiative, which apparently wanted a political theorist to reformulate plans for covert operations in Southeast Asia (my boss, however, kept rejecting my above-board recommendations to challenge the Marcos regime in the Philippines). Back on the streets, I became impressed by the millions of people marching, worldwide, against nuclear madness, and I noticed in particular that the anti-nuclear movement attracted great numbers of women, and that most of its leaders were women—Helen Caldicott, Randall Forsberg, Petra Kelly, Mary Kaldor, Pam Solo, Christa Wölf, Katya Komisaruk, the Women's Action for Nuclear Disarmament (WAND), and the Greenham Common Camp. Eventually I wrote my laser-printed dissertation on such matters. By 1989, a bunch of men were crediting nuclear weapons for bringing down the Berlin Wall, but I remembered a different post–Soviet history altogether. For the remainder of the century, my own theoretical efforts correlated inversely with the rise of the stock market: in the greedy 1980s, I invested heavily in irony, trying to sell it as the trope of that decade; in the millennialist rush toward riches in the 1990s I wrote about death instead, another self-mocking master trope that never quite caught on with my professional colleagues.

In Great Britain by the end of the century, a sheep was cloned. In Japan, the toilet-paperless turbo-toilet was introduced. Back home, my elderly father never found a hearing aid that would stop the background ringing in his ears, and we await even further miniaturization of the digital revolution.

Political theorists seldom agree these days about the proper nature and uses to which political theory ought to be put. Nonetheless, it is probably fair to say that most political theorists attempt to look at politics, at least part of the time, from broad, large-scale, long-range points of view—informed by history, comparative analysis, textual exegesis, philosophical reflection, and imaginative projection. The word *theory* derives from an ancient Greek practice whereby city officials sent emissaries to neighboring cities to observe their rival religious practices—and reportedly such information was not put to any immediate, urgent use but was considered illuminating nonetheless.

For my present purposes, if I may assume some generous license based on the example of the ancient theorist's spectatorial wanderings and musings, I suggest that the century we just concluded was one of *massification*. It was a century featuring fast-paced change and monumental events. These events and changes conspired to bring people's fates colliding together, so that large human population blocs would be *massed* together, their destinies increasingly intertwined. It was a century of world wars, both hot and cold; of major revolutions and sweeping social movements; of assembly-line production, economic expansion, and widespread consumption; of breathtaking technological advances in travel, communication, and destruction. Human institutions had to adapt on large scales to these massive changes. It was a century wherein we witnessed the spread of communism, the spread of Islam, the spread of democracy; of nationalism and multinationalism; of imperialism and postcolonialism; of the population explosion; of space travel and exploration; of natural resource depletion and global pollution; of scientific and medical breakthrough discovery.

From afar or in retrospective repose, one would think that political theory's general knack for breadth would have been especially helpful in comprehending twentieth-century major trends toward massification, but it is as yet unclear how well political theory fared along these lines. Some notable theorists—Hannah Arendt, Sheldon Wolin, and Michel Foucault—examined this issue in various ways and drew troubling conclusions that may shed some light on the role of political theory in the twentieth century. All three questioned whether political theory was at all *useful* in the twentieth century, and yet their disparately skeptical appraisals of theory's uneven role may lead to the unexpected conclusion that theory's perverse benefit after all was to call into tacit question, to hold such a question at least in reserve, whether "usefulness" under terms of societal massification should be championed as a standard for critical evaluation at all.

By almost any measure, the Second World War represented nothing less than a watershed event in human affairs. It was a war that introduced the world to totalitarianism—the practice whereby an organized state attempts to exert total control over the thought and behavior of its subjects. It was a war that featured atrocities the likes of which the world hitherto had not experienced on the scale now exhibited: national fascism, Stalinism, concentration camps, systematic genocide, firebombs, nuclear bombs. Hannah Arendt, the German-educated émigré who fled to America, saw the war as signifying a profound turn in human affairs, a crisis of consciousness for which there could be no turning back nor any easy repair for the future. As she wrote in the final passage of the preface to her 1951 book, *The Origins of Totalitarianism*,

> We can no longer afford to take that which was good in the past and simply call it our heritage, to discard the bad and simply think of it as

a dead load which by itself time will bury in oblivion. The subterranean stream of Western history has finally come to the surface and usurped the dignity of our tradition. This is the reality in which we live. And this is why all efforts to escape from the grimness of the present into nostalgia for a still intact past, or into the anticipated oblivion of a better future, are vain.[1]

The war revealed a dirty secret about our Western civilization.[2] For all of our vaunted progress, for all of our enlightened practices and democratic institutions, for all of our material comforts and technological gizmos, we found that we could commit calculated acts of cruelty unto one another—and somehow not be utterly shaken at the horror of it all. That we prided ourselves on our advanced techniques and rational science of large-scale social organization—our constitutions and our cars—should have made it even worse, but the world moved on, as if with a click of the remote. For Arendt, the Holocaust was symptomatic of a much larger malaise potentially afflicting the entire Western world, spilling beyond totalitarian movements into the "non-totalitarian" world.[3] People could now commit atrocities, or rather participate in bureaucratic structures that waged cruelties on their behalf, and yet such complicit participants could no longer quite recognize themselves or their actions or the effects of their actions as cruel. Surely they were intelligent enough people, yet apparently they were not *thinking* about the evil they were effecting. How could this be?

In her 1953 essay, "Understanding and Politics," Arendt approaches this question by asking whether we can understand totalitarianism when it, in practice and by definition, robs us of our independent critical resources. Earlier forms of radical state evil, she notes, were lumped together under the term *imperialism*. Totalitarian government, on the other hand, is a *new* phenomenon, historically unprecedented, and so maybe we cannot understand it by making empirical recourse to past historical models. In fact, it may be, she suggests, that our methods of "political science" are inadequate to grasp the uniqueness of modern totalitarian government. This is because totalitarian dynamics may continue to operate sub rosa or may have their functional equivalents elsewhere. Totalitarian logic, for instance, characteristically appeals to the dictates of scientific causality, the ostensibly absolute authority of which essentially preempts and eliminates dissent. Similar appeals to the authority of science in nontotalitarian venues may not violently rob us of our independent critical faculties, but they can provide all-too-convenient excuses for letting our vigilance lapse. Or, Arendt submits, reliance on the magic of the market and the concomitant appeal to "self-interest" for organizing almost all of our collective affairs, making ourselves thus gullible to the advertising industry's manipulations, has made us more "stupid" in the twentieth century. It was a century, according to Arendt, marked by "the growth of meaninglessness," accompanied by "the loss of common sense" and "the increasing stupidity" of nearly everybody, intellectuals and non-intellectuals alike.

A remedy to this unhappy or vicious condition, if an internal diagnosis is even still possible, may spring from the evidently ineradicable and ever-recurring human tendency toward creative initiative and new beginnings—which may in turn inspire the lesson that we must always try to understand the world anew. At the least, Arendt suggests, we must remind ourselves that science, for all of its insights and accomplishments, cannot provide us with adequate self-understanding, because science can never truly apprehend unprecedented newness. Arendt seems to recommend the classical theorist's occasional stepping away from the prevailing norms, practices, and categories of the day in order to gain a "distanced" perspective on things. Theory *means* thinking, as a separation from worldliness. She ends her essay by appealing, strangely enough, to a faculty of "imagination" whose distance from reality might actually afford greater clarity on reality than straight empiricism can ever offer. But she warns that if we humans ever want to be at home on this earth, the price might involve never being "at home" in the twentieth century. Clearly, in Arendt's eyes, the twentieth century was a misbegotten one, and perhaps her theoretical followers should not be too disheartened over political theory's alleged shortcomings and failures in that context.

Arendt's sweeping analysis of totalitarianism in the twentieth century, along with its backhanded estimation of the role of theory as foil, did not win the day. Instead, reflections on the significance of World War II grew into a chorus that actually blamed theory for the ills and evils of that period. Hitler supposedly had read Nietzsche, and the Nazis took other cues from German idealism. Communism owed its intellectual origins to Marx, whose dictates had been put into practice by Lenin's theoretical vanguard. America, in contrast, had achieved its stability and success supposedly by eclipsing theory's prominence in favor of can-do pragmatism and a checks-and-balances proceduralism. Madisonian America had stayed above the fray of old-world tumult, because it did not seek to reinvent human nature but instead accommodated people's foibles and interests.

The postwar suspicion toward theory grew into an animus. During the 1950s and 1960s, a general movement developed that not only decried theory's earlier collaborative role in fostering communism and fascism but also proclaimed that theory would be and should be forever discredited. Theory was pronounced dead or dying.[4] Let the people choose their fates for themselves instead of having some high-minded, monomaniacal egghead ponder the universe on their behalf. Governments and officials should follow suit. Theory on this view was associated with idealism, ideology, abstraction, metaphysics, utopianism, romanticism, normative thinking, and social engineering. Even some political theorists during this time, apparently swept up into the mood of the day, publicly advocated that political theorizing should come to an end, lest there be any lingering doubts among their colleagues. Theory, they told their fellows, should cease and desist all operations, because it had become dangerous or at least presumptuous or simply irrelevant and thus unnecessary.

Many of these anti-theory theorists were outspoken advocates of political liberalism, a system that supposedly does not require much theoretical intervention or oversight. Liberalism as a governmental system observes a strict, practical distinction between the public and private realm. The point of respecting and enforcing that distinction, for many of these anti-theory liberals, is to give the private sector its due and to restrict public regulation of private activities as much as possible. The underlying assumption of anti-theory liberalism is that private autonomy does not require theoretical articulation. It runs more or less by itself. Accordingly, state regulatory influence should be limited. Private rights should be protected, and private interests should be freely expressed and pursued. Liberalism does not aspire to deliver perfect societies or heroic individuals, but it certainly does better than fascism or communism in avoiding outright cruelty, its advocates assert.

Before World War II, writers whom we now have canonized as professional political theorists (Machiavelli, Locke, Rousseau, Burke, Mill, Du Bois, Beauvoir, and so on) often occupied nonscholarly positions of note. Many of them were employed as diplomats, envoys, court officials, social rebels, pamphleteers, poets, preachers, or journalists. After the war, however, almost all political theorizing receded to university settings. Political theory increasingly became a delimited, specialized branch of academic discourse, to be housed in a discipline called "political science." But such a place offered little sanctuary from a hostile or an unappreciative world. Even here, political scientists did not entirely welcome their war-torn colleagues, for they not so secretly shared much of the suspicion leveled at large against political theory. In fact, in the decades following the war, in political science departments almost everywhere, political scientists and political theorists retreated into separate camps and defined themselves in opposition to one another. Political scientists, as their name would suggest, largely emulated the methods of natural science now applied to political phenomena: observation, hypothesis testing, empiricism, data collection, objectivity. Wary of becoming political partisans or advocates, political scientists often labored to limit their analytic purview to human "behavior" as they saw it. New battle lines were thus drawn: political theory versus behaviorism. Political theory in the latter part of the twentieth century again found itself on the defensive.

Sheldon Wolin's 1969 essay, "Political Theory as a Vocation," emerged out of this context. Political theory had become almost entirely a species of academic inquiry, now situated within the discipline of political science, and political theorists found that on a daily basis they had to contend with the methodism of their science-minded departmental colleagues. Since Wolin's essay harks back to the work of German sociologist Max Weber, a brief digression on Weber's writing would be helpful to provide some background to Wolin's piece.

In 1904, Weber predicted that the twentieth century would likely become "disenchanted." By "disenchantment," Weber meant that the magic of religiosity and the mysteries of spirit, so influential in earlier epochs, would now be subjected to strictly secular scrutiny. Rationality, in turn, eventually would dominate all aspects of human life. A newly modern economic order of machine production would "determine the lives of all the individuals who are born into this mechanism, not only those directly concerned with economic acquisition, with irresistible force."[5] Such individuals would be capable of calculating only the means, not the ends, of life. They would know not where they were going (nor would they think much about it anymore), but they would attempt to get there fast. "Material goods," Weber warned, would gain an "increasing and finally an inexorable power"[6] over the lives of such blindly ambitious people. They will become materialists and consumers. They become careerists and bureaucrats ("specialists without spirit, sensualists without heart"[7]). In the United States, the place with the highest development of capitalism, according to Weber, the pursuit of wealth would assume the character of sport. Such sportive individuals simply abandon any attempt to justify their competitive activity by relating it to higher spiritual and cultural values. They are simply carried along by the momentum of their wealth-getting activity, and little else seems to matter in life. A "mechanized petrification" thus goes hand in hand with "convulsive self-importance."[8] Weber's prophetic work, *The Protestant Ethic and the Spirit of Capitalism*, provided an early analysis that capitalism eventually would win—but at a spiritual cost, as it were.

Weber's dark outlook for the future of the twentieth century contained a few bright notes. Withstanding the century's tendencies toward secularization, rationalization, utilitarianism, technicism, scientism, bureaucratization, and materialism would be a kind of epic individual who still regarded his or her work as if it were a religious calling—a vocation—even though such a person would no longer be a believer in old-time faith. Against the backdrop of the forces of disenchantment such a person would stand up to the times and attempt to reinvest his ordinary work with, as it were, greater meaning and larger purpose, or at least with plain and simple integrity. Scholars who pursue scholarship as a vocation would attempt to bring a kind of moral clarity to their workaday academic strivings, even though modern science largely eschews such reflective broodings.[9] Weber suggested that there might even be a kind of person who pursues latter-day politics as a vocation, even though modern politics requires at times cold calculation and ruthless manipulation.[10] Indeed, Weber explicitly recommends that only a person who can combine ethics and pragmatism, pursuing politics with both the heart and the head—someone who is not altogether "spiritually dead"—has a genuine "calling for politics" in the modern world.[11]

Taking his main cue from Weber, Wolin issued a similar call for political theory to be pursued as a vocation—a vocation that would somehow conjoin the roles of scholar and citizen that Weber had kept functionally separate. Vocational political theory would engage the hearts and minds of its practitioners, abandoning the pretense of disinterest that informed the methodism of political science in the postwar/Cold War period. Wolin in fact saw the triumph of methodism as presenting a "crisis" in political education. Political theory as a vocation furnishes and preserves *tacit* political knowledge, based on deep historical understanding and sharp awareness of the complexities of political experience—and only such an enlarged view of the political condition provides discriminating judgment adequate to our contemporary predicaments. Scientific methods alone do not and cannot provide sufficient grounds for making informed political decisions.

Political scientists, when they do venture forth with something like a theory about the proper role of political theory, often attempt to contain its influence to "normative" affairs—as if theory's one comparative occupational advantage is to sermonize about remotely utopian fantasies. Or, political scientists will see theory's proper role as generating "hypotheses" and "models" for quasiscientific testing and falsification. Wolin shifts the burden of explanation back to theory's detractors and trivializers. Methodism, he contends, cannot offer a well-rounded perspective on itself, especially one that is critical. The behaviorist boasts that his methods are not theory driven or value laden, but that braggadocio lacks the resources to prove itself, even empirically. By default, according to Wolin, the methodist's purview remains ensconced within, and therefore tethered to, and therefore in service of, the status quo. Small wonder that under century-wide terms of massification, political scientists should observe patterned regularities of human conduct, but they lack the historical and cultural resources to be able to assess whether such regularities are indeed lawful or merely law-like because of mass mimicry or other humanistic variables.

Especially in times of crisis—or even in times of wide-scale mediocrity or collective dumbing down—Wolin claims that there is a need for "epic" political theorists who can break radically with the paradigms of the day. Such theory is "epic" because of the magnitude of its scope and claims. It has the audacity but also the intellectual reach to challenge society's fundamental assumptions, if need be. It has the vision to suggest alternatives that may be available, even if such possibilities appear distant and foreclosed under current conditions. Epic theory is "extraordinary," Wolin says, borrowing from Thomas Kuhn, because it "inaugurate[s] a new way of looking at the world, which includes a new set of concepts, as well as new cognitive *and* normative standards." The methodist can hardly postulate beyond observable facts and trends, and such a modest outlook can hardly keep pace with the shifting realities of politics over the long run. (Latter-day case in point: few, if any, political scientists predicted the 1989 collapse of the Soviet empire, whereas theorists familiar with Marx were saying all along that the Soviet Union had been operating on precarious theoretical grounds.) The epic theorist, on the other hand, steeped in the contingencies of the human condition, "aims to grasp present structures and interrelationships, and to re-present them in a new way." But even as he outlines the need for epic theory in today's world, Wolin invokes Weber's nightmare scenario and suggests that it has come true:

> In a fundamental sense, our world has become as perhaps no previous world has, the product of design, the product of theories about human structures deliberately created rather than historically articulated. But in another sense, the embodiment of theory in the world has resulted in a world impervious to theory. The giant, routinized structures defy fundamental alteration and, at the same time, display an unchallengeable legitimacy, for the rational, scientific, and technological principles on which they are based seem in perfect accord with an age committed to science, rationalism and technology. Above all, it is a world which appears to have rendered epic theory superfluous.[12]

For some contemporary students of political theory, Wolin's cry for epic theory was soon heeded. In 1971, John Rawls published A Theory of Justice, which some admirers hailed as restoring the moribund field of political theory to some level of respectability and currency.[13] Artfully conjoining a Hobbes-like state of nature with a Kantian overlay, Rawls concocted a grand thought experiment about politics that captured the imagination of many of his readers. His "original position" provided a way to connect "normative" philosophical gambits with real-world concerns about distributive economics, and thus it seemed to speak to generational anxieties about the welfare state. At bottom, the book seemed to answer the tricky question about how a liberal state could be "just" without being socialist, and an entire publishing industry devoted to Rawlsian analysis and explication grew in the decades following.

Yet at the same time, Rawls's book failed to reflect and address many of the political realities of his day. Feminism was enjoying tremendous waves of resurgence during the 1960s, 1970s, and 1980s. The civil rights movement and the growing matter of racial politics were similarly not well covered in his lengthy volume. The protracted antagonisms of the Vietnam War; the pressures on the liberal state due to nationalist postcolonial uprisings; the international threats of nuclear conflagration and arms escalation; sexual and cultural revolutions and the coming out of the gay and lesbian movement; assassinations, high crimes and misdemeanors, and other political corrup-

tions—all of these realities that formed the living context for Rawls's w
somehow did not find their way into his vision and at best became relegat
in the book to the "non-ideal" world. While many academics argued at
length about his abstract designs for achieving justice, Rawls's actual influence
on electoral politics or judicial decision making was nugatory. A *Theory of
Justice* owed its eventual popularity more to political thinkers residing in
philosophy departments than to political theorists operating in political science departments. Although its scope was clearly "epic" in Wolin's general
sense of the term, the book failed to provide the "tacit knowledge" based on
historical experience and empirical understanding that Wolin claimed was
central to the crafty insights of political theorizing.

While analytic, mostly American political philosophers reveled in Rawls's
rhapsody, a countermovement was gaining ground within Continental circles.
In the late 1960s, structuralist theory—the idea that social systems follow
regular patterns of development issuing from constant cultural, historical,
psychological, anthropological, linguistic, or economic determinants—confronted a serious challenge by a movement later known as poststructuralism.
Poststructuralists rejected the investigative assumption that societies or individuals necessarily follow fixed rules or patterns of behavior and instead
shifted focus to the specific workings of power within particular societies.
One of the leading figures of this movement was Michel Foucault, whose
own work over the course of his career migrated from structuralism to
poststructuralism.

It may be a bit awkward to include Foucault in this brief survey of epic
contributions to twentieth-century political theory, if only because he explicitly disclaimed that his aim was ever to construct a general "theory." He
repeatedly voiced a suspicion about the Enlightenment project of seeking
universal truths about human nature, and he associated most Western political philosophy with that universalistic aspiration. For Foucault, the hallmark
of such political theory has been its devotion to idealist abstractions, first
principles, and utopias.[14] But Foucault's contention was that precisely that
attempt to achieve foundational clarity and theoretical elegance deflected
attention away from the way power actually operates. He thus shifts the focus
away from the traditional concerns of theory and toward specific historical
studies of particular institutional practices that seem to reveal an alternative
view of how power functions.

Yet Foucault's avid readers could scarcely resist the temptation to cull his
many investigations into what might be called a "new theory of power." The
old theory of power saw power as located within sites, issuing outward from
centralized states or from strong intentional subjects, such as kings or governmental officials, and the power of such centered authorities presumably
derived from their right to threaten their subjects with violence and death.
But power in the modern world does not operate very often in this crudely

coercive way. Instead, it is dispersed throughout society instead of being situated in one vested body. People are slowly disciplined over time into the prevailing order of things, until they become self-disciplining. No cold-blooded commander in chief need threaten them anymore with bodily injury for them to become civilly compliant. Modern power, for Foucault, is thus "decentered" and hails from multiple sources. In fact, it often is invisible or "masked," to the extent that the modern exercise of power passes as normal and normalizing for all parties involved. Now taken for granted, power stakes a claim over our entire living existence. According to Foucault, modern power is organized around the management of life, not the menace of death. As he argues in "The History of Sexuality," the study of power must therefore shift from an "analytics of blood" to an "analytics of sexuality."[15] Power in the modern world, operating on live bodies not just dead or soon-to-be dead ones, exercises itself primarily through the administration of sexuality. Contemporary political theorists, following Foucault, must therefore study sex as the royal road toward understanding power.

In the 1970s and 1980s, a number of sexualized studies indeed followed Foucault's lead. Queer studies became a mainstay in academic circles. Feminism experienced what some called a "third wave of resurgence." Identity politics, focusing on the intersecting dynamics of race, class, sex, and gender, became extremely influential. Poststructuralists in general were concerned with the capacity of power to construct identities and to erect boundaries within specific contexts, and they applied most of their efforts toward exposing and deconstructing the hold that particular disciplinary practices have over concrete lives—stopping short, à la Foucault, of generating any unified field theory of power.

Postmodernism, as opposed to poststructuralism, was an amorphous term that many associated with any reaction against modernity. "Modernity" was understood as the project of seeking rational progress for the good of humanity everywhere, but in-the-know postmodernists also associated modernity with a tendency to periodize history, especially according to a linear trajectory that defines "modernity" as having escaped the forces of "tradition." All "moderns," the beneficiaries of such progress, see themselves as having graduated from an earlier dark period—thus the postmodern pronouncement of entering into a new phase beyond modernity was itself ironic. The term postmodern was therefore deviously self-subverting. That is where the fun begins.

Jean-François Lyotard defined postmodernism—too baldly, as he knew— as "incredulity toward metanarratives."[16] The main metanarratives informing the modernist period would probably be those of historical progress, liberation, universalism, legitimacy, coherence, individualism, democracy, nationalism, enlightenment, science, and utility. Unrelenting incredulity over these tropes and metanarratives probably yields various reactive tendencies that subsequently have been associated with various postmodern moods: playfulness, eclecticism, polyvocality, incommensurability, hybridity, instability, and contestation. Characteristically, the postmodern practitioner would not assume that rival discourses could be reconciled via a mediating third term, thus the clash of differences must be allowed to play itself out. Difference would be showcased. In general, then, postmodernism applied to political analysis seemed to foster a growing sensitivity toward pluralized practices and manifold, protean, transgressive identities. It helped prepare the way for new multicultural and globalized investigations while bracketing the assumption that such pursuits are necessarily leading toward a humane future. Critics of postmodernism, in turn, complained that it led to political listlessness and playful paralysis.

Although postmodernism attracted few zealous devotees, its lingering influence probably will continue to inform political theory's future. Political theory at the *fin de siècle* was left without a unifying mission, direction, or mandate. Today it is marked by robust diversity, or call it "fragmentation." Political theorists, now operating almost exclusively as academicians, go about their separate projects wherever and however they see fit, to whatever end as well. They pursue a wide variety of topics, texts, methods, manners, periods, and people. Given such scattershot efforts, political theory's overall usefulness to the rest of society is doubtful, a question that probably should remain open and unsettled. Whether the field's diversity is, on balance, a good thing is subject to ongoing debate. Therewith, such debates can now occur in numerous contexts, not simply one, all-confining public agora. New voices are finding creative expression in political theory, whereas in the ancient world, only white male citizens could speak. For pestering his fellows, Socrates was executed, whereas political theorists today surely need not worry about succumbing to that dire conclusion. Nevertheless, gadflies can be swatted or one can shoo them away, but they also can be simply ignored by the slumbering beast that they attempt to sting.

12

America Goes to College

A Manifesto of Sorts

Thirty years after writing his famous call-to-arms essay, "Political Theory as a Vocation," Sheldon Wolin recently penned a recantation.[1] Back in the 1960s, the world, both within and outside the walls of academe, was "undertheorized," he then contended. Political theorists were therefore needed to step forward and provide forthright examples of wide-ranging, well-rounded, critical and visionary education crucial to the operation and vitality of modern democracy, Wolin believed. Today, however, the world is marked by "overtheorization," a condition wherein erudite academic enterprise becomes so insular that it actually erodes belief in the idea that intellectuals can have an overall salutary effect in producing a thoughtfully engaged populace. Scholars have become great careerists but poor exemplars (let alone teachers) of vigilant citizenship—and political theorists are as guilty or as remiss as any other egghead in the academy. What happened to make the high-minded Wolin lose heart?

The number of academics claiming to be "theorists" or to do "theory" today is extraordinarily high; conversely, few scholars dare publicly to eschew theory altogether. Many journals, books, and other publications are devoted to the promulgation of "theory"—and almost all of these theoretic productions claim for themselves a "politics" or "political" relevance. As such, Wolin observes, "political theory" is ubiquitous, even if the number of formal academic positions in traditional political theory has diminished over the last few decades.

Yet along with the apparent proliferation of political theorizing, we have witnessed an ever-greater differentiation of function among current self-anointed practitioners—theorists have become more and more specialized in their outlooks, and therewith they serve smaller and more focused constituencies. The triumph of theory has been accompanied, according to Wolin, by an intellectual pluralism and a robust heterogeneity. While many postmoderns, multiculturalists, and interest-group liberals celebrate such diversified purviews and approaches, Wolin warns that as a consequence of their fascination with multiplicity, contemporary political theorists have retreated from, and have even abandoned, a bygone aspiration toward *generality*, both intellectual and political. Although now "ubiquitous," the practice of theorizing today is, for Wolin, also "indeterminate" and altogether "incoherent." Its fragmentation, its relentless focus on heterogeneous publics, decentered constituencies, and shifting identities, reflects but also reinforces a wider, woefully fragmented world. In that regard, Wolin issues an unmistakable rebuke: Such "theory"—more concerned with "theoretic theory" than anything else— is not really "political," though it often goes by that name. Most notably, "postpolitical" theory obscures its own complicity in a structure of academic hierarchy, underwritten by corporate sponsorship, which allows it to flourish unchecked while rendered innocuous. Professional theorists hypocritically "deconstruct" power relations but are gainfully ensconced within them. Democrats in rhetoric only, they identify "not with the elevation of the brawny, but with the care and feeding of the brainy classes."[2]

If one pokes at Wolin's stinging analysis, however, one starts to notice that he reserves his ire for those theorists operating within the "heavily subsidized research university."[3] Secure in their posts, they ignore "class divisions" within their own ranks, namely, at research institutions that employ "gypsy" instructors and teaching assistants. The "fragmented academy" of which he speaks, the main target of his lament, cannot be the typical liberal arts college, the vast majority of which employ no teaching assistants and resist hiring adjuncts. Implicitly he signals this exception, for instance, when he rails against the particularizing purview of the overtheorized academy that now displaces "the plane of generality, once represented by ideals of a liberal or humanistic education."[4] Wolin, in his harshest words about the modern world, a world that now co-opts and even rewards radical theorists, does not insist overtly on the distinction between the research university versus the small liberal arts college, but nevertheless he seems to rely implicitly on that invidious comparison:

> The crisis of democracy is also a crisis for the intellectual, especially for the academic intellectual in most of the social sciences and humanities. A climate of opinion is being developed in which tenure, academic freedom, and faculty role in university governance are likely to be changed in favor of even more managerial control. At the same time, the ideal of the "virtual university" tailored to the needs of a technologically driven

society is gaining support, not least because it offers the hope, mainly illusory, that by a severely practical curriculum its students can climb the wall separating the dystopian from the utopian side. When scrutinized according to such measures as cost-effectiveness, the bottom line, and productivity, the ideals of the humanistic liberal arts education cannot survive, except as an appendage to the culture industry or as a Potemkin village where the sons and daughters of the rich and infamous receive a polish unobtainable elsewhere. Otherwise, from the point of view of our utopia managers, there is no justification for the remainder of traditional scholarly and intellectual activities.[5]

Wolin, it seems, has downplayed or underestimated the persistence of numerous small liberal arts colleges across the country, or else he has dismissed them out of hand as Potemkin villages for the elite only. At the same time, however, his words betray an evident nostalgia for the small liberal arts college ethos: an academic community that aspires toward a sense of common mission, even while celebrating plurality and individuality; a latter-day *Gemeinshaft* instead of a *Gesellschaft*[6]; a place that champions liberal and humanistic education, wherein members earnestly attempt to organize their affairs through democratic self-governance, where to speak is to act; and a place to which members dedicate themselves, because they view their enterprise foremost as a calling, not a career. The question is thus raised: What if all along Wolin's background political theoretic ideal, his referent and foil to the corruptions of the rest of modern society as he sees them, his worldly utopia, is not the Greek agora, the Paris commune, the New England township, or Rawls's original position but rather something that looks like Oberlin College? What if we started to reread the rest of his political theory with this idealized site now in mind, valorizing rather than repressing such formative undergraduate interactions? What if we started to refract much of the rest of our prominent political theory models, concepts, and paradigms through the prism of the prototypical liberal arts college as norm and practice? How would that change our theory? How would that change our politics? How would that change our educational outlooks and practices?

First, however, I would like to offer my own quick retrospective on one of the first chapters of this book, on Stanford's Great Books program. Fifteen years have passed since I taught in the program. At the time, the controversy generated a lot of consternation for the many parties involved—but now I, for one, perversely miss the fireworks. The controversy has died down, in fact, it has died away. An eerie silence has overtaken colleges and universities across the nation regarding such curricular debates. No one argues about curricular content much anymore. We do not argue about which is better for first-year students, Shakespeare or Paulo Freire. Accommodating diversity, former opponents across the canonical divide have made a pact with one another—we pedagogues will agree to disagree, or rather, we just will not meddle with one another's courses, texts, and students. Many institutions have dispensed, therefore, with general education requirements and have found ways to diffuse and displace substantive debates over what constitutes an excellent college education, for one or many. Pragmatic college officials now frequently promote multiple distributional "skills" as the key to liberal education, or else they simply abandon any pretense toward liberal learning in favor of quasivocational training. The decentering of the curriculum, however, did not settle any arguments—it just shut down the debate altogether.

To repeat, I now miss those arguments. I do not believe my newfound nostalgia is due simply to the weary passing of time and the failures of selective memory. The Stanford crisis prompted, or maybe it was a pretext for bringing forward, a newly held, widely shared, if ever-precarious, propensity toward enacting a campus-wide community, albeit an uneasy and unexpected one. Stanford professors and instructors had to take time out from writing our long-winded treatises, in pursuit of beautiful careers and noble purposes, in order to talk with one another, along with concerned students. Meetings regarding the debate were passionate and probing. Today, the core curriculum draws scant controversy, and professors seldom need to bother with one another, a collective standoff replicated at universities across the country. Wolin is dead-on correct about the widespread fragmentation of the academy, along with the retreat from a commitment toward generality. How can it be that so many persons writing cutting-edge commentaries about contestability cannot apparently find cause to carry on spirited conversations with their immediate colleagues? (Lobbing verbal grenades via printed texts does not require quite the same kind of courage or care.)

Over the last fifteen years, I have also adjusted my views about the late Allan Bloom's critique of the Stanford decanonization and similar campaigns at other universities. Mind you, I still object strongly to the overall, if somewhat buried, premise of Bloom's *The Closing of the American Mind*,[7] namely, that the opening of American higher education to women and minorities has been mainly responsible for an alleged decline in educational standards and an erosion of higher education's higher mission. I do not agree with Bloom's background belief, on which the argument turns, that an inborn aristocracy of certain men is naturally better suited for intellectual pursuits, and thus the democratic masses simply should not go to college. I do agree now, however, with his early assessment—which seems prophetic in retrospect—to the effect that the American academic campaign for openness and inclusion has ironically resulted in a profusion of particularistic dogmatisms, an entrenched condition that has not fostered on-campus cross-fertilization but rather mute and multitudinous indifference. The kicker is, no one wants to revisit the debate. Should undergraduates be required or expected to have read the Bible and the Koran at some point before leaving college? Do not even bring up the issue; do not go there. Faculty may not be especially eager to talk about diversity in good faith, but the current generation of students knows or suspects that something is amiss—if one can get them to open up about it. Surprisingly, I have found that a great many students, even liberal and/or secular ones when given the choice, would prefer to talk about their "souls" in Bloomian fashion rather than their "identities," "subject-positions," or postmetaphysical "performances."

Small undergraduate seminar classes are not unique at small Pomona College, but they were unusual at large Stanford, and thus they assumed a special cache in that context. Yet as I mentioned previously, I valued the Great Books classes at Stanford not simply because of the small class structure—the course content, the purported greatness of the books themselves, framed and informed our precious interactions. My own political theory courses at Pomona and elsewhere have featured tremendously diversified syllabi over these past fifteen years, but I am not sure that any of my subsequent teaching experiences have ever quite matched the magic of those Great Books discussions. Sadly, I have not had the courage of my own convictions, conflicted though they may be, to offer a dedicated Great Books course in my post–Stanford years. On my own behalf, I need also say that it was not just the structure or content of those classes that made them extraordinary. I want to add and emphasize, inasmuch as the course was the only course required of all Stanford frosh, it drew attention and gained significance (for supporters and opponents alike) because much of the campus, wholly one-fourth of the undergraduate population, and not just my particular isolated classes, was reading the same book during the same week, week in and week out, over an entire year. We had created an extended reading community, 1,600 readers of the same text at any one time. That did not create a community of consensus or unity. We argued bitterly about most of the books, but by the end of the week, we could revel in each other's company, while knowingly respecting—not just repressing—our differences. I remember one year, during *The Divine Comedy* week, one Stanford dorm threw a Dante party—a progressive party. It was a three-story dorm, and each floor played its appropriate part in the trilogy, featuring decorations, costumes and libations from the *Inferno*, the *Purgatorio*, and the *Paradiso*, floor to floor, respectively. In contrast, at Pomona College (and I would imagine at Stanford today as well), our college-wide curriculum never—to say the least—forms the basis for intelligent, student-initiated partying. With nothing in common at stake, in such a supercharged, pressure-cooker, get-ahead place, such resident go-getting persons simply can and usually will go their separate ways.

In the 1970s and 1980s, deconstruction, poststructuralism, and postmodernism became important movements in the American academy. Jacques Derrida and others contributed immensely valuable lessons about the self-contained, self-promulgating importance of the written word. The word, they taught, is not necessarily reducible to an author's intentions, as if the putative "intended" word could control or exhaust the possibilities of its multivalent import. Moreover, written words are not simply imperfect copies of the spoken word, as if the latter has an immediacy and a vitality lacking in, because allegedly not fully arrested by, the former. Such lessons eventually would lend some momentum to the proliferation of the written word through new electronic technologies and altogether would, by implication, tend to eclipse the importance of traditional face-to-face learning. Human capital thus invested in the virtual university and Internet distance learning would seem to be on the rise, whereas recent intellectual and technological innovations would seem to imply that the eyeball-to-eyeball method of education, the former comparative advantage of the residential liberal arts college, has become outmoded. In some circles, speaking as a method of education has been rendered almost passé, a waste of valuable time, an inefficient communicative transaction, a skewed power dynamic, all based on a discredited metaphysics that gives undue priority to human subjects.

Reading materials abound in multiple formats today. With a click of the mouse, one can avail oneself of vast libraries of digitized information. Readers have become avaricious consumers in a mind-bogglingly vast marketplace of materials, yet another click of the mouse takes one into a Byzantine world of chat room after chat room, where solo computer operators attempt to reach across electronic divides to communicate interactively with other terminal-bound souls. The last few decades have provided mounting evidence to suggest that reading experiences conducted completely away from the presence of others fail, in the fullness of time, to satisfy completely. Oprah Winfrey, the media mogul whose book recommendations have helped galvanize an untapped readership among her television viewers and beyond, apparently knows this. Her book club readers could, on their own, choose to read anything from a postmodern panoply at their behest, yet presumably they appreciate receiving recommendations from someone they think they know and trust—and it took a media-savvy, "tele-friendly" celebrity to step into that lonely breach. Evidently, a good many literate persons are not satisfied simply to read and learn in relative isolation, devoid of direct human contact and discussion.[8] The University of Phoenix is expanding and reportedly making good money, but applications to the top residential liberal arts colleges also are at an all-time high. Numerous students and their parents are willing to pay top dollar so that, basically, such students can sit around a conference or lunch table and chat about books and such. Why?

Liberal arts practitioners and proponents need to be clearer about the joys, magic, or chemistry of the classroom—and the overall benefits (to use, infelicitously, such economic language) of spending a good number of years in such an intimate setting. We need to get the message out that one of America's greatest assets or privileges is its unaligned network of small liberal arts colleges. Political theorists often draw a distinction between "positive" and "negative" forms of freedom. Applying that distinction to liberal arts college life, we might suggest that the liberal arts classroom provides its members with opportunities for both kinds of freedom—a freedom to enact, and a shelter against encumbrances. The key in both cases is that the liberal arts classroom structures its affairs according to a minimalist agenda, adopting thereby a noninstrumentalist view and mode of education. One reads his or her books, comes to class, and then talks, listens, and explores. Individuals in the class have nearly absolute freedom to raise whatever issues come to mind, a free license that provides—sometimes immediately, sometimes obliquely, sometimes in deferred fashion—its own internal joys, justifications, and risks. My own data set includes only two decades' worth of students, but I would venture to conclude at this point that the liberal arts classroom potentially holds a democratically expansive appeal. Most college-inclined individuals I have encountered, when given the right setting, find that they enjoy examining ideas, exchanging views, challenging one other, whetting their curiosities, questioning their texts, discovering new points of view, learning from others, and plumbing old and new mysteries. It also may be that the activity within the so-called "ivory tower" provides a real-world comparative foil to what Hannah Arendt called "the social world," the "world of necessity" as opposed to freedom. She sweepingly characterized all of modernity as being afflicted by "the instrumentalization of the whole world and the earth, this limitless devaluation of everything given, this process of growing meaninglessness where every end is transformed into a means."[9] Accustomed otherwise to, or poised for, a future of discharging private tasks and meeting worldly needs, liberal arts classmates seem to revel in the rarefied context that grants them the time, space, and luxury to interact on the terms that they largely decide among and for themselves.[10]

Diversity is, to be sure, a crucial part of the experience—the more, the better. John Stuart Mill's classic statement on liberalism—*On Liberty*—still provides the foundational statement on the uses and pleasures of diversity. For Mill, liberal diversity requires more than a formal expression or a formal toleration of dissent and conflicting points of view. A vibrant liberal society, and by extension the terms and practices of liberal learning, requires an atmosphere, cultivated through both official and unofficial means, that protects but also promotes, that encourages and actively seeks out, oppositional, idiosyncratic, and even offensive views. The only kind of free speech that needs protection is offensive speech, and speech rights do not mean a thing if they do not protect speech at the extremes—that is a commonplace of liberal theory. Less appreciated is Mill's dictum that liberal individuals and liberal institutions must go out of their way to withstand conformity and to foster and celebrate discursive diversity and individual waywardness. Better to be Socrates dissatisfied than a fool satisfied, Mill proffered; but he also wanted to contend that such provisional Socratic "pleasures" were both qualitative *and* quantifiable, both intrinsic and extrinsic, both individual and societal. He ran into trouble when he claimed that the social benefits of schooled diversity somehow could be calculated in utility-maximizing terms.

So, too, I submit, contemporary advocates for classroom diversity, many of today's multiculturalists and identity advocates, make a similar mistake—one that reflects a larger misunderstanding about liberal learning. They argue for classroom diversity essentially in utilitarian terms, evidently viewing the classroom as a training ground for extrinsic civic, social, and cosmopolitan agendas, and in the process, they effectively undermine the benefits, attractions, and freedoms that the noninstrumentalist classroom can offer. As a case in point, one of my recent seminars, a course called "Political Freedom," served up a wonderfully revelatory classroom encounter. We had read some feminist literature on the Muslim practice of veiling and the controversies surrounding it.[11] One (unveiled) woman revealed that she was a devout Muslim, and she made that disclosure in order to counter, with some sympathies expressed as well, the views of another (veiled) classmate. Our discussion of the controversy thus became very personal and very political, not only theoretic. Let me say that I do not believe that that exchange would have happened at all had I advertised the class and its readings in advance as feminist; I do not believe that these two women in particular would have both enrolled in the same such course. The conversation, serendipitous rather than preengineered, never would have happened, if I may be permitted a counterfactual speculation. If I had advertised the class in advance as an exercise in diversity, I do not think that these two women would have risked a mutual confrontation; they simply would have accepted each other's point of view—that is, quietly. ("Whatever!" is the sneering motto of the diversity generation.) The vague but cryptically solvent rubric of "political freedom," I believe, initially attracted them to the course, welcomed their contributions, and sponsored their interactions. "Diversity"—the exchange of diverse views among diverse persons—was a hugely valuable by-product or dividend of the course, not its overt premise and advertised purpose.

I pause here. I know I have probably lost some readers. Skeptics and cynics will accuse me of romanticizing college life and covering up its shortcomings (and I am[12]). Get real, they will snap: liberal arts programs are being eliminated across the country. How could one possibly, with a straight face, tout the perversely precious virtues of noninstrumentality in a world that demands results—a world that is not going to change anytime soon?[13]

An anecdote to the point: a few years ago, a colleague asked me to help conduct a few sessions of an "Alumni College" for Pomona College alums. For a few intensive summer days, alumni would return to campus to participate in short-course college classes. As a favor to my colleague, I agreed to be one of the participating professors—but I came with a bad attitude. Most of these alums were retirees in their seventies and eighties, and I expected to be babysitting Grandma while she subjected me to rambling ambles down memory lane. Attempting to overcome such initial ageist prejudices, I indeed sat down next to an elderly grandma-looking woman during our first get-acquainted breakfast. Instead of finding myself sitting next to an amiable bingo player, I discovered that here was a woman who recently had learned how to fly a four-seater airplane, whose knowledge on geopolitics was extensive, and who wanted to press me on my views of Eric Voegelin. And yes, she had four children and twelve grandchildren. I guessed that such a person must be an anomaly. Yet, shortly, the entire table of wrinkled eminences had started a heated debate over some hot-button issue. They did not defer to my professorial authority, and I had to work to get my two-cents' worth on the table.

In the formal sessions I found myself facing eighty such folks, and I proceeded with my earlier plan to present a prepared lecture to them. Almost as soon as I started speaking, hands flew up. A cane-wielding fellow challenged some of my premises right away. Another such hip-replacement refugee referred to literature that I seemed to be overlooking. Some persons were taking copious notes. Side conversations started to bypass me altogether. I quickly abandoned my script in order to carry on an impromptu seminar. The raucous group continued the conversation well into the evening—a couple of participants had even taken their break time to rush to the library to track down some citation in order to adjudicate some dispute. That night, my mind was racing. It was exciting, it was fun, it was challenging. I learned a great deal about the subject under review. Afterwards I even sent a few of the participants, none of them professional scholars, one of my manuscripts for critical feedback. Only later did it hit me: why would an eighty-some-year-old person take copious notes in such a setting?

Inspired by such apparently unadulterated enthusiasm for learning, I began my regular fall classes telling my young students about my summer experience, and I gave them a charge: we were going to act as if we were eighty-year-old students of the liberal arts. We would thus attempt to pursue ideas, as it were, for their own sake. Were we to find ourselves taking copious notes, it surely would not be in order to cram for a test. Throughout the semester, we would put our concerns about grades in abeyance. I had met old persons much like themselves, I assured them, who obviously relished an experience that they, as eighteen year olds, had perhaps already taken for granted: reading, thinking, and talking with each other. The real "payoff" for a liberal arts education perhaps would come only after they retired: they themselves could look forward to becoming such persons, eventually able to take advantage of the leisure time afforded by retirement.[14] Well-rounded liberal arts graduates, I tantalized, are more likely to retain their wits, wherewithal, confidence, and curiosity after a lifetime of workaday work.

Why wait, however, for retirement to partake of such pleasures? Young students, fresh out of high school, are as yet unable to compare the freedoms of college with the rival freedoms of the "real world" that still await them. (Typically, at Pomona College, about a year after graduation, alums get weepy eyed and yearn to return, even many of those who had been eager to get out.) Persons who disparage liberal arts college life as an "ivory tower," claiming to prefer instead to reside exclusively in the "real world," must (from my ivory tower vantage) be living in bad faith or partial ignorance about the three-dimensional virtues of these little heavenly oases—little country clubs that offer even more services than tennis, golf, and massage. One can throw clay with one's peers, perform lab experiments, take nature walks, study the stars, perform in an orchestra, take in a play, play on a team, crunch numbers, volunteer for a cause, attempt to solve global problems, or study and ponder the universe. One can research and discuss and argue about religion, biology, sociology, art history, Russian, or African-American affairs. People can choose to work diligently in such a setting—and most do, because they are doing what they want to do. Since someone else usually is paying the tab, or they are taking out loans against their own gainfully employed futures, most residential liberal arts college students enjoy for a time the utter luxury of not needing to sell their labor or products as the basis for their industrious endeavors at hand. Such free-ranging liberty makes getting a job, even a productive, challenging one, look rather confining in contrast. Indeed, for those in the know, one wishes that all of one's friends could participate as citizens at some point in such a lavishly engaging "ivory tower" existence.

Returning to Wolin, I insinuated earlier that his background conceptions of visionary politics and the vocational enterprise of political theory emanate from, or uncannily resemble, buried and blurred notions of the liberal arts classroom, situated within the residential liberal arts college community. I would go further to suggest that much of contemporary political theory performs, unacknowledged, a similar displacement or transference, shifting and substituting often back and forth, abstracted and extrapolated from the terms of life that theorists know in the classroom versus life at large, projected onto what John Rawls calls the "non-ideal" world. In more fashionable parlance, we would say that a binary separating the "ivory tower" from the "political" world insidiously informs and animates much theorizing—much of which also purports to make a successful translation applicable from the former to the latter. However, I would suggest that political theorists, Wolin included, should attempt to flip the equation, or some of its terms, around, reassessing the new result. Instead of defining the political "Other" as operating somewhere in contradistinction to the rarefied, reputedly depoliticized workings of the undergraduate classroom, I suggest that we hypostasize that the classroom constitutes ground zero of many of our normal and normative conceptions of politics, and that the rest that passes for "politics" is a deformation, and not the real deal.[15] Many "political" models in currency today—deliberative democracy, Socratic citizenship, contestatory agonism, communicative rationality, township republicanism, Rawlsian originalism, deconstruction, multiculturalism, postmodern pluralism—were indeed hatched in academic laboratories but have only rhetorically left such incubating nests. Most attempt to introduce some aspect of noninstrumentality into the allegedly debased interactions of modern politics—but they quit the classroom in bad faith and concede too much to the debasements, aligning those with politics as such. Wolin's recent woes could be explained along these lines.

To help retain Wolin's more youthful visionary outlook, the rest of us should cleave to our lived convictions. Instead of seeing college as merely prefatory to an outside, adult world—for instance, college as a place where we inculcate lessons in "civic" education whose reforming agents we deliver to a society in waiting, or, for another example, college as a place where we conduct transgressive thought experiments that we hope will send revolutionary ripples outward—we should attend to our matters at hand and patiently invite the rest of the world to adopt our practices and conform to our terms, rather than junking ours for theirs (thereby taking seriously Dewey's adage that education is not preparation for life, but life itself). Immodestly and grandiosely, I would like all of America to have the chance to go to college, as depicted above. I do not believe that liberal arts learning should be or need be reserved for the privileged few, nor need it be mutually exclusive with other forms of education, pursued in other venues. In truth, I would like all of America to become more collegelike, a raised-bar democratic vision that has been promoted variously by Thomas Jefferson, John Dewey, Jane Addams, W. E. B. Du Bois, and Grant Wood and that has been practiced viably by diversity-minded institutions such as Amherst College, Pomona College, and others.

What would it take to enact that vision, to take our democracy back to school? I write under no illusions; the liberal arts probably will not see a renaissance any time soon in a commodity-driven world, but a few practical measures could be undertaken toward that end.

1. *Expand access and exposure for liberal arts colleges by opening and encouraging enrollment by persons of all ages and backgrounds.* Even at those well-to-do colleges that are sufficiently affluent to offer "need-blind" admissions and generous financial aid packages in order to promote socioeconomic diversity in the classroom, the resulting student populations that claim to be "diverse" are still heavily skewed toward an eighteen-to-twenty-two-year-old demographic profile. How could older folks be enticed to live and learn for a few years in a residential college setting? A welcoming climate would help, and material sup-

port would enable. Some colleges currently offer "reentry" programs for older students, and a rare few offer scholarships for such individuals based on need. It would be wonderful to expand the number of such programs across the country—but generational diversity campaigns also should encourage well-heeled individuals to seek admission into the classroom. Wealthy individuals could pay their own way at institutions that open their doors to them (if their qualifications meet the criteria for admission). Businesses could offer liberal arts sabbaticals as perks in compensation packages. Philanthropic donors and foundations could help provide the assistance for "nontraditional" student scholarships. The point is not to tear down the wall separating the "ivory tower" from the outside world but instead to install something like a revolving door at the gate.

I would be thrilled to see in my lifetime a widespread transvaluation of values so that money would be freely flowing into college coffers helping to make the liberal arts experience more available to persons of all ages. While waiting for pigs to fly, however, individual professors can take a few small, practical, positive steps to help work toward that wistful vision. Almost every professor at almost every college currently enjoys the academic freedom to admit "auditors" into their classes. It would not take much to regularize and publicize this practice, reserving a few spaces in each class for "community participants." My hunch, which is based on local experience, is that once younger college students see the benefits of interacting with older persons *as peers*, all operating under the equalizing conditions of the classroom, they subsequently will want every classroom encounter to include a broadened array of perspectives. For older folks, the experience sells itself—and maybe the word will slowly get out that college, not the boardroom or the golf course, is truly the place to live life to the fullest.

2. *Sing loudly the praises of noninstrumentalist ideals and modes of education; protect and reinforce institutional practices conducive to such classroom encounters.* Limiting admission to the young perpetuates the notion that the main point of going to college is to get a good job and thus to prepare illiberally for the future—rather than to instill a love for learning for its own sake. Finding ways to deemphasize (short of eliminating altogether) the meritocratic importance of grades and degree credentialing would help withstand the gradual corruption or hostile takeover of the liberal arts mission. For instance, those of us who have taught at institutions that use "narrative evaluations" instead of grades know from firsthand experience that telling adverbs and tailored adjectives produce more creative and motivated students than the crude A-B-C-D-F grading system. The main pressure on such

institutions for abandoning the narrative evaluation system and re-
sorting back to grades comes from medical and other graduate schools
that want quantifiable data for admissions. True, it cannot be ignored
that many liberal arts students will be attending graduate schools in
the future, yet if curricular planners give too much weight to such
preprofessional considerations, the liberal arts mode of education is
not just squeezed and compromised but invaded and violated. College
officials should likewise resist "accountability" campaigns which seek
implicitly, though sometimes overtly, the veritable destruction of the
liberal arts.

Every college faculty member in today's litigious environment
should be protected (materially and psychologically) by professional
educators' liability insurance. The point is not to prompt lawsuits or
undermine trust; rather, an insurance policy that pays lawyers' fees
and court costs helps ensure and facilitate the *free exercise* of free
speech rights and privileges. Faculty members, especially those who
push the envelope or operate in gray zones, if accused of verbal mis-
conduct cannot rely on their institutions to rally to their defense.
Administrators, rightly or wrongly, often are more concerned about
protecting the endowment than protecting extreme or questionable
speech. Knowing that they might be cut loose to fend legally for
themselves, professors are liable to start erring on the side of caution
in their classrooms—in which case, the free exercise of free speech is
not simply chilled, it is dead thereafter, for all practical purposes.
Liberal arts institutions could take the national lead, making a bold
statement on behalf of academic freedom, by offering to pay (the
modest fees) for these individual policies for faculty members. Such
structural mechanisms for academic freedom are crucial to supporting
the overall mission of liberal education—as Richard Rorty says, the
whole purpose of granting academic tenure, for instance, is to allow
faculty the freedom to become loose cannons, because students *need*
to see freedom enacted before their eyes by actual human beings.[16]

3. *College presidents, development officers, and trustees should press donors
proactively and unapologetically for funding for the liberal arts* qua *the
liberal arts.* In ancient Greece, the work of slaves and women afforded
male citizens the time and leisure to interact freely in the space of the
agora. In the modern economy, liberal arts education requires money.
The intensive period of residential repose, away from the distractions
and obligations of the outside world, necessarily requires funding from
external sources; liberal arts institutions are anxiously dependent, or
call it slavishly parasitic, upon the munificence and goodwill of others. Research universities usually can offer potential donors a more
tangible bang for their bucks; they can attach names to highly visible

initiatives and grand causes. Liberal arts institutions cannot promise such reciprocating or ostentatious results, but a fair number of small liberal arts colleges have indeed become relatively affluent, not through corporate sponsorship or government soft money but mainly because right-minded alumni know personally the lifelong benefits of liberal learning and want to make that rare privilege available to others. By giving, they continue to participate in the extended community of their beloved colleges. The trick is to get more private benefactors to see the light—especially since publicly mandated funding for the liberal arts probably will not be freely forthcoming any time soon. The late composer, poet, sage (and former Pomona College liberal arts student), John Cage, contended that it is no longer folly to propose in earnest that the modern technological economy can yield sufficient surplus capital, so that "our common wealth/in order to bring about continuous elevation of human dignity/we will be able to afford to give everyone student fellowships in any subjects they elect."[17] But what kind of catholic pitch for the liberal arts could conceivably generate broadened appeal, reaching beyond the affective ties of any one college?

My own sense is that American small colleges need to take public-relations advantage of their unique status as bastions of unabashed freedom.[18] It is a freedom that operates separately from, though not entirely at odds with and ultimately is materially reliant upon, the freedom gained through the "free enterprise" system—which does not practice or endorse the liberal ethos. The classic quip, which reflects a deeper tension between commerce and academe, that is, between the marketplace of goods versus the market-place of ideas, is, "If you're so smart, why aren't you rich?" My matter-of-fact reply has always been, "If I were rich, I'd still be teaching—in fact, I can't imagine being any place for an extended period that's better than being in a college environment." Yet I do not wish such an existence for myself only. If I made a lot of money I would want to bring my grown-up friends and associates back together so that we could do many of the activities, serious and silly, that college kids enjoy doing. You cannot just *buy* that kind of community, though, no matter how much money you make. Free individuals want to be with other free individuals, on free terms—and it takes a special kind of institutional arrangement to support all of that sovereign activity. I suspect that my views are shared, though not as yet widely, by those philanthropic individuals who work their entire lives to the point that they have acquired the means so that they can give back something to society, and instead of running for plutocratic political office (an increasingly exercised option these days), they turn away from the limelight and support education instead. Once you have a billion bucks in the bank, you might realize that what you really want to do with your life is not vacation endlessly in the Cayman Islands but go (or go back) to college. We should, and could, encourage that latent wish, making the option more acceptable and available. Open up the colleges, therefore. Found new colleges as they are needed. Get the message out: Viva the American liberal arts college!

As a political theorist, I would add that those participants in and practitioners of liberal arts education are indeed contributing, behind the scenes and with each other, perhaps unawares and only remotely, to the strengthening and improvement of American democracy, albeit from within rather than at large.[19] Wolin ends his recent essay thus: "It would be nice to end on an uplifting note and invoke political theory to come to the aid of democracy, but besides being fatuous that call may be too late in the day."[20] Sadly, Wolin may be right that these are dark times for both democracy and political theory, although his mood might have turned a little less morose about those dire matters had he requested political asylum at a small liberal arts college somewhere. Nonetheless, heeding his new broadside, all political theorists would do well, especially those who still feel somehow impelled toward democratic-minded political theory, to set themselves to the liberal task of living, thinking, feeling, exploring, and crafting well-rounded lives first, and then to generate specialized scholarship not as their vocation but as a derivative pursuit.

Of course there is a portion of reading quite indispensable to a wise man. History and exact science he must learn by laborious reading. Colleges, in like manner, have their indispensable office—to teach elements. But they can only highly serve us when they aim not to drill, but to create; when they gather from far every ray of various genius to their hospitable halls, and by the concentrated fires, set the hearts of their youth on flame. Thought and knowledge are natures in which apparatus and pretension avail nothing. Gowns and pecuniary foundations, though of towns of gold, can never countervail the least sentence or syllable of wit. Forget this, and our American colleges will recede in their public importance, whilst they grow richer every year.

—Emerson, "The American Scholar"

Notes

INTRODUCTION

1. Eva T. H. Brann does advance an argument to this point; see Eva T. H. Brann, "The American College as the Place for Liberal Learning," in *Distinctively American: The Residential Liberal Arts Colleges*, ed. Steven Koblik and Stephen R. Graubard (New Brunswick: Transaction, 2000), 151–71.

2. For detailed analyses of some of the threats to liberal arts colleges, especially economic threats, see Gary Bonvillian and Robert Murphy, *The Liberal Arts College Adapting to Change: The Survival of Small Schools* (New York and London: Garland, 1996); Paul Neely, "The Threats to Liberal Arts Colleges," in *Distinctively American*, 27–45; Michael S. McPherson and Morton Owen Schapiro, "The Future Economic Challenges for the Liberal Arts Colleges," in *Distinctively American*, 47–75.

3. Of the 3,500 colleges and universities in the United States, about 800, according to one source, can claim a liberal arts identity and at the same time qualify as "independent" and "residential" (Eugene M. Lang, "Distinctively American: The Liberal Arts College," in *Distinctively American*, 133–34). Yet the latest Carnegie classification lists only 125 colleges as baccalaureate (Liberal Arts I) institutions (*Chronicle of Higher Education* 23 [October 1998]). A 1987 Carnegie study put the number of residential liberal arts colleges at 212, a number still often cited; see David W. Breneman, *Liberal Arts Colleges: Thriving, Surviving, or Endangered?* (Washington, D. C.: The Brookings Institution, 1994).

4. Some have tried. See *The Small American College: A Vital National Asset* (Washington, D. C.: The Council of Independent Colleges, 1983); Burton Clark, *The Distinctive College: Antioch, Reed and Swarthmore* (Chicago: Aldine, 1970), reissued with a new introduction by Burton Clark, *The Distinctive College* (New Brunswick: Transaction, 1992); *Distinctively American*.

5. Alexander W. Astin and Calvin B. T. Lee, *The Invisible Colleges* (New York: McGraw-Hill, 1972).

6. Clark Kerr referred to the American research university as a "City of Intellect" and contrasted it to the liberal arts college as a "village." See Clark Kerr, *The Uses of the University* (Cambridge and London: Harvard University Press, 2001), 199.

7. In the ten-year period, from 1992 to 2001, 4.6 percent of the grants awarded in the United States and Canada competition were awarded to persons with a

liberal arts college (Baccalaureate I) affiliation. While this figure alone does not prove bias or discrimination, the fact that 40 percent of those liberal arts college recipients hail from New York colleges does suggest that visibility is indeed a key variable in the selection process.

8. I agree with not everything, but indeed much of Michael Oakeshott's views on education; yet I question whether his view of the British university applies to its American counterpart. Hence, I insist on drawing a sharp distinction between university life versus small college life (in America). See Michael Oakeshott, "The Idea of a University," *The Voice of Liberal Learning: Michael Oakeshott on Education*, ed. Timothy Fuller (New Haven and London: Yale University Press, 1989), 95–104.

9. Kant's phrase. See Isaiah Berlin, *The Crooked Timber of Humanity: Chapters in the History of Ideas*, ed. Henry Hardy (New York: Knopf, 1990).

10. See Hannah Arendt, "The Crisis in Education," *Between Past and Future: Eight Essays in Political Thought* (New York: Viking, 1954), 3–15.

11. Between 1990 and 1998, only 40 percent of the placements in political science ended up in Ph.D. departments; see table 3, Sue Davis, "The Job Market for Political Scientists in 1998: The Good News and The Bad," *PS* 33: 3 (September 2000): 675–77. A Pew Charitable Trust survey of eleven other disciplines found that only 27 percent of full-time faculty holds appointments at research universities. See "Graduate Education Flawed, Study Finds," *Academe* 87: 4 (July–August 2001): 14.

12. A countervailing trend: University of California, Irvine, has lost women faculty over the last ten years, and one explanation is that the liberal arts college environment is more congenial to many women than the research university. "I believe I would have a better chance of balancing work and family life at a small liberal arts college, particularly since I may well want to have children before I come up for tenure at age 40," reported Catherine Clark, a chemistry professor at Chapman University. See Gary Robbins, " 'UCI Short of Female Faculty'," *Orange County Registrar* (July 15, 2001): 1.

13. Benjamin R. Barber, *An Aristocracy of Everyone: The Politics of Education and the Future of America* (New York: Ballantine Books, 1992); Patrick J. Deneen, *The Odyssey of Political Theory: The Politics of Departure and Return* (Lanham: Rowman and Littlefield, 2000), 21.

14. Daniel W. Conway and John Seery, "The Demise of Western Culture," *Curricular Reform: Narratives of Interdisciplinary Humanities Programs*, ed. by Mark E. Clark and Roger Johnson Jr. (Chattanooga, Tenn.: Southern Humanities Council Press, 1991), 89–113.

15. Page Smith, *Killing the Spirit: Higher Education in America* (New York: Viking, 1990).

16. Austin Sarat and Dana R. Villa, eds., *Liberal Modernism and Democratic Individuality: George Kateb and the Practices of Politics* (Princeton: Princeton University Press, 1996).

17. Jürgen Habermas, *The Structural Transformation of the Public Sphere*, trans. Thomas Burger and Frederick Lawrence (Cambridge: MIT Press, 1989). Habermas does turn his attention toward the form and functions of a university, and even the American university system in particular, and addresses the discursive ideal of the classroom seminar or of a communicative community of researchers. But he does

not take up the question of the unique character of the American small, residential liberal arts college and its internal relations or its larger relationship to society. Jürgen Habermas, "The Idea of the University: Learning Processes," in *The New Conservatism: Cultural Criticism and the Historians' Debate*, Shierry Weber Nicholsen, ed. and trans. (Cambridge: MIT Press, 1990), 100–127.

18. John Seery, "Moral Perfectionism and Abortion Politics," *Polity* 33: 3 (spring, 2001): 345–64.

19. John Seery, "What, Exactly, Is 'Sacred' in a Life?" *Los Angeles Times*, August 18, 1996, p. 5.

20. Daniel W. Conway, *Nietzsche's Dangerous Game: Philosophy in the Twilight of the Idols* (New York: Cambridge University Press, 1997); also see John Seery, "Nietzsche Contra Nietzcheanism: Philosophy in the Twilight of an Idol," *Journal of Nietzsche Studies* 16 (fall 1998): 80–86.

21. See Friedrich Nietzsche, *On the Future of Our Educational Institutions: Homer and Classical Philology*, trans. J. M. Kennedy (New York: Macmillan, 1924).

22. Tracy B. Strong, *Friedrich Nietzsche and the Politics of Transfiguration* (Berkeley: University of California Press, 1975).

23. Friedrich Nietzsche, *Thus Spoke Zarathustra*, trans. Walter Kaufmann (New York: Viking Penguin, 1978), 137–38.

24. John Seery, "Grant Wood's Political Gothic," *Theory and Event* (Baltimore, MD: Johns Hopkins University Press, Muse Project), vol. 2, no. 1 (March 1998): 1–36.

25. John Seery, "Castles in the Air: An Essay on Political Foundations," *Political Theory*, 27: 4 (August 1999): 460–90.

26. John Seery, "Twentieth Century Context," *Contemporary Political Theories: A Reader and Guide*, ed. Alan Finlayson (Edinburgh: Edinburgh University Press, forthcoming 2001).

27. Hannah Arendt, "Preface: The Gap between Past and Future," *Between Past and Future*, 3–15.

CHAPTER 1

1. The Great Works track was one of eight tracks in the Western Culture Program at Stanford. Most of the other tracks were affiliated, loosely or officially, with departments or other ongoing programs, whereas the Great Works track, the largest of the eight, was entirely unaligned.

2. For example, I noticed that professors from the Stanford Political Science Department and the Hoover Institute started writing articles on the matter, even though absolutely no one from the Department or Hoover had ever taught in the program or had previously shown the slightest teacherly interest in the course as long as I had been there. One political scientist, who has since published his sweeping views about how to reform the entire educational system in America, confessed to me that he had never heard of the Western Culture Program at Stanford—which I found to be an alarming oversight, since this professor had been teaching at Stanford for many years, the program was debated on a daily basis, and the Political Science Department was housed in the same building right next to the Western Culture Program.

3. The relationship with surrounding businesses is still cozy (*author's note*: this essay was originally written in 1990). For instance, a number of businesses subscribe to regular Stanford courses and participate in them via the closed-circuit television network. Students have microphones behind their desks, which they are supposed to use (for the benefit of their television viewers) in the event that they need to pose a question to the lecturer. If employees of IBM (for instance) want to ask a question from their remote-control vantage, they can interrupt the proceedings via a speaker system that operates from the back of the classroom. Students hear a voice from IBM coming from a box. No real human being ever need appear as a classmate.

4. I am disappointed with the growing contention that Socrates was the classical exemplar of rationalistic, male-dominated, mastery-seeking discourse and as such represents the problem with subsequent Western discourse. This thesis seems to derive from a particular reading of Socrates and Plato through particular readings of Hegel, Nietzsche, and Heidegger. I hope that this reading does not pass uncontested, but this chapter is not the place to attempt to dispel those notions.

5. All sorts of statistics are available, and all sorts of questions were asked of students (and I have these figures at my disposal), but the most comprehensive question on student evaluations—"At the end of the year, do you think your Western Culture sequence was a positive experience?"—broke down as follows: on a scale of 1 (no) to 5 (yes), the program approval rating (4s and 5s) for the years 1985 through 1988 was 80 percent, and the negative (1s and 2s) was 6 percent. For the Great Works track in particular, these figures were 86 percent approval, 4 percent negative (only 1 percent of the students expressed a 1 rating during the three years).

6. At one point during the years of the Western Culture debate, neighboring East Palo Alto had the highest murder-per-capita rate in the United States, another point that never factored into our canon disputes.

7. I will not attempt to elaborate on a definition of irony here. Elsewhere I have tried to do just that, and if I did not succeed there, I am afraid that I will not be able to answer it any better here. See John Evan Seery, *Political Returns: Irony in Politics and Theory from Plato to the Antinuclear Movement* (Boulder: Westview Press, 1990).

8. This Great Books issue divided the campus racially, starkly though not strictly, along color lines, and by trying to understand these divisions that seemed to correspond roughly to skin color, I am not offering or advocating racialist explanations. My own view of race as an analytic category is that I regard it as a floating signifier, an unstable sign that individuals can and do imbue with various and multiple meanings. All sorts of strategies of dealing with race are possible: one individual may regard race as a badge of honor, another may feel defensive about it, another may be bored by it, or all of the above. Race may or may not be an important and importantly contested sign, depending on context. What cannot be shoved under the rug is that at Stanford during those three years, race emerged as a hot issue, as it has at many universities across the country in recent years. I realize that in attempting to understand this phenomenon I am running the risk of being perceived as stereotyping and generalizing, and one does not want to brand individuals. I hope that I have sufficiently qualified my remarks in this chapter, and in my own teaching I would never treat an individual student as if she or he were simply an actor of some general class. But I do want to address the dynamics of how

individuals appropriate to themselves class designations, how they may try to avoid them, distance themselves from them, react to them, and so on in myriad ways. Thus my use of "white" versus "black" or "male" versus "female" is extremely provisional, and I do not mean to ascribe some necessary import to these terms. Finally, however, my economical designations of white versus minority student bespeak not so much skin color as the difference between dominant and marginalized groups (for instance, gay and lesbian groups expressed discontent with the program as well).

9. Here I might mention that my experience at Stanford does not confirm Shelby Steele's general portrait of blacks in American universities. Where he saw an "inferiority complex," I saw an initial ambivalence—a strong desire to take advantage of the opportunities that Stanford had to offer, and yet a self-questioning of that desire. Ability, confidence, and opportunism were seldom lacking at Stanford.

10. A problem, however, with departing from a loosely chronological ordering of books is that an alternative approach necessarily has to be organized according to some (i. e., someone's) alternative agenda and set of questions, themes, and so forth. Then we must confront the problem of whether these new themes subject students to new forms of ideological straitjacketing and privileging. Chronology can be burdensome, but often I prefer it once I hear the new agenda actually proposed.

11. As a beneficiary of a diversity campaign, I am sympathetic to affirmative action policies in hiring and admissions. Times change—fifteen years ago (author's note: add at least ten more years now), I was recruited by Northeastern colleges in an all-out effort to bring Midwestern students to the East in order to expand "geographical" diversity (I wore overalls and flannel shirts, and I sort of liked the idea that people thought that my being from Iowa made me a member of a disadvantaged group). But many of the arguments for these programs are off-putting, except to those bound to benefit directly. I do not think a proponent should suggest that there is any necessary epistemological or even sociological connection between ideas and personal background, and this approach should be abandoned. I rather like Mill's argument, namely, that the *indirect* effects of governmental policy (in his case, democracy) are more important that the direct effects—and one can apply this reasoning to academic policy. Democracy raises and expands the standards of an entire society; it activates people *generally* (which was Mill's response to a Burkean argument about the alleged advantages of a benign dictator, or the noblesse oblige of an aristocratic ruling class). Even if you had a bunch of white men who actually made a heartfelt effort to diversify their ideas, present alternative modes of explanation, and try to see the world from nonwhite points of view, and who were successful in this effort, this resultant situation would not be desirable. Diverse ideas would flourish, but they would not be perpetuated by a general populace. The point applied to university life is not that the standards of the university are to be leavened and "lowered," but rather that if one wants activated minds generally, a democratic education, reaching as many constituencies as possible, is most likely to tend in that direction (though it does not ensure the result). A critic may say that this pragmatic approach panders to human shortcoming, and the response to that criticism is not that only a black person (for instance) can teach or learn from another black person but rather, as Mill argues, that it is prudent to let people look after their own interests (which is not to concede that black people will necessarily support or

represent "black" interests, as if such exist). Diversity is the best *policy*, a good rule of thumb—especially in contrast to the alternative, entrusting a minority group of white men to cover the vast range of possible ideas.

12. In my own political theory classes, I have mixed up the course material— I include Chinese, Indian, and Islamic texts, for instance, and my courses are preoccupied with feminist issues and feminist deconstructions; I also try to pay attention to issues of class and race. I am designing a course in non-Western political theory, to supplement or offset my courses in traditional Western theory, as well. So the above argument does not really apply to my political theory "canon." In disciplinary courses, however, the point is not really the same as what we were attempting at Stanford.

13. Another way that Western literature often adopts internally a "voice from without" is to include characters who are clearly marginalized or extreme: madmen, exiles, suicides, monsters, slaves, knaves, fools, savages, doubles, or demons.

14. In *Political Returns*, I argue that Orphic irony tends in the direction of creating an anticonsequentialist communitarianism.

15. In the last few years of the program, a few instructors experimented with dorm-based sections, and there was some minimal self-selection into the various tracks, but for the most part, these decisions were blind.

16. In the pages of the *New York Times*, Bloom vilified my former colleague, Charles Junkerman, for arguing for the teaching of Frantz Fanon's *The Wretched of the Earth*, but Bloom seemed completely unaware of the particular controversy surrounding the book at Stanford (it was never really a question of teaching Fanon as opposed to John Locke).

17. *Author's note*: gay and lesbian issues, not to mention postcolonial issues, are occluded in this chapter, which reflects the discourse at the time. Even though I was hired by two men who soon became prominent and outspoken activists and writers on gay issues, the canon debate in the late 1980s did not engage issues of homophobia and heteronormativity, at least not on the Stanford campus. It might be noted that Judith Butler's highly influential *Gender Trouble* was published in 1990.

CHAPTER 2

1. The "Blue Room" is a large room in one of the dining halls at Pomona College, which can be converted into a lecture-style venue.

2. René Girard, *The Scapegoat*, trans. Yvonne Freccero (Baltimore: Johns Hopkins University Press, 1986).

3. Gustave Flaubert, *Madame Bovary*, ed. and trans. Paul de Man (New York and London: Norton, 1965), 5.

4. Michael Rogin, *Ronald Reagan, the Movie; and Other Episodes in Political Demonology* (Berkeley: University of California Press, 1987), 30.

5. Banana slug, Jumbo elephant, and Sagehen are the totems or school mascots for UC Santa Cruz, Tufts University, and Pomona College, respectively.

6. Abraham Lincoln, "Second Inaugural Address," *Speeches and Writings 1859– 1865* (New York: The Library of America, 1989), 686–87.

7. Hannah Arendt, *The Human Condition* (Chicago and London: University of Chicago Press, 1958), 236–43.

8. Sheldon S. Wolin, *The Presence of the Past: Essays on the State and the Constitution* (Baltimore and London: Johns Hopkins University Press, 1989).

9. Ibid., 145.

10. Ibid., 145–46.

CHAPTER 3

1. "Presumably, authority is a permanent institution, whereas any given student soon passes forever beyond the status of student. And a teacher only teaches: if he does anything more than instruct, he influences." See George Kateb, "Disguised Authority," *Democracy* 2: 3 (July 1982): 122.

2. Friedrich Nietzsche, *Twilight of the Idols*, trans. Walter Kaufmann, *The Portable Nietzsche* (New York: Viking, 1959), 532.

3. *Author's note*: this chapter was written well before Kateb's book on Emerson was published. See George Kateb, *Emerson and Self-Reliance* (Thousand Oaks: Sage, 1995).

4. George Kateb, "Thinking about Human Extinction (2): Emerson and Whitman," *Raritan* 6: 3 (winter 1987): 4.

5. George Kateb, "Thinking about Human Extinction (1): Nietzsche and Heidegger," *Raritan* 6: (fall 1986): 23.

6. Ibid., 25.

7. George Kateb, "Democratic Individuality and the Meaning of Rights," in *Liberalism and the Moral Life*, ed. Nancy Rosenblum (Cambridge: Harvard University Press, 1989), 206.

8. George Kateb, "Nuclear Weapons and Individual Rights," *Dissent* (spring 1986): 166.

9. Kateb, "Democratic Individuality and the Meaning of Rights," 198.

10. Virginia Woolf, *To the Lighthouse* (San Diego: Harcourt Brace Jovanovich, 1927), 106, 247, 284, 301.

11. Hannah Arendt, *On Revolution* (New York: Penguin, 1963), 255.

12. Walt Whitman, *Democratic Vistas* (St. Clair Shores: Scholarly Press, 1970), 16.

13. Ibid., 18.

14. Ibid., 31.

15. Ibid., 28.

16. Ibid.

17. Ibid., 36.

18. Ibid., 50.

19. Ibid., 33.

20. Judith Shklar, "Emerson and the Inhibitions of Democracy," *Political Theory* 18: 4 (November 1990): 614.

21. Kateb tries to implicate Whitman in the Emersonian quest for solitude. He contends that Whitman is finally a theorist of solitude, not one who proclaims the "adventures of human connectedness." He draws upon one particularly religious citation from *Democratic Vistas* (p. 47), but I am uncertain whether such religious ecstasies are to be linked to Whitman's passages on identity. Also note, as mentioned above, that the paragraph immediately following the solitude citation is the passage

exhorting young persons to enter into politics. See George Kateb, "Walt Whitman and the Culture of Democracy," *Political Theory* 18: 4 (November 1990): 570.

22. Kateb grants this point as well, only to reject any compromise position, again on the basis of an either/or distinction between individualism and communitarianism: "I do not mean to be intransigent. I concede that the terrible features of modern life are not what they are because of recent anti-individualist idealism. Rather, the anti-individualist theorists have been insufficiently attentive to the possibility that their studied anti-individualism lessens their ability to protest and resist these features, or to do so consistently. I also concede that it is plausible to hold that some terrible features of modern life seem to come from some type of individualism, whether economic individualism or another. . . . Anti-individualist ideals are meant to mitigate or end these troubles. But the potential cost is intolerably high. Nothing is worse than the horrors that do or would come from the unqualified prestige of participation in sovereign politics, the society wide bond of Community, the solidarity of the armed group, and the project of socialized self-realization." See Kateb, "Democratic Individuality and the Meaning of Rights," 204.

23. Whitman, *Democratic Vistas*, 47–48.

24. Arendt ends *The Human Condition* with a quote from Cato that suggests a recurring Katebian point, namely, that democratic inclusion is best achieved through solitary thinking: "Never is he more active than when he does nothing, never is he less alone than when he is by himself" (p. 325).

25. George Kateb, "Appendix: The Life of the Mind," *Hannah Arendt: Politics, Conscience, Evil* (Totowa, NJ.: Rowman & Allanheid, 1984), 189–97.

26. George Kateb, *Utopia and Its Enemies* (New York: Free Press, 1963), 4.

27. Whitman, *Democratic Vistas*, 35–36.

CHAPTER 4

1. Max Weber, "Science as a Vocation," *From Max Weber: Essays in Sociology*, trans. and ed. by H. H. Gerth and C. Wright Mills (New York: Oxford University Press, 1946), 150.

2. Ralph Waldo Emerson, "The American Scholar," *Selections from Ralph Waldo Emerson: An Organic Anthology*, ed. by Stephen E. Whicher (Boston: Houghton Mifflin, 1957), 63–80.

3. George Shulman, "American Political Culture, Prophetic Narration, and Toni Morrison's *Beloved*," *Political Theory* 24: 2 (May 1996): 295–314.

4. Weber, "Science as a Vocation," 155.

CHAPTER 5

1. Of course, every term is loaded, containing and occluding various linguistic economies of signification, exclusion, emphasis, and oversight, and the terms "pro-choice" and "pro-life" are certainly no exception in that regard, for they represent particular histories, strategies, compromises, and so forth. The term *pro-choice* surely shifts the emphasis toward a woman's right to choose and thus probably grants operational privilege to proceduralism over substantive contestation, and this chapter will call that privilege into question. Yet I, for one, much prefer that term over

proposed alternatives, such as N. Ann Davis's suggestion of "permissive" (versus "restrictive"). See Davis, "The Abortion Debate: The Search for Common Ground," Part 1, *Ethics* 103 (April 1993): 516–36.

2. For a superb recent exposition on varieties of perfectionism and their relation to politics, see George Sher, *Beyond Neutrality: Perfectionism and Politics* (Cambridge: Cambridge University Press, 1997), esp. 9–11. Sher distinguishes between and among the various claims to perfectionism, a necessity because, he points out, "perfectionism" has no canonical meaning. Yet I might also point out that Sher discusses almost exclusively *contemporary* formulations of perfectionism, or those moderns who draw upon, for instance, Aristotle or Aquinas, but he neglects an explicit discussion of religious perfectionism, notably the long tradition of Christian perfectionism. See also Thomas Hurka, *Perfectionism* (New York and Oxford: Oxford University Press, 1993).

3. See *The New Civil War: The Psychology, Culture, and Politics of Abortion,* ed. Linda J. Beckman and S. Marie Harvey (Washington, D. C.: American Psychological Association, 1998).

4. John Rawls simply does not recognize the validity or "reasonableness" of the moral-theological case against abortion, especially as it pertains to public debate. He asserts, for instance, that prohibiting abortions in the first trimester is clearly "unreasonable." He does not think that a theological objection to abortion presents a viable "limit" on public reason, since citizens can vote their "nonpolitical" values and try to convince other citizens accordingly, hence, such theological claims do not "transcend" the claims of public reason. See John Rawls, *Political Liberalism* (New York: Columbia University Press, 1993), 243n, 246.

5. For foundational statements on the neutrality principle see, in addition to Rawls, Robert Nozick, *Anarchy, State, and Utopia* (New York: Basic Books, 1974); Bruce Ackerman, *Social Justice in the Liberal State* (New Haven: Yale University Press, 1980); Ronald Dworkin, *A Matter of Principle* (Cambridge: Harvard University Press, 1985).

6. John Rawls, *A Theory of Justice* (Cambridge: Harvard University Press, 1971), 329.

7. See Stanley Cavell's attempt to reconcile Emersonian Perfectionism with the claims of liberal democracy, *Conditions Handsome and Unhandsome: The Constitution of Emersonian Perfectionism* (Chicago and London: University of Chicago Press, 1990).

8. Rawls, *A Theory of Justice*, 327.

9. In her 1989 challenge to Rawls, Susan Okin barely discusses abortion, and only in passing: "There is bitter opposition between those who assert that women, like men, have the right to control their own bodies and those who assert that, from the moment of conception, fetuses, like human beings, have the right to life. We have no currently 'shared understandings' on abortion, partly because *both* basic liberal rights cannot be universalized to fetuses as well as to women." See Susan Moller Okin, *Justice, Gender, and the Family* (New York: Basic Books, 1989), 66n. Susan J. Hekman, to cite another example, does not mention abortion at all in her critique of Rawls by way of Gilligan. See *Moral Voices, Moral Selves: Carol Gilligan and Feminist Moral Theory* (University Park: Pennsylvania State University Press, 1995).

10. Michael Sandel, *Democracy's Discontents: In Search of America's Public Philosophy* (Cambridge: Harvard University Press, 1996), 17.

11. Naomi Wolf, "Our Bodies, Our Souls," *The New Republic* (October 16, 1995): 26.

12. Ibid., 34.

13. Roy Rivenburg, "A Decision between a Woman and God," *Los Angeles Times*, May 24, 1996, p. E1.

14. Ronald Dworkin, *Life's Dominion: An Argument about Abortion, Euthanasia, and Individual Freedom* (New York: Knopf, 1993).

15. Ibid., 25.

16. Drucilla Cornell, *The Imaginary Domain: Abortion, Pornography & Sexual Harassment* (New York and London: Routledge, 1995), 80.

17. Wendy Brown forcefully chastises liberals for their degendering rights talk, and in the particular case of abortion, she contends that "gender neutral" discourse may reinscribe by rendering invisible women's subordination. While Brown's point is entirely well taken here, I might mention that a similar erasure or deflection occurs in her analysis, namely, a detheologizing about abortion politics, an apparent nervousness about discussing rival metaphysical positions on abortion and similar topics. See Wendy Brown, *States of Injury: Power and Freedom in Late Modernity* (Princeton: Princeton University Press, 1995), esp. 140–41. In that regard, I find Kirstie McClure's insistence that Lockean political rights must be viewed within a theistic order to be particularly helpful. See Kirstie M. McClure, *Judging Rights: Lockean Politics and the Limits of Consent* (Ithaca and London: Cornell University Press, 1996). Oddly, some liberal theory that attempts to rethink the place of religion nonetheless manages to steer clear of any discussion of the abortion issue; see *Obligations of Citizenship and Demands of Faith: Religious Accommodation in Pluralist Democracies*, ed. Nancy L. Rosenblum (Princeton: Princeton University Press, 2000).

18. William E. Connolly also questions the terms of Rawls's secularism and wishes to reintroduce religious discourse into liberal politics, but I have not included his most recent book in this brief opening survey, because he does not explicitly connect Rawls's critiques to the abortion issue. See *Why I am Not a Secularist* (Minneapolis and London: University of Minnesota Press, 1999), 22, 64–70.

19. Compare this challenge to Rawlsianism with Bonnie Honig's call for greater agonistic vigilance—a politics of virtú rather than virtue—with respect to abortion and other legal decisions. For the most part, Honig seems to brand most flights and forays into metaphysics as retreats from or "displacements" of political contestation, so one might suspect that my project would be incongruent with hers. But by providing an alternative, modified, perfectionist theology, I actually see my own double-crossing challenges to Rawls and to Christianity as being compatible with her agonistic aims, even if it enacts that contest on putatively "metaphysical"—rather than "judicial" or properly "political"—terrain. See Honig, *Political Theory and the Displacement of Politics* (Ithaca and London: Cornell University Press, 1993), 14–15.

20. Rawls recognizes only in passing the difficulties of the abortion issue with respect to legitimating values of political liberalism. See Rawls, *Political Liberalism*, 243–44.

21. Dworkin, *Life's Dominion*, 77.

22. Ibid., 78.

23. Ibid., 79.

24. "It is not my present purpose to recommend or defend any of these widespread convictions about art and nature, in either their religious or secular form. Perhaps they are all, as some skeptics insist, inconsistent superstitions. I want only to call attention to their complexity and characteristic structure, because I hope to show that most people's convictions about abortion and euthanasia can be understood as resting on very similar, though in some important ways different, beliefs about how and why *individual* human life, in any form, is also inviolable" (Dworkin, *Life's Dominion*, 81).

25. Ibid., 101.

26. William E. Connolly, *The Ethos of Pluralization* (Minneapolis: University of Minnesota Press, 1995), xxix–xxx. I should note that Connolly's main project in *Why I am Not a Secularist* is "to rework the secular problematic" rather than to interrogate the terms of the sacred, so my task herein departs a bit from his later emphasis on secularism and its discontents. See *Why I am Not a Secularist*, 4.

27. Rawls, *A Theory of Justice*, 258.

28. Georges Bataille, *The Accursed Share: An Essay on General Economy*, vol. 1, trans. Robert Hurley (New York: Zone Books, 1988), 9.

29. Bataille's work is influencing several contemporary accounts, notably: Jean Starobinski, *Largesse*, trans. Jane Marie Todd (Chicago and London: University of Chicago Press, 1997); Jacques Derrida, *The Gift of Death*, trans. David Wills (Chicago and London: University of Chicago Press, 1995); Alan D. Schrift, ed., *The Logic of the Gift* (New York: Routledge, 1997).

30. Georges Bataille, "The Notion of Expenditure," *Visions of Excess: Selected Writings, 1927–1939*, ed. Allan Stoekl (Minnesota: University of Minnesota Press, 1985), 116–29; see also Georges Bataille, *Inner Experience*, trans. Leslie Anne Boldt (Albany: State University of New York Press, 1988).

31. Bataille, *The Accursed Share*, vol. 1, 38–41.

32. Georges Bataille, *Death and Sensuality: A Study of Eroticism and the Taboo* (New York: Walker and Company, 1962), 97.

33. Dworkin, *Life's Dominion*, 179.

34. Georges Bataille, *Theory of Religion*, trans. Robert Hurley (New York: Zone Books, 1989), 43.

35. Bataille, *Death and Sensuality*, 119–20. I might clarify here that Bataille claims that Christianity posits an eternal, continuous soul; but that characterization may be more Greek than pan-Christian. I thank Lee McDonald for insisting on this (and other) qualifications to the above account of Christianity.

36. Bataille, *Theory of Religion*, 43.

37. Ibid., 49.

38. Jean Reith Schroedel has examined the policy implications of treating the fetus as a person once it is born. See *Is the Fetus a Person? A Comparison of Policies across the Fifty States* (Ithaca: Cornell University Press, 2000).

39. Congregation for the Doctrine of the Faith, "Declaration on Abortion" (Vatican City: Vatican Polygot Press, November 18, 1974); cited in Tom Poundstone, "The Catholic Debate on the Moral Status of the Embryo," *The Silent Subject: Reflections on the Unborn in American Culture*, ed. Brad Stetson (Westport and London: Praeger, 1996), 169–75.

40. Bataille, *Death and Sensuality*, 100–101.

41. Ibid., 102.

42. Ibid., 31.

43. Ibid., 120.

44. Ibid., 121.

45. Ibid., 120.

46. Bataille, "The Notion of Expenditure," 127.

47. This formulation could be productively challenged as being overly individualistic, whereas several variants of Christianity have traditionally viewed salvation as a collectivist enterprise. Below, however, the Japanese case suggests how a concern with the fate of the souls of individual fetuses can relate to a shared sense of social good.

48. Abstinence would not do the trick theologically—presumably one needs the creation of an informed soul via conception in order to require a redemption and to make a sacrifice.

49. Cf. Stanley Cavell on perfectionism versus "end-time" theology. See his *Conditions Handsome and Unhandsome: The Constitution of Emersonian Perfectionism* (Chicago: University of Chicago Press, 1990), 129–33.

50. Malcolm Potts, "Foreward to the Second Edition," in S. Chandrasekhar, *India's Abortion Experience: 1972–1992* (Denton: University of North Texas Press, 1994), xv.

51. Georges Bataille, *The Accursed Share*, vols. 2 and 3, trans. Robert Hurley (New York: Zone Books, 1991), 261–430; on applying Bataille's analysis to twentieth-century communism, see Robert Meister, "Beyond Satisfaction: Desire, Consumption, and the Future of Socialism," *Topoi* 15: 2 (spring 1996): 189–210.

52. Max Weber, *The Protestant Ethic and the Spirit of Capitalism*, trans. Talcott Parsons (New York: Charles Scribner's Sons, 1958), 232–33, n. 66.

53. See, for instance, Leonard Binder, *Islamic Liberalism: A Critique of Development Ideologies* (Chicago: University of Chicago Press, 1988), 198–203.

54. Bataille, *The Accursed Share*, vol. 1, 76–76; vol. 2, 39–58; "The Notion of Expenditure," 121–24; *Death and Sensuality*, 204–207.

55. Bataille, *The Accursed Share*, vol. 2, 56.

56. Ibid., 58.

57. Strathern, in her seminal work on women and gift giving, does not explore abortion; see Marilyn Strathern, *The Gender of the Gift: Problems with Women and Problems with Society in Melanesia* (Berkeley: University of California Press, 1988).

58. Derrida, *The Gift of Death*, 112; cf. Bataille, "The Notion of Expenditure," 122.

59. "It is, after all, quite possible to argue that abortion is beneficial for society. It is difficult to imagine that the world would be a better place if the forty million to fifty million fetuses legally aborted each year grew up to reproduce themselves at the frightening rate that adult humans seem to do." See Mary Gordon, "Abortion: How Do We Think About It?" *Good Boys and Dead Girls and Other Essays* (New York: Viking, 1991), 131.

60. Cornell, *The Imaginary Domain*, 32, 84; Amartya Sen, "More Than One Hundred Million Women Are Missing," *New York Review of Books* 37 (Christmas issue, December 1990), 61–66.

61. See Mira Dana, *Abortion and the Emotions Involved* (London: Women's Therapy Center, 1984); Miriam Claire, *The Abortion Dilemma: Personal Views on a Public Issue* (New York and London: Plenum Press, 1995).

62. The politics of abortion in Japan are a bit more complicated than simple acceptance and easy accessibility. See William R. LaFleur, *Liquid Life: Abortion and Buddhism in Japan* (Princeton: Princeton University Press, 1992), 193–96. For more of a multireligious perspective on mizuko kuyō, especially Shinto and neo-Shintoist views, as well as major Buddhist opposition, see Helen Hardacre, *Marketing the Menacing Fetus in Japan* (Berkeley: University of California Press, 1997).

63. LaFleur, *Liquid Life*, 12.

64. Ibid., 182.

65. Ibid., 183.

66. Ibid., 26.

67. Ibid., 85.

68. Ibid., 150.

69. Ibid., 216.

70. See, for instance, Laurence H. Tribe, *Abortion: The Clash of Absolutes* (New York: Norton, 1990).

71. Rawls favors a "present entry theory of interpretation" for the original position but alters that "motivational assumption" in order to effect an inter-generational outlook that can ensure a fair scheme of material resources, an appropriate rate of capital savings, respect for the environment, and a perpetuation of just institutions. But nowhere is he concerned with constructing a just family, in the way that LaFleur describes mizuko kuyō. See Rawls, *A Theory of Justice*, 137, 140, 286, 292.

72. Derek Parfit attempts, by a "nonreligious ethics," to address one's commitments to people temporally removed from one's immediate context (i. e., one's commitments to dead people). While his rationalist approach to issues of suicide, population growth, and war prevention is admirable, I have my doubts about whether a protracted temporal scheme involving absent parties can avoid metaphysics entirely. See Derek Parfit, *Reasons and Persons* (Oxford: Clarendon Press, 1984).

73. John E. Seery, *Political Theory for Mortals: Shades of Justice, Images of Death* (Ithaca and London: Cornell University Press, 1996).

74. Cornell calls for "imaginary projection" that helps women articulate their rights to individuation and bodily integrity, yet she seems to have a hard time imagining the fetus's rights except as future "imaginary children." See *The Imaginary Domain*, 32. For a fascinating history of the construction of the "fetus," see Barbara Duden, *Disembodying Women: Perspectives on Pregnancy and the Unborn*, trans. Lee Hoinacki (Cambridge: Harvard University Press, 1993).

75. Seery, *Political Theory for Mortals*, 190.

76. Carol Gilligan, *In a Different Voice: Psychological Theory and Women's Development* (Cambridge: Harvard University Press, 1982).

77. "Claire's inability to articulate her moral position stems in part from the fact that hers is a contextual judgment, bound to the particulars of time and place, contingent always on 'that mother' and that 'unborn child' and thus resisting a categorical formulation. To her, the possibilities of imagination outstrip the capacity

for generalization. But this sense of being unable to verbalize or explain the rationale for her participation in abortion counseling, an inability that could reflect the inadequacy of her moral thought, could also reflect the fact that she finds in the world no validation of the position she is trying to convey, a position that is neither pro-life nor pro-choice but based on a recognition of the continuing connection between the life of the mother and the life of the child." See Gilligan, In a Different Voice, 58–59. Gilligan seems to slip here, namely, by calling the fetus a "child," but it remains unclear how Claire continues a relational, caring connection with an unborn or an aborted fetus.

78. Hardacre begins her book with a long passage from Ann Rice's The Witching Hour, which describes a number of movies with a "Fetuses in Hell" motif. Note, however, that a male character, Michael, is brooding about the death of an aborted fetus and, unable to forget it, he starts remembering movies with images of fetuses in them.

79. See my description of the Final Position in Political Theory for Mortals. That position, I contend, avoids the outright masculinism of Rawls's Original Position by sketching a relational notion of face-to-face, discursive accountability among "shades" in a land of the dead: "Shades can recognize other shades in their former personhood—or at least their former gender and racial attributes are discernible— since their former bodies have not been abstracted into lifeless souls but rather, as shades, bear the accumulated marks of past lives" (Political Theory for Mortals, 160).

80. Hardacre is probably right to worry that "fetocentric discourse" usually works to the detriment of women's choice in abortion (e. g., the essays in The Silent Subject), but I do not think that a Gilliganesque imaginary conversation with the dead must be necessarily haunting to women. LaFleur, for a counterexample, points out that gift giving to the dead can often accrue benefits to the givers, so that guilt and gratitude shade into one another. See Hardacre, Marketing the Menacing Fetus in Japan, 3–6; LaFleur, Liquid Life, 143.

81. Or what Connolly calls "the spiritualization of enmity." See Why I am Not a Secularist, 161.

82. "Politics does not now become reducible to metaphysical debate . . . and often enough this dimension can be placed in abeyance to defuse a political debate or negotiate a difficult settlement. But it is often pertinent to place such questions on the register of public debate when issues appear such as the right to die, abortion, gender politics. . . . For in these domains today some parties to the debate already assert a general metaphysical orientation as if it were unquestionable, while a variety of liberals and secularists hesitate to contest the certainty of these assumptions actively" (ibid. 185).

CHAPTER 6

1. Daniel W. Conway, Nietzsche's Dangerous Game: Philosophy in the Twilight of the Idols (Cambridge: Cambridge University Press, 1997).

2. Daniel W. Conway, "Solving the Problem of Socrates: Nietzsche's Zarathustra as Political Irony," Political Theory 16: 2 (May 1988): 257–80; John E. Seery, "Politics as Ironic Community: On the Themes of Descent and Return in Plato's Republic," Political Theory 16: 2 (May 1988): 229–56; "The Demise of Western Culture," with

Daniel Conway, *Curricular Reform: Narratives of Interdisciplinary Humanities Programs*, 89–113; *The Politics of Irony: Essays in Self-Betrayal*, ed. and intro. Daniel W. Conway and John E. Seery (New York: St. Martin's; London: Macmillan, 1992).

3. Friedrich Nietzsche, *Beyond Good and Evil*, ed. and trans. Walter Kaufmann (New York: Viking Penguin, 1982), 205.

4. Conway, *Nietzsche's Dangerous Game*, 95.

5. Weber, "Science as a Vocation," *From Max Weber: Essays in Sociology*, 156.

CHAPTER 7

1. Jean Baudrillard, *America*, trans. Chris Turner (London and New York: Verso, 1988), 85.

2. Of course, there are those academics, including some keen to irony, who seem to believe that almost everything they write is of great political consequence, hence, some purport to make a transition from irony to politics too smoothly for my tastes. Such is my worry about Linda Hutcheon's book—which in many respects is superb— yet her notion of politics seems too textually precious. See Linda Hutcheon, *Irony's Edge: The Theory and Politics of Irony* (London and New York: Routledge, 1995).

3. Richard Rorty, *Contingency, Irony, and Solidarity* (Cambridge: Cambridge University Press, 1989).

4. Paul Rudnick and Kurt Andersen, "This Is the Irony Epidemic," *Spy Magazine* (March 1989); Alex Ross, "The Politics of Irony," *The New Republic* (November 8, 1993): 22–31.

5. Beth Pinsker, "Sonnenfeld's 'MiB' Takes Walk on the Wry Side," *Inland Daily Bulletin*, July 9, 1997, p. A6.

6. Thomas Mann, *Reflections of a Nonpolitical Man*, trans. Walter D. Morris (New York: Frederick Ungar, 1983).

7. See my "Political Irony and World War: A Rereading of Thomas Mann's *Betrachtungen*," *Soundings* 73: 1 (spring 1990): 5–29.

8. Readers might want to suggest other contenders for the title, and I have no problem with that. Grant Wood appeals to me as an American political ironist, because *American Gothic* is so prominent and yet so apparently misunderstood— which suggests that the irony, always risky, also is somehow working. A more obvious example of an American irony advocate is Randolph Bourne. See his "The Life of Irony," in *Youth and Life* (Cambridge: Riverside Press, 1913), 106–17. For a wonderful analysis of Bourne's own self-masking, see Leslie J. Vaughan, *Randolph Bourne and the Politics of Cultural Radicalism* (Lawrence: University of Kansas Press, 1997), esp. 42–56.

9. I tried to define irony in "Irony: A Politics of the Page," in *Political Returns: Irony in Politics and Theory from Plato to the Antinuclear Movement* (Boulder, San Francisco, and Oxford: Westview Press, 1990), 161–225; more recently, see Leslie Paul Thiele, "Ideology and Irony," in *Thinking Politics: Perspectives in Ancient, Modern, and Postmodern Political Theory* (Chatham: Chatham House, 1997), 213–38.

10. Of the three, Benton, Curry, and Wood, only Wood worked in the Midwest.

11. Robert Hughes also contends that the term *regionalism* is dubious, based on a slipshod history; see *American Visions: The Epic History of Art in America* (New York: Knopf, 1997), 437–38.

12. Note that in the most recent Wood exhibition in Davenport, the curators present Wood as a "master" of European influences; see Brady M. Roberts, James M. Dennis, James S. Horns, Helen Mar Parkin, *Grant Wood: An American Master Revealed* (San Francisco: Pomegranate Artbooks, 1995). James M. Dennis recently has published a book about the dubious term *regionalist*. See James M. Dennis, *Renegade Regionalists: The Modern Independence of Grant Wood, Thomas Hart Benton, and John Steuart Curry* (Madison: University of Wisconsin Press, 1998).

13. "His transformation from an all-purpose painter to a dedicated regionalist was a slow, meandering process spread over a period of three or four years." See Wanda M. Corn, *Grant Wood: The Regionalist Vision* (New Haven: Yale University Press, 1983), 25.

14. Darrell Garwood, *Artist in Iowa: A Life of Grant Wood* (New York: Norton, 1944), 88.

15. Grant Wood, "Wood, Hard-Bitten" *The Art Digest*, (February 1, 1936): 18. Wood once explained that by the cow comment he simply meant that he preferred working with his hands.

16. Grant Wood, *Revolt against the City* (Iowa City: Clio Press, 1935); republished in James M. Dennis, *Grant Wood: A Study in American Art and Culture* (New York: Viking, 1975), 229–35. Most scholars believe that Wood's friend, Frank Luther Mott, probably had a hand in writing a good part of the essay (see Corn, *Grant Wood*, 153, n. 85).

17. "Grant Wood Denies Reputation as Glamour Boy Painter" *Los Angeles Times*, February 19, 1940, Part II, p. 1; in Wood scrapbooks, Archives of American Art, Smithsonian Institution (hereafter referred to as AAA), 1216/8.

18. The main exception is *Stone City*, although Wood once said that he never liked that piece.

19. Robert Hughes, "American Visions," *Time* magazine, (Special Edition 1997): 22.

20. Nan Wood Graham quotes her brother on his move toward Gothic painters: "Here I was on dangerous ground, because story-telling pictures can so easily become illustrative and depend on their titles." See Nan Wood Graham, with John Zug and Julie Jensen McDonald, *My Brother, Grant Wood* (Iowa City: State Historical Society of Iowa, 1993), 67.

21. "Open Forum," *Des Moines Sunday Register*, December 21, 1930. AAA, 1216/286.

22. Wanda M. Corn, "American Gothic: The Making of a National Icon," *Grant Wood: The Regionalist Vision*, 129–42.

23. Ibid., 131. Hughes repeats (without attribution) this same line, apparently from Corn, but the evidence does not seem to fit the claim. The *New York Herald Tribune*, on November 23, 1930, described *American Gothic* as imbued with "genuine feeling" and a "sincerity" (AAA, 1216/284); the *Chicago Daily News*, on October 29, 1930, called the painting "one of the finest records of Americana that has ever been painted" (AAA, 1216/284). Corn cites New York criticism of Wood's "too sweet charm and decorative mannerisms." All of the Iowa letters to editors voicing outrage at the painting would suggest that they saw the satire and social criticism in the painting and felt it was directed at them—and they did not like it. Corn

seems to conflate Midwestern admirers and defenders of Wood with an anti-satire or oblivious-to-satire crowd. See Corn, *Grant Wood*, 46, 153, n. 88.

24. Matthew Baigell, *The American Scene: American Paintings of the 1930's* (New York: Praeger, 1974), 110.

25. Dennis, *Grant Wood*, 78.

26. Adeline Taylor, "Easterners Look Wistfully at Midwest," *Cedar Rapids Gazette*, October 21, 1943 cited in Dennis, *Grant Wood*, 135.

27. Hughes, "American Visions," 22.

28. "Gertrude Stein Praises Grant Wood," *Montrose* (Iowa) *Mirror*, July 17, 1934.

29. Ibid.

30. Dorothy Dougherty, "The Right and Wrong of America," *Cedar Rapids Gazette*, September 6, 1942.

31. Ibid.

32. Ibid.

33. Garwood, *Artist in Iowa*, 124.

34. "Iowans Get Mad," *The Art Digest* (January 1, 1931): 9.

35. Graham, *My Brother, Grant Wood*, 76.

36. Garwood traces Wood's interest in Gothic architecture to an early period of study at the Minneapolis Handicraft Guild, where Ernest Batchelder promoted a revival of the Gothic in America. See Garwood, *Artist in Iowa*, 33.

37. Gothic references in other works by Wood include the Veterans Memorial stained glass, a window in *Stone City*, a window in *Honorary Degree*, and a 1928 pen-and-ink drawing; Wood also installed a Gothic window in the Green Mansion near Stone City. Nan Graham Wood reports that Wood showed her pictures of old Gothic stone carvings from a cathedral in France before he asked her to pose for *American Gothic* (AAA, 1216/286).

38. Edward B. Rowan, "The Artists of Iowa," November 7, 1930; AAA, 1216/285.

39. Grant Wood seemed to suggest at one point that *American Gothic* was merely a study in verticality, and that he intended to do a companion piece in the horizontal lines of the mission-style bungalow. While it might well have been true that Wood initially was attracted to the Gothic style for those vertical lines, it would be reductive to see the final product as merely such a formal study. Letter to the editor from Grant Wood, printed in "The Sunday *Register's* Open Forum," *Des Moines Register*, December 21, 1930, AAA 1216/286.

40. Ibid.

41. Dennis, *Grant Wood*, 239, n. 19.

42. Corn points out that Wood's best friends in Iowa City were writers, not artists. See *Grant Wood*, 44.

43. Matthew Baigell, "Grant Wood Revisited," *Art Journal* 26: 2 (winter 1966–1967): 117.

44. Corn, *Grant Wood*, 133.

45. Brady M. Roberts, "The European Roots of Regionalism: Grant Wood's Stylistic Synthesis," *Grant Wood: An American Master Revealed* (San Francisco: Pomegranate Books, 1995), 41.

46. *The Des Moines Register*, March 22, 1996. In her own book, Corn cites all second-hand reports, from sister Nan, Arnold Pyle, and Park Rinard, about Wood's intentions to paint a daughter, not a wife. Wood, however, might have had reasons to desexualize the painting in conversations with all three of these people. See Corn, *Grant Wood*, 157.

47. See especially, Jacques Derrida, "Restitutions," in *The Truth in Painting*, trans. Geoff Bennington and Ian McLeod (Chicago: University of Chicago Press, 1987), 255–382.

48. See, for instance, "American Gothic Is Explained to Grant High Pupils" (publication unknown), March 6, 1931, AAA, 1216/289.

49. "An Iowa Secret," *Art Digest* 8 (October 1933): 6; cited in Roberts, "The European Roots of Regionalism," *Grant Wood*, 41. My only question about this document is that when sister Nan posed for *American Gothic* she wasn't a "maiden" at the time. The slipup could perhaps reflect poorly on the authenticity of the quotation, but it also could indicate an interesting erasure or memory lapse on Wood's part: he perhaps remembers his sister as a spinster sitting in for another spinster. James Dennis cites the same passage as sufficient proof to establish that Wood's intent was simply to portray the woman as a wife. It should be noted that while Wood refers to a husband, he does not call the woman a wife in the passage. See Dennis, *Renegade Regionalists*, 101.

50. Graham, *My Brother, Grant Wood*, 75.

51. Again, the citation is *Des Moines Register*, December 30, 1930, AAA, 1216/286. That interview could be based on another document that I have not recovered, yet the aforementioned newspaper clipping was part of Nan Wood Graham's scrapbook collection.

52. Also note that Nan Wood Graham, a lifelong advocate of the "daughter" interpretation, reveals in her book that Grant Wood felt that writer Arthur Millier had the "best understanding of the painting," and in the quotation she cites, Millier refers to the "farmwife's apron." See Graham, *My Brother*, Grant Wood, 75–76.

53. For references to Suckow and Sigmund, see Corn, *Grant Wood*, 133, 156, n. 15, 157, n. 17.

54. Or at least that is the speculation between Nan and her mother, but they do not ask Grant point blank about their "Cedar Rapids spinster" theory. See Graham, *My Brother*, Grant Wood, 74.

55. Corn, *Grant Wood*, 133.

56. Sylvester O. Ogbechie has suggested to me that the woman's head etched on the brooch, echoing the questionable hair theme in the painting, seems to recall the theme of Medusa, which would underscore the double-crossing lines of gender trouble in the painting—since Medusa turned men into stones. Dennis claims that the brooch represents Dianna, the antique symbol of untainted feminine youth. See Dennis, *Renegade Regionalists*, 99–101.

57. Garwood explains the evolution of *American Gothic* thus: "So what had started out to be a farmer and his wife became a small-town businessman and his daughter." Yet earlier Garwood recalls that Wood had been fascinated with a story about a farmer whose wife had died. See *Artist in Iowa*, 100, 124.

58. I have presented *American Gothic* to three classes of Upward Bound high school students from Pomona, California, and students from all three classes

mentioned almost immediately that they saw "abuse" in the woman's eyes in the painting.

59. Ruth Suckow, "Best of the Lot," *Smart Set* 69 (November 1922): 5–36, cited in Corn, *Grant Wood*, 156.

60. I am deeply grateful to Joseph Acorn of Alamo, California, for alerting me to the possibility of a "Lot" allusion in *American Gothic* that might tie into the spinster theme, and also for all of his inspired commentary on the subject, generously and freely volunteered.

61. Garwood, *Artist in Iowa*, 112.

62. Corn is very good at revealing sexual motifs in the painting, and she points out that political and sexual themes pop up in the second life of the painting as a national icon, but she tends to suggest that the latter phenomenon does not derive from the former, or at least such commentaries and parodies do not follow from Wood's intentions: "What commentators saw in the image and what the artist had in mind when he made the painting were not exactly the same." If, however, the painting is "about" suppression in its first iteration, then popular ventilation could be more intimately related to the author's understanding of the painting. See Corn, *Grant Wood*, 132.

63. Hughes, "American Visions," 439; Hughes also repeated this claim in his interview with Brian Lamb on C-SPAN, July 20, 1997; the interview can be accessed at http://www.booknotes.org.

64. Hughes, "American Vision," 442.

65. *Author's note*: since this writing, I have been in correspondence with Henry Adams, who has uncovered other rumored evidence of Wood's homosexuality.

66. At the least, Hughes would need to explore the *American Gothic* references in the *Rocky Horror Picture Show*.

67. "Grant Wood Denies Reputation As Glamour Boy of Painters," *Los Angeles Times*, Feb. 19, 1940, AAA 1216 (no frame number; see scrapbook #4, 1939–1947).

68. Derrida rightly warns against lending too much authority to such interpretative substitutions; see "Restitutions"; also see my discussion of his analysis, in John E. Seery, *Political Theory for Mortals: Shades of Justice, Images of Death* (Ithaca and London: Cornell University Press, 1996), 129–31.

69. "A topic of conversation of many tea tables and boudoir babbles is Grant Wood, Cedar Rapids artist. But he paints on and on and maintains a discreet silence about marriage"; "There Have Been Brides and Brides but Bachelors Still Elude the Fair Sex." (AAA, 1216/245).

70. Nan claims that her brother left the great love of his life behind in Paris, a woman named Margaret, but then Nan expresses confusion about why there is not a single reference about Margaret in any of Grant's correspondence. See Graham, *My Brother, Grant Wood*, 45–46. Moreover, Nan speculates that the main reason that Wood did not marry Margaret was financial; likewise, the main grounds she cites for her brother's divorce from Sara are financial (ibid., 149). Corn skims over the "bachelor" issue, explaining that "Wood never took time for romance." See *Grant Wood*, 47.

71. Garwood, *Artist in Iowa*, 60. In Nan's account, Frances Prescott quickly overcomes her skepticism about Wood, and the Pied Piper comment is presented as perfectly innocent. See Graham, *My Brother, Grant Wood*, 30–31.

72. Garwood, *Artist in Iowa*, 73.

73. Ibid., 91.

74. Ibid., 221.

75. Ibid., 79; Nan explains that Wood bought the cameo for his mother because it reminded him of Nan. See Graham, *My Brother, Grant Wood*, 68.

76. "Wood's stern and rigid father lurks behind some of the artist's most memorable images, all of which are, in some way, tenuous in their affections. The gaunt, humorless man in *American Gothic* . . . reflect Wood's memories of his authoritarian father." See Corn, *Grant Wood*, 3. On his deathbed, Wood talked about wanting to paint his father's portrait as a companion piece to *Woman with Plants*. See Garwood, *Artist in Iowa*, 246.

77. Nan ends her book: "Grant had been both brother and father to me." See *My Brother, Grant Wood*, 181.

78. Corn, *Grant Wood*, 3.

79. At the beginning of the Brian Lamb interview, Hughes explains that he has been to a therapist for the first time in his life in order to treat depression. After finishing the PBS series and the book *American Visions*, he suffered from a bout during which he felt that he had not accomplished much in his life. Immediately the conversation turns to a subject of Grant Wood's alleged homosexuality.

80. For the photographic citations in *American Gothic*, see Corn, *Grant Wood*, 129–30.

81. Corn, *Grant Wood*, 139.

82. Ibid., 136.

83. Ibid. Paul Newman features an American Gothic image on the packaging of some of his food products. It is probably worth mentioning that early in this design campaign, the image included likenesses of Newman and his wife, Joanne Woodward; in the more recent version, however, the wife is replaced by Newman's daughter, Nell.

84. Ibid., 141.

85. Jeffrey Toobin, "American Gothic: What Rushes into the Newsless Void?" *The New Yorker* (July 28, 1997): 4–5.

86. Hughes, "American Visions," 422.

87. Garwood says that Wood had been a Democrat all his life who gloated over the reelection of Woodrow Wilson; Nan says that he had been a political independent who had become a Democrat by the end of his life. Garwood's claim that Wood talked freely about his politics only within a very small group seems to account for his sister's misreading of his enthusiasm for politics. Dennis, who interviewed Graham about such matters, says that Wood had no clear-cut partisan convictions in politics, but that he remained "essentially a liberal despite the antiprogressivist mood in the 1920's." See Garwood, *Artist in Iowa*, 134; Dennis, *Grant Wood*, 240 n. 13, 241, n. 22.

88. Garwood attributes this comment to Hazel Barnes. See Garwood, *Artist in Iowa*, 135.

89. Dennis, *Grant Wood*, 241 n. 6. In 1939, Wood painted a poster for the British War Relief but later refused to do one for America First. See Garwood, *Artist in Iowa*, 233.

90. "Grant was so isolated politically that he had grown accustomed to keeping silent on the subject—so much so that many of his friends thought he wasn't interested in politics." See Garwood, *Artist in Iowa*, 135.

91. Dennis, *Grant Wood*, 109.

92. Ibid., 112.

93. Ibid.

94. "This War to Give America Art Leadership, Wood Says," *Milwaukee News Sentinel*, January 7, 1940, cited in Dennis, *Grant Wood*, 112.

95. Michel Foucault, *The Order of Things: An Archaeology of the Human Sciences* (New York: Random House, 1970).

96. Paul de Man associated irony with *parabasis*. See "The Rhetoric of Temporality," *Interpretation: Theory and Practice*, ed. Charles S. Singleton (Baltimore: Johns Hopkins University Press, 1969), 199–200.

97. Cf. my analysis of the "comic reflexivity" of the prisoner in Plato's allegory of the cave and also Freccero's similar analysis of Dante the pilgrim standing before the gates of Hell. Seery, *Political Theory for Mortals*, 64, and John Freccero, "Infernal Irony: The Gates of Hell," *Dante: The Poetics of Conversion* (Cambridge: Harvard University Press, 1986), 93–109.

98. Cavell, *Conditions Handsome and Unhandsome*, 2ff.

99. Survival issues (e. g., *Victorian Survival*) and the passing of time are clearly recurring motifs in Wood's work. Psychoanalysts might ask of the above account whether Wood was trying to father the future out of his own spinsterdom. Along those lines, I might point out that Wood refused to adopt Sara's son after they married.

100. Hughes is therefore right, I believe, to read some distance between *American Gothic* and himself, but he takes that distance to be geographical, whereas I suggest it is temporal.

101. Death figures prominently in other ways in Wood's career. Wood received his first job after high school by answering an ad for a mortuary night watchman. Hazel Brown reports that young Wood was fascinated with burial places in Europe, and he lingered in cemeteries at other times too. Later, David Turner called upon Wood to help with the job of turning Sinclair House into a mortuary. The Turners supported Wood, and John B. Turner is featured as a "pioneer" in Wood's painting of him. See Graham, *My Brother, Grant Wood*, 19; Brown, *Grant Wood and Marvin Cone* (Ames; Iowa State University Press, 1972), 15, 32.

102. Harry L. Engle, *The Palette and Chisel*, January 1931, AAA, 1216/297.

103. Graham, *My Brother*, Grant Wood, 125.

104. Corn, *Grant Wood*, 101.

105. Baigell, "Grant Wood Revisited," 116.

106. The memorial features the goddess Republic presiding over six figures of the country's major wars.

107. *The Overmantel* seems to be spoofing a suburban drive to affect an early American heritage.

108. *Arbor Day* was painted to commemorate two Cedar Rapids schoolteachers.

109. Dennis links this painting to colonial motifs. See *Grant Wood*, 116.

110. A painting about modern technology.

111. From Lewis's *Main Street* description of the "booster" character: "Mr. Blausser . . . a born leader, divinely intended to be a congressman but deflected to the more lucrative honors of real-estate."

112. A painting of the executive secretary of the Cedar Rapids Chamber of Commerce.

113. A war relief poster.

114. Dennis makes an excellent case for the political context of the "maternalism" of this painting and for maternalist themes running throughout Wood's career. See Dennis, *Renegade Regionalists*, 97ff.

115. Wood, "Revolt against the City," 234.

116. Corn explains that Wood had been very taken with an article by Howard Mumford Jones on the consequences of debunking American traditions. Jones called on artists and writers to develop a new kind of patriotism that would bring back the great legends and myths, albeit without "romanticizing" them. Wood's response, suggests Corn, was to treat the fables as fables, so that a more informed public might be able to navigate for itself between debunking and romanticism and yet still "accept" these tales in a neopatriotic manner. See Corn, *Grant Wood*, 121–22; Howard Mumford Jones, "Patriotism—But How?" *Atlantic Monthly* 162 (November 1938): 585–92.

117. Dennis, *Grant Wood*, 109.

118. Adeline Taylor, "Grant Wood's Penetrating Eye and Skillful Brush to Deal Next with Some of America's Pet Institutions," *Cedar Rapids Gazette*, September 25, 1932; AAA, 1216/357.

119. Kathy E. Ferguson, *The Man Question: Visions of Subjectivity in Feminist Theory* (Berkeley and Los Angeles: University of California Press, 1993), 30–35.

120. "Grant Wood Explains Why He Prefers to Remain in the Middle West," *Cedar Rapids Sunday Gazette and Republican*, March 22, 1931; cited in Dennis, *Grant Wood*, 197.

121. Wood, "Revolt against the City," 235.

122. Gregory Vlastos, *Socrates, Ironist and Moral Philosopher* (Ithaca: Cornell University Press, 1991), 44.

123. "Grant . . . had a firm belief that if you expose people of average intelligence to good art and good taste, they will react appropriately, and they are completely sold when they are convinced the discovery is entirely their own. Grant played this gentle trick in many ways, many times." See Hazel E. Brown, *Grant Wood and Marvin Cone*, 65. One wonders what Wood would say about *Men in Black* and David Letterman, whether today's "pop" irony would satisfy his desire for a democratic art form "with the possibilities of living through the ages."

124. Corn, *Grant Wood*, 25.

125. Corn tends to periodize these tendencies, claiming that by the late 1930's, Wood presented his art as reflecting American democracy, mainly therefore as a response to criticism that regionalism was parochial and xenophobic.

126. See Dennis on the dangers of misreading the "mimetic" ironies of Lewis and Wood. *Grant Wood*, in Dennis, 128–29. Hutcheon warns that the risks of misinterpretating irony frequently reinforce its conservative character; I think, however, that she is insufficiently appreciative of those risks and of ironically created communities. See Hutcheon, *Irony's Edge*, 27 ff. For an analysis of the ways in which

parodic repetitions sometimes can become politically disruptive, see Judith Butler, *Gender Trouble: Feminisim and the Subversion of Identity* (London and New York: Routledge, 1990), esp. 139–49.

127. Brown, *Grant Wood and Marvin Cone*, 100–101.

CHAPTER 8

1. Brian Stonehill, associate producer and translator, "Francois Truffaut: 25 Years, 25 Films," Laser on disc (Voyager: The Criterion Collection, 1993).

2. Brian Stonehill, *Understanding D. W. Griffith* (Claremont: Pomona College/Stonehill Multimedia, 1998).

3. Michael Rogin, "The Sword Became a Flashing Vision: D. W. Griffith's The Birth of a Nation," Ronald Reagan, the Movie and Other Episodes in Political Demonology (Berkeley: University of California Press, 1987), 190–235.

4. Ibid., 199.

5. Marshall McLuhan, *The Medium Is the Massage* (New York: Bantam Books, 1967).

6. Stanley Cavell, *The World Viewed: Reflections on the Ontology of Film* (New York: Viking, 1971).

7. Alexander Nehamas, "Serious Watching," *The Interpretive Turn: Philosophy, Science, Culture*, ed. David R. Hiley, James F. Bohman, and Richard M. Shusterman (Ithaca: Cornell University Press, 1991).

8. Brian Stonehill, "Media Literacy Means Better, Smarter TV Viewing," *The Christian Science Monitor*, July 26, 1996, p. 18.

9. Jürgen Habermas, *Between Facts and Norms: Contributions to a Discourse Theory of Law and Democracy*, trans. William Rehg (Cambridge, MIT Press, 1996).

10. Jacques Derrida, *Spectres of Marx*, trans. Peggy Kamuf (New York: Routledge, 1994).

11. Brian Stonehill, "Slow Motion Dangerous in Courtroom," *The Christian Science Monitor*, February, 23, 1993, p. 19.

12. Brian Stonehill, "Take It From Aristotle," *Los Angeles Times*, February 20, 1995, p. 5.

13. Edmund Newton, "A Need to 'Watch Out for What We Watch,'" *Los Angeles Times*, March 25, 1990, p. J1.

14. Brian Stonehill, "It Wouldn't Hurt Films to Make Presidents Life-Size," *Newsday* March 7, 1996.

15. Brian Stonehill, "The Mickey Moused Media," *Los Angeles Times*, p. B9

16. Brian Stonehill, "The Poets of Pasadena," *Los Angeles Times*, July 9, 1997, p. B7.

17. John Cage, "Art and Overpopulation" (unpublished piece).

18. Pomona College refers to its general education skills curriculum as the PAC (Perception, Analysis, and Communication) system.

19. Brian Stonehill, *The Self-Conscious Novel: Artifice in Fiction From Joyce to Pynchon* (Philadelphia: University of Pennsylvania Press, 1988).

20. Daniel Wood, "Aristotle Had TV Pegged 23 Centuries Ago," *Los Angeles Times*, November 8, 1989, p. 11.

21. Kathleen Fitzpatrick, "The Exhaustion of Literature: Novels, Computers, and the Threat of Obsolescence." *Contemporary Literature* 43.4 (forthcoming winter 2002).

CHAPTER 9

1. The comedian, John Cleese, received an honorary degree and gave a short address at Pomona's graduation ceremony on the day following Class Day.

2. Karl Kohn, "Sax, for 4," (Claremont: Karl Kohn Music Prints, 1996).

3. Ralph Waldo Emerson, "Friendship," *The Essays of Ralph Waldo Emerson* (Cambridge and London: Harvard University Press, 1979), 111–27.

4. The legendary Penny Lee Dean, holder of thirteen world swimming records, coaches the women's swim team at Pomona. See her *Open Water Swimming: A Complete Guide for Distance Swimmers and Triathletes* (Champaign, Ill: Human Kinetics, 1998).

5. Claremont, the home of Pomona College and the Claremont Colleges, is baseball home-run hitter Mark McGwire's hometown.

6. We had compared Pinsky's *An Explanation of America* to Whitman's *Leaves of Grass*. See Robert Pinsky, *An Explanation of America* (Princeton: Princeton University Press, 1979) and Walt Whitman, *Leaves of Grass*, ed. Malcolm Cowley (New York: Penguin, 1959).

7. William Wordsworth, "Lines, composed a few miles above Tintern Abbey on revisiting the banks of the Wye during a tour," in *The Complete Poetical Works of William Wordsworth* (New York: Thomas Y. Crowell, 1892), 239–44, lines 30–35.

CHAPTER 10

1. Judith Butler, "Contingent Foundations: Feminism and the Question of 'Postmodernism,' " *Praxis International* 11: (July 1991): 150–65. The paper was first presented in a different version at the Greater Philadelphia Philosophy Consortium in 1990.

2. Judith Butler and Joan W. Scott, eds., *Feminists Theorize the Political* (New York and London: Routledge, 1992), 3–21; Seyla Benhabib, Judith Butler, Drucilla Cornell, and Nancy Fraser, with introduction by Linda Nicholson, *Feminist Contentions: A Philosophical Exchange* (New York and London: Routledge, 1995), 35–57; see also *Twentieth Century Political Theory: A Reader*, ed. Stephen Eric Bronner (New York and London: Routledge, 1997), 248–58, It should be noted that Butler subsequently has distanced herself from the original essay. See Butler, "For a Careful Reading," *Feminist Contentions*, 127–43, esp. 127.

3. Butler, "Contingent Foundations," in Butler and Scott, *Feminists Theorize the Political*, 3.

4. Ibid., 7.

5. Ibid., 16.

6. Butler later clarifies that she is not presenting a "theory of the self" but is more interested in gender identities. See "For a Careful Reading," 133.

7. Butler, "Contingent Foundations," 7.

8. Butler, "For a Careful Reading," 131.

9. Butler, "Contingent Foundations," 7, 17.

10. Butler, "For a Careful Reading," 131.

11. Butler, "Contingent Foundations," 16; "For a Careful Reading," 131.

12. "To call a presupposition into question is not the same as doing away with it; rather, it is to free it up from its metaphysical lodgings in order to occupy and to serve very different political aims." See Butler, "Contingent Foundations," 17.

13. Robert B. Reich, *The Work of Nations: Preparing Ourselves for 21st Century Capitalism* (New York: Alfred A. Knopf, 1991).

14. Kirstie McClure, "The Issue of Foundations: Scientized Politics, Politicized Science, and Feminist Critical Practice," in Butler and Scott, *Feminists Theorize the Political*, 341–68, esp. 365.

15. See, for example, Evan Simpson, ed., *Anti-Foundationalism and Practical Reasoning: Conversations between Hermeneutics and Analysis* (Edmonton, Alberta, Canada: Academic Printing, 1987); Stephen Crook, *Modernist Radicalism and Its Aftermath: Foundationalism and Anti-Foundationalism in Radical Social Theory* (London and New York: Routledge, 1991); Barbara Herrnstein Smith, *Belief and Resistance: Dynamic of Contemporary Intellectual Controversy* (Cambridge: Harvard University Press, 1997).

16. Stanley Fish, "Anti-Foundationalism, Theory Hope, and the Teaching of Composition," *Doing What Comes Naturally: Change, Rhetoric, and the Practice of Theory in Literary and Legal Studies* (Duke and London: Duke University Press, 1989), 342–55; esp. 342.

17. Ibid., 342–43.

18. Ibid., 343.

19. Ibid., 345.

20. Ibid., 344.

21. Ibid., 345.

22. Evan Simpson, "Colloquimur, ergo sumus," *Anti-Foundationalism and Practical Reasoning: Conversations between Hermeneutics and Analysis*, (Edmonton: Academic Printing and Publishing, 1987), 1–2.

23. Richard Rorty, *Philosophy and the Mirror of Nature* (Princeton: Princeton University Press, 1979), 159.

24. Ibid., 162–63.

25. Ibid., 163.

26. Ibid., 12–13, 39, n. 6, 159, n. 40.

27. Ibid., 159.

28. Ibid., 161.

29. Charlene Haddock Seigfried, "Like Bridges without Piers: Beyond the Foundationalist Metaphor," *Antifoundationalism Old and New*, ed. Tom Rockmore and Beth J. Singer (Philadelphia: Temple University Press, 1992), 143–64.

30. C. S. Peirce, *Collected Papers of Charles Sanders Peirce*, ed. Charles Hartshorne, Paul Weiss, and Arthur Burks (Cambridge: Harvard University Press, 1960), 1:1.

31. William James, *The Principles of Psychology*, in *The Works of William James*, ed. Frederick H. Burkhardt, Fredson Bowers, and Ignas K. Skrupskelis, 3 vols. (Cambridge: Harvard University Press, 1981), 2:656–57.

32. Seigfried, "Like Bridges without Piers: Beyond the Foundationalist Metaphor," 144.

33. With some minor tweaking, I am borrowing the term *political constructivism* largely from Rawls. The tweaking is needed, insofar as his original position still resembles an Edenic form of prepolitical theorizing. For instance, Rawls insists that "political constructivism also holds that if a conception of justice is correctly founded on correctly stated principles and conceptions of practical reason, then that conception of justice is reasonable for a constitutional regime" (p. 126). As I attempt to show from the discussions of Christine de Pizan and Hannah Arendt below, political construction materials can be based on *poiesis*, not simply *phronesis*. See John Rawls, *Political Liberalism* (New York: Columbia University Press, 1993), 89–129.

34. Butler, "Contingent Foundations," 19.

35. Ibid., 17, 16.

36. Ibid., 129, 133.

37. Ibid., 12, 20, n.1.

38. Richard Rorty, *Consequences of Pragmatism (Essays: 1972–1980)* (Minneapolis: University of Minnesota Press, 1982), 144.

39. Christine de Pizan, *The Book of the City of Ladies*, trans. Earl Jeffrey Richards (New York: Persea Books, 1982), 16.

40. Margaret Brabant and Michael Brint make the point that whereas Augustine identifies spiritually with Aeneas's quest, Christine identifies with Dido as the architect and builder of a great city. See Brabant and Brint, "Identity and Difference in Christine de Pizan's *Cité des Dames*," in Margaret Brabant, ed., *Politics, Gender, and Genre: The Political Thought of Christine de Pizan* (Boulder: Westview Press, 1992), 209–10.

41. Giovanni Boccaccio, *Concerning Famous Women (De Claris Mulieribus)*, trans. Guido A. Guarino (New Brunswick: Rutgers University Press, 1963).

42. Patricia A. Phillippy, "Establishing Authority: Boccaccio's *De Claris Mulieribus* and Christine de Pizan's *Le livre de la cité des dames*," in *The Selected Writings of Christine de Pizan*, ed. Renate Blumenfeld-Kosinski (New York: Norton, 1997), 329–61.

43. De Pizan, *The Book of the City of Ladies*, 66.

44. Phillippy, "Establishing Authority," 344.

45. John Freccero, *Dante: The Poetics of Conversion* (Cambridge: Harvard University Press, 1986).

46. See Kate Langdon Forhan, "Reflecting Heroes: Christine de Pizan and the Mirror Tradition," *The City of Scholars: New Approaches to Christine de Pizan*, ed. Margarete Zimmermann and Dina De Rentiis (New York: Walter de Gruyter, 1994), 189–96.

47. See Dana R. Villa, "Hannah Arendt: Modernity, Alienation, and Critique," in *Hannah Arendt and the Meaning of Politics*, ed. Craig Calhoun and John McGowan (Minneapolis: University of Minnesota Press, 1997), 179–206.

48. Arendt also discusses Virgil and the *Aeneid* in connection with Herman Broch's *Death of Virgil*. See Arendt, "No Longer and Not Yet," *The Nation*, September 2, 1946, pp. 300–302; Arendt, "Herman Broch: 1886–1951," trans. Richard Winston, in *Men in Dark Times* (San Diego: Harcourt Brace Jovanovich, 1955), 111–51.

49. Hannah Arendt, *The Life of the Mind* , *Part I*, *Thinking* (San Diego: Harcourt Brace Jovanovich, 1977), 152. Some careful readers of Arendt might insist that I should qualify this statement to read the purest form of *Roman* politics, but that historicizing slant would elide the importance of this particular passage. Especially noteworthy here is that Arendt distinguishes between early Roman philosophy, which she says is exclusively political, the purest form of which she finds in Virgil, and later Roman philosophy, which becomes ossified, thus extinguishing the element of surprise that apparently is crucial to Arendt's sense of politicalness. Virgil's novelly creative appropriation of the Greeks is to be distinguished from later Roman, that is, quasiscientific or sacred appeals to Greek authority. In contrast, Virgil makes only a cameo appearance in Arendt's earlier essays on Roman authority. In focusing on Arendt's fascination with the pure politics of Virgil, I am not suggesting that she advocates some contemporary emulation of or imitative reliance on Virgil—but I do want to recover the buried idea that the past can be imaginatively embraced.

50. Hannah Arendt, *On Revolution* (New York: Penguin, 1963), 202.

51. Ibid., 202–203.

52. Ibid., 203.

53. Ibid., 204.

54. Ibid.

55. Arendt, *The Life of the Mind, Part 2, Willing*, 200–203; Arendt, *On Revolution*, 204–205.

56. Arendt, *On Revolution*, 205; *Willing*, 203.

57. Arendt, *Willing*, 206.

58. Arendt, *Willing*, 210; *On Revolution*, 206.

59. Arendt, *Willing*, 204; *On Revolution*, 205.

60. Arendt, *Willing*, 208; *On Revolution*, 206.

61. Arendt, *Willing*, 208; *On Revolution*, 206.

62. Arendt, *Willing*, 208.

63. Ibid.

64. Ibid., 208–9.

65. Arendt, *Willing*, 210; *On Revolution*, 206.

66. Arendt, *Willing*, 211; *On Revolution*, 209.

67. Arendt, *Willing*, 211.

68. Ibid., 214.

69. Ibid., 213.

70. Arendt, *On Revolution*, 210.

71. Arendt, *Willing*, 215.

72. Arendt, *On Revolution*, 208.

73. Ibid.

74. Ibid.

75. Arendt, *Willing*, 204; *On Revolution*, 209.

76. Arendt, *On Revolution*, 213.

77. Ibid., 211.

78. Ibid.

79. Arendt, *Willing*, 207; *On Revolution*, 212.

80. Arendt, *On Revolution*, 212.

81. Ibid.

82. Arendt, *Willing*, 216.
83. Arendt, *Willing*, 217; *On Revolution*, 211.
84. Arendt, *On Revolution*, 213–14.
85. Ibid., 214.
86. Arendt, *Willing*, 217.
87. See Dana R. Villa, *Arendt and Heidegger: The Fate of the Political* (Princeton: Princeton University Press, 1996).
88. Hannah Arendt, "What Is Authority?" *Between Past and Future* (New York: Viking, 1961), 140. I am aware that in her preface, Arendt denies that the subsequent essays contain any practical prescriptions: "The following six essays are such exercises, and their only aim is to gain experience in *how* to think; they do not contain prescriptions on what to think or which truths to hold. Least of all do they intend to retie the broken thread of tradition or to invent some newfangled surrogates with which to fill the gap between past and future" (p. 14; also see p. 141).
89. Ibid., 136.
90. Ibid., 95.
91. Ibid.
92. Ibid.
93. Ibid.
94. Arendt ended the original version of her essay with this paragraph on shifting groundworks. See Hannah Arendt, "What Was Authority?" in *Authority*, ed. Carl Friedrich (Cambridge: Harvard University Press, 1959), 81–112.
95. Hannah Arendt, "On Hannah Arendt," *Hannah Arendt: The Recovery of the Public World*, ed. Melvyn A. Hill (New York: St. Martin's Press, 1979), 336–37; see also 314.
96. Ibid., 336.
97. Arendt betrays her Edenic tendencies when writing about foundational walls; city walls are built in relation to nature, as a hedge against the encroachments of nature. See *Between Past and Future*, 286, n. 18.
98. Stan Spyros Draenos makes the important suggestion that perhaps we can emulate Arendt's example of thinking without a ground without, however, merely following in her footsteps. But that elusive exemplification still provides little political direction, whether direct or oblique. See Stan Spyros Draenos, "Thinking without a Ground: Hannah Arendt and the Contemporary Situation of Understanding," in *Hannah Arendt*, ed. Hill, 209–24.
99. Richard Rorty wishes that leftist academics would stop so much claptrap theorizing and attend instead to real political concerns. While I welcome his incisive critique of a visionless academic Left, his own political recommendations remain hamstrung by his inability or unwillingness to argue for his particular version of a less cruel, more egalitarian, anticommunist, pro-American style of liberal democracy. To him, such foundational requests smack of metaphysics, so he avoids explaining himself; yet he betrays and undercuts his own positive contributions when he keeps slipping back into the kind of academic infighting of which he so disapproves. My point is that there are alternative ways of establishing political foundations that may prove more effective at large than Rorty's personally passionate reliance on Dewey. See Richard Rorty, *Achieving Our Country: Leftist Thought in Twentieth-Century America* (Cambridge: Harvard University Press, 1998).

100. See Max Weber, "Politics as a Vocation," *From Max Weber: Essays in Sociology*, 128.

101. Most of Arendt's political "spaces" appear to be modeled on open-air, outdoor images, with the exception of the town hall, and her recurring discussions of "worldlessness" and "homelessness" only exacerbate that tendency. But Seyla Benhabib's discerning eye detects an interior design that informs the relations in Rahel Varnhagen's salon: "the salon is a fascinating space: unlike an assembly hall, a town square, a conference room, or even simply the family dinner table, the salon, with its large, luxurious, and rambling space, allows for moments of intimacy; in a salon, people are with each other but must not always be next to each other. Salons are amorphous structures with no established rules of entry and exit for those who have formed intimacy; in fact, it may be a sign of good manners to foster and to allow the formation of intimacy among members of the salon. What is important here is the fluidity of the lines between the gathering as one and the gathering as many units of intimacy, and how the salons can be both public and private, both shared and intimate." See Seyla Benhabib, *The Reluctant Modernism of Hannah Arendt* (Thousand Oaks: Sage, 1996), 16.

102. Hannah Arendt, *The Human Condition* (Chicago: University of Chicago Press, 1958).

103. Arendt, *Between Past and Future*, 36–37, 108, 111, 129–33; "The Image of Hell," *Commentary* 2/3 (September 1946): 291–95; *The Human Condition*, 233; *Men in Dark Times*, 233, 245.

CHAPTER 11

1. Hannah Arendt, *The Origins of Totalitarianism* (New York: Harcourt Brace Jovanovich, 4th ed. 1973), ix.

2. I have benefited in this section by reading Tracy B. Strong's "Nihilism and Political Theory," in John S. Nelson, ed., *What Should Political Theory Be Now?* (Albany: State University of New York Press, 1983), 243–63.

3. Hannah Arendt, "Understanding and Politics," *Partisan Review* 20: 4 (1953): 379.

4. David Easton, *The Political System* (New York: Alfred A. Knopf, 1953); Alfred Cobban, "The Decline of Political Theory," *Political Science Quarterly* 68: 2 (September, 1953), 321–337; T. D. Weldon, "Political Principles," *Philosophy, Politics and Society*, first series, ed. Peter Laslett (Oxford: Basil Blackwell, 1956), 22–34; Leo Strauss, "What Is Political Philosophy?" *Journal of Politics* 19 (August 1957): 343–68; Judith N. Shklar, *After Utopia: The Decline of Political Faith* (Princeton: Princeton University Press, 1957); Robert A. Dahl, "Political Theory: Truth or Consequences," *World Politics* 11 (October 1958): 89–102; Daniel Bell, *The End of Ideology: On the Exhaustion of Political Ideas in the Fifties* (New York: Free Press, 1960); Isaiah Berlin, "Does Political Theory Still Exist?" in Peter Laslett and W. G. Runciman, eds., *Philosophy, Politics and Society*, second series (Oxford: Basil Blackwell, 1962), 1–33.

5. Max Weber, *The Protestant Ethic and the Spirit of Capitalism*, trans. Talcott Parsons (New York: Charles Scribner's Sons, 1958), 181.

6. Ibid.

7. Ibid., 182.

8. Ibid.
9. Weber, "Science as a Vocation," in *From Max Weber*, 129–54.
10. Weber, "Politics as a Vocation," in *From Max Weber*, 77–128.
11. Ibid., 127.
12. Sheldon S. Wolin, "Political Theory as a Vocation," *American Political Science Review* 63: 4 (December 1969): 108.
13. John Rawls, *A Theory of Justice* (Cambridge: Harvard University Press, 1971).
14. Paul Rabinow, "Introduction," in Michel Foucault, *The Foucault Reader*, ed. Paul Rabinow (New York: Pantheon Books, 1984), 5.
15. Michel Foucault, *The History of Sexuality: Volume I: An Introduction*, trans. Robert Hurley (New York: Vintage Books, 1980), 148.
16. Jean-François Lyotard, *The Postmodern Condition: The Power of Knowledge*, trans. Geoff Bennington and Brian Massumi (Minneapolis: University of Minnesota Press, 1984), xxiv.

CHAPTER 12

1. Sheldon S. Wolin, "Political Theory: From Vocation to Invocation," *Vocations of Political Theory*, ed. Jason A. Frank and John Tambornino (Minneapolis and London: University of Minnesota Press, 2000), 3–22.
2. Ibid., 21.
3. Ibid., 9.
4. Ibid., 13.
5. Ibid., 20–21.
6. Ibid., 8.
7. Allan Bloom, *The Closing of the American Mind* (New York: Simon & Schuster, 1987).
8. See Darnton on reading communities: "When the *philosophes* set out to conquer the world by mapping it, they knew that their success would depend on their ability to imprint their world view on the minds of their readers. But how was this operation to take place? What in fact was reading in eighteenth-century France? Reading still remains a mystery, although we do it every day. The experience is so familiar that it seems perfectly comprehensible. But if we could really comprehend it, if we could understand how we construe meaning from little figures printed on a page, we could begin to penetrate the deeper mystery of how people orient themselves in the world of symbols spun around them by their culture." See Robert Darnton, "Readers Respond to Rousseau: The Fabrication of Romantic Sensitivity," *The Great Cat Massacre and Other Episodes in French Cultural History* (New York: Basic Books, 1984), 215–16.
9. Arendt, *The Human Condition*, 158.
10. I realize that this pristine depiction is vulnerable to the kind of (instrumentalist) critique that Hanna Pitkin once directed toward Hannah Arendt: "What is it they talked about together in that endless palaver in the agora? What does she [Arendt] imagine was the *content* of political speech and action, and why is this question so difficult to answer from her text?" See Hanna Pitkin, "Justice: On Relating Public and Private," *Political Theory* 9/3 (August 1981): 327–52.

11. See Nancy J. Hirshmann, "Eastern Veiling, Western Freedom?" *The Review of Politics* (summer 1997): 461–88.

12. To cite just two glaring problems: liberal arts institutions are not, in fact, run as democracies, even if "self-governing" faculties at many institutions enjoy relative autonomy and academic freedom in most curricular and scholarly matters. At the same time, many institutions are being increasingly subjected to top-down, top-heavy administrative encroachments that threaten to undermine any semi-autonomous sphere of academic freedom that teachers and students may have appropriated for themselves within an otherwise hierarchical scheme of things. Administrators at private schools especially can get away with many illiberal policies, and even if they violate the legally protected civil freedoms of their members, it often is hard for a lone maverick teacher to fight, or risk fighting, a legal battle against a well-endowed corporation. Second, most schools cannot afford need-blind admissions policies that permit low- and middle-class students into the classroom, hence, in fact, most liberal arts colleges remain elite, homogeneous, bourgeois institutions—though their hearts or lips might say something else.

13. Louis Menand, worried about the fate of liberal arts colleges after the end of their Golden Age as he sees it, calls for a return to "relevance" with non-liberal fields but, in my view, makes too many concessions toward that end without attending sufficiently to the intrinsic virtues and ulterior benefits of noninstrumentalized education. Louis Menand, "College: The End of the Golden Age," *The New York Review of Books* (October 18, 2001): 44–47.

14. "Reading implies time for reflection, a slowing-down that destroys the mass's dynamic efficiency." See Paul Virilio, *Speed and Politics: An Essay on Dromology*, trans. Mark Polizzotti (New York: Semiotext(e), 1986), 5.

15. Cf. Kateb on Arendt: "One way into these questions is to notice that Arendt is intent on determining the essence of what she often calls (especially in *On Revolution*) the authentically political. Her premise is that if the authentically political can be conceptualized properly, it will present itself as something so attractive, as well as so advantageous, that in the minds of her readers, and of others by a radiating influence, the dignity of politics will be on the way to being restored. The irony is that for Arendt the dignity of politics has nothing to do with using government as a weapon or instrument of social reform or even adaptation to social change." See George Kateb, "Political Action: Its Nature and Advantages," *The Cambridge Companion to Hannah Arendt*, ed. Dana Villa (Cambridge: Cambridge University Press, 2000), 131.

16. Richard Rorty, *Philosophy and Social Hope* (New York: Penguin, 1999), 125.

17. John Cage, "Overpopulation and Art," unpublished work, presented at the Stanford Humanities Center, 1991.

18. There is a dangerous movement afoot, however, to substitute individual notions and practices of "academic freedom" with corporate versions, that is, the right of an institution to set its own internal policies and procedures so that individual freedoms can be abridged with legal impunity. See *Urofsky v. Gilmore*, 98–1481, U. S. Court of Appeals for the 4th Circuit; Harvey A. Silverglate, "Freedom Seems Academic," *National Law Journal* (September 11, 2000). I regret to say that my own institution, promoted by the college's lawyers and top administration, has contributed significantly to this movement; see *Pomona College v. Superior Court*, 45 Cal.App.4th 1776 (1996).

19. "Democracy cannot flourish where the chief influences in selecting subject matter of instruction are utilitarian ends narrowly conceived for the masses, and, for the higher education of the few, the traditions of a specialized cultivated class." See John Dewey, *Democracy and Education* (New York: Macmillan, 1916), 226.

20. Wolin, "Political Theory: From Vocation to Invocation," 21.

Index

abortion politics, 17, 91–96, 220n59
    and Christian theology, 97–102
    and death, 92–93, 97, 99, 101–3, 105–6
    and feminism, 93, 101, 218n17, 221n74
    and liberalism, 92–96, 218n20
    in Japan, 102–4, 221n62
academic freedom, 48, 204–5. *See also* freedom
    dangers to, 239n18
Adams, John, 171
Addams, Jane, 203
Aeschylus, 26, 38
America
    and social contract, 58
    and the redemption genre, 51, 82
    as a multiracial society, 31, 49, 52, 60, 77
    as New World experiment, 69
    dealing with the past, 57–58
    origin stories about, 51
American Council of Learned Societies, 2
American founding, 10, 73, 170–72
American Gothic, 53. *See also* Wood, Grant
    ambiguity of, 123, 125–26, 129–30
    as political irony, 132–33
    as regionalist commentary, 120–22
    as satire, 120–22, 224–25n23
    connection to politics, 131–34
    history of, 121–22, 131
    husband and wife controversy, 123–25, 226n49, 226n52, 226n57, 228n83
    sexualized dimensions of, 126–30, 226n46, 227n62
American small colleges, 1, 6. *See also* liberal arts colleges
    as bastions of freedom, 65, 198–99, 202, 206. *See also* freedom
    versus research university, 2–3, 8, 64–65, 194, 205–6
Amherst College, 11, 15–16, 18, 56, 63–67, 75, 77, 86, 89
    commitment to diversity, 66, 68, 203
anti-foundationalism, 153, 159–63, 233n15. *See also* Butler, Judith; Fish, Stanley; Rorty, Richard
    Antigone. *See also* Sophocles

Aquinas, Thomas, 36, 97, 99, 165, 217n2
Arendt, Hannah, 18, 43, 58, 72, 75, 77, 145, 169, 176, 182–84, 199
    and birthing metaphor (natality), 173–74
    as exemplar of the liberal arts, 10, 12
    as leading theorist of her generation, 10
    connection to Virgil, 19, 170–73, 234n48, 235n49
    Life of the Mind, 171–73
    on Augustine, 173–74
    on bannister metaphor, 175–76
    on constitutions, 170
    on imagination, 20, 184
    on Jefferson's America, 72
    On Revolution, 170–73
    on the American founding, 73, 170–71
    on theory, 184
    Origins of Totalitarianism, 172, 182–83
    "Understanding and Politics," 183–84
Aristotle, 8–10, 25, 38–39, 73, 77, 98, 142, 145, 165, 217n2
Augustine, 35, 38, 45, 97, 166–67, 173–74, 234n40
    and Arendt's birthing metaphor, 173–74
    and confession, 50, 59
    City of God, 173
Austin, J.L., 111

Baigell, Matthew, 121, 123, 143
Barber, Benjamin, 9–10, 135, 210n13
basketball, 56, 72
    as American activity, 73
Bataille, Georges, 81, 91, 96–101
    and potlatch, 100–1
    on Christianity, 91, 97–99, 106
    on death, 98, 101
    on procreative sexuality, 98
    restricted versus general economy, 96
    The Accursed Share, 96
Baudelaire, Charles Pierre, 117
Baudrillard, Jean, 117
Beauvoir, Simone de, 185
Bellah, Robert, 10

Printed in the United States
86841LV00004B/77/A